Tim

a1

Consciousness Literature & the Arts 21

General Editor:
Daniel Meyer-Dinkgräfe

Editorial Board:
Anna Bonshek, Per Brask, John Danvers,
William S. Haney II, Amy Ione,
Michael Mangan, Arthur Versluis,
Christopher Webster, Ralph Yarrow

Time, Memory, Consciousness and the Cinema Experience

Revisiting Ideas on Matter and Spirit

MARTHA BLASSNIGG

Amsterdam - New York, NY 2009

Cover design:
Aart Jan Bergshoeff

The paper on which this book is printed meets the requirements of "ISO
9706:1994, Information and documentation - Paper for documents -
Requirements for permanence".

ISBN: 978-90-420-2640-7
E-Book ISBN: 978-90-420-2641-4
ISSN: 1573-2193
© Editions Rodopi B.V., Amsterdam - New York, NY 2009
Printed in the Netherlands

Contents

Introduction

Let us suppose that we have to do a piece of intellectual work, to form a conception, to extract a more or less general idea from the multiplicity of our recollections. A wide margin is left to fancy, on the one hand, to logical discernment on the other hand; but, if the idea is to live, it must touch present reality on some side; that is to say, it must be able, from step to step, and by progressive diminutions or contractions of itself, to be more or less acted by the body at the same time as it is thought by the mind.

(Henri Bergson 1991: 173)

The origins of this research project go back a long way with some faint roots in a cross-fertilisation between cultural anthropology and philosophy in a study of the intrinsic qualities of spiritual practice and conceptions of immanence mainly in a contemporary European context. This interest led to an interdisciplinary study of the phenomenon of angels through an ethnographic fieldwork study in Vienna of clairvoyants' perceptual processes in connection with experiences of angelic apparitions, in a comparison of the multi-sensorial experience of what could be called mystic experiences with the treatment of the spiritual in film. This research suggested that, both the cinema[1] experience and the perception of apparitions could be understood as phenomena of an extended spectrum of amplified and enhanced qualities of ordinary perceptual processes.[2] This study subsequently led to a

---

[1] The term 'cinema' in this book is understood as a *dispositif,* defined as a network of imperatives including the basic cinematographic apparatus; in case it is applied in a different sense it will be identified in the text. The term 'Cinématographe' is used when refering to the patented Lumières apparatus or technological device; it appears as 'cinematograph' or 'cinematic apparatus' when the term refers to a generality of moving image apparatuses and practices or the technological concept.

[2] This study resulted in the thesis 'Seeing Angels and the Spiritual in Film: an Interdisciplinary Study of a Sensuous Experience' (2000). Some core aspects are synthe-

fuller consideration of the philosophical aspects relating to the processes of the mind in the context of audio-visual environments, drawing on a pathway through Gilles Deleuze's cinema books to an extensive re-reading of Henri Bergson's original writings, which were conceived in the very period when the emerging projection technologies were introduced to the public. This had to be seen against the intellectual background of extensive discussions around issues such as time, movement, memory, consciousness and the unconscious, etc.

The initial conceptualisation of this book was informed by the hypothesis that if there existed a 'spiritual dimension' in relation to human consciousness[3] that is not dependent on, or restrained by, the concept of belief or imagination, it must be possible to situate its validation independently of religious or cultural institutions. Before approaching the theme of *l'esprit*[4] in Bergson's works, it should be pointed out that etymologically the term 'spirit' derives from the Latin, *spiritus* ('breathing'), and also relates to the Greek term *psukhê* (psyche = 'breath', 'life', 'soul', 'mind'), which stands for the principle of animation, or life.[5] Both roots reveal an ontological dimension of the term that bridges an apparent distinction between inside and outside, and in the following segue an understanding of the 'spiritual' dimension as experience, embedded in the cognitive processes and in 'being', defining the subject-object relationship. In this sense, it relates most closely to Bergson's use of the term *esprit*, best translated as 'mind'. This definition of 'spiritual' or 'spiritual dimension', as it will be used here, excludes any references to religious practices or institutionalised and personal belief systems. It is probably best ex-

---

sised in a chapter published with the title 'Clairvoyance, Cinema and Consciousness' (Blassnigg 2006a/b).

[3] The term consciousness is here used according to Bergson who seemed not to adhere to a strict definition of it, when he admitted that: "… for want of a better word we have called it consciousness" (1998: 237). He further proposed that: "… life is connected either with consciousness or with something that resembles it" (1998: 179).

[4] *L'esprit* is translated in *Matter and Memory* (1991) as the 'mind' or 'spirit', a translation that Henri Bergson in 1908 approved. Bergson (1991: 11) in few occasions also related the terms 'soul' and 'mind' with one another, in the original terms *ame* and *esprit*.

[5] This original definition still reflects in the current use of the term, among other things as: "(1) The animating or life-giving principle in humans and animals", or: "(5) The active power of an emotion, attitude, etc., as operating on or in a person; an inclination or impulse of a specified kind" (Shorter Oxford English Dictionary 2002, 5th edn.).

pressed through the common conception of a vital principle: an active power of an emotion, attitude, or impulse. A similar definition of the term 'spiritual' is provided in the introduction of Allan Kardec's *The Spirit's Book*, originally published in 1857:

> Strictly speaking, Spiritualism is the opposite of Materialism; every one is a Spiritualist who believes that there is in him something more than matter, but it does not follow that he believes in the existence of spirits, or in their communication with the visible world. Instead, therefore, of the words SPIRITUAL, SPIRITUALISM, we employ, to designate this latter belief, the words SPIRITIST, SPIRITISM, which, by their form, indicate their origin and radical meaning, and have thus the advantage of being perfectly intelligible; and we reserve the words *spiritualism, spiritualist*, for the expression of the meaning attached to them by common acceptation. (Kardec 1989: 21)

Kardec reflects Dilthey's distinction a century earlier between 'natural sciences' and 'sciences of the spirit' (literally translated from the German term *Geisteswissenschaften)*. In his *Introduction to the Human Sciences* (1883), Dilthey acknowledged the shortcomings of the notion of 'spirit' in that it does not "separate *facts of the human spirit* from the *psychophysical unity of human nature"* (1883, second chapter — emphasis in the original). The critical reflection on the problematic of the psychophysical relationship in Dilthey's acknowledgement foreshadowed the way the term 'spirit' featured in Bergson's innovative approach to metaphysics in philosophy and, in a contemporary reading, opens an entry to the discipline of anthropology, constituting one of the disciplinary foundations for this book.

Bergson's work will be approached and applied in the following chapters in two distinct ways: first through a re-reading of Bergson's philosophy in the historical context of the emerging cinema and, secondly, in an application to a current understanding of the emerging cinema and its spectatorship. The latter is particularly significant to the way Bergson's philosophy today stimulates a particular way to rethink the emergence of the cinema as a philosophical *dispositif,*[6]

---

[6] The term *dispositif,* initially applied to the cinema by Jean-Louis Baudry (1975) and translated in English into the term 'apparatus', is here and further on mainly used in its French meaning which, as Frank Kessler (2004) reminds us, indicates an arrange-

whereas in terms of its material manifestations at the time he hardly took up this dimension directly in his work and only scarcely refers to it explicitly — for very obvious reasons as we shall see later.

Initially it may seem arbitrary that Bergson's philosophy of perception and consciousness has been chosen for a treatment of the subject matter of 'spirit' in this book, but in the course of the following elaborations it will become evident that the focus on Bergson's thinking is interrelated with many key issues around the metaphysical implications of the emerging cinema. His work can be regarded in this context as both a nexus and catalyst for certain ideas and aspects that are relevant for this subject area. On the one hand, being its contemporary, his thinking crystallised the intersection of forces that impacted on the way photographic recording and projection technologies were understood at the time of their initial diffusion which led to their rapid, widespread and popular reception (and which also reflect on the cinema's enduring popularity today). On the other, his philosophy stimulates and triggers critical reflections around the issues of 'consciousness' and 'intuition' in contemporary as well as current debates, especially as his philosophy offers an alternative to static, analytical and atomistic approaches to consciousness. As such it bears a particular relevance to the way an ontological dimension of cinema spectatorship can be addressed with bearings on an understanding of the continuous fascination and appeal of the cinema as philosophical *dispositif*.

The starting point for this research draws on new-historicist research and cinema theory, which have revealed how the technological transformations of the cinema, especially in its emerging stages, have been shaped through the audiences' engagement and interpretation (Punt 2000). Increasingly interdisciplinary studies of the late 19th century have shifted the predominant explanatory model for the popularity of the cinema from a focus on 'realism' and straight-forward preoccupation with movement to a wider spectrum of concerns with

---

ment or assemblage of heterogeneous elements, as well as a certain 'tendency' that the connections between the elements bring forth, resulting in a specific historical formation through their interplay. The term 'apparatus' is used in the sense of either the technological assemblage or devices: originally from Latin *apparare* ('make ready'), *parare* ('prepare'). In the Oxford English Dictionary it is defined as: "(1) The things collectively necessary for the performance of some activity or function; the equipment used in doing something; a machine, a device" (Shorter Oxford English Dictionary 2002, 5th edn.).

the immaterial and occult not only in film content but also as intrinsic dimension to, and driving force of, popular culture. As Michael Punt (2005a/b, 2004, 2003a/b, 1998b), Tom Gunning (2007, 2003, 1995), and John Durham Peters (1999), among others have demonstrated, these dimensions are particularly evident in the complex network of forces that impinged on the emerging cinema. Scientists' and technologists' interests in invisible forces, conjuring practices and conjurer filmmakers and producers, the ubiquity of spiritist séances and occupations with the occult, and the audiences' awareness of the deception of the cinema illusion in play with their own cognitive processes, all constituted significant strands that intersected in the cinema *dispositif*. This extended perspective together with the recent critical deconstruction of the concept of representation and the refiguring of subjectivity in the Humanities, particularly in philosophy, anthropology and film and media theory, has provided the ground for a reconsideration of certain ideas around matter, mind, consciousness, time and spirit. This has been called for in particular by their persistent resurfacing in the preoccupation with perceptual issues around media technologies.

Whereas in discussions on the so-called 'spiritual' dimension the literature predominantly features a focus on the 'virtual', in the sense of phenomenological or 'transcendental' dimensions of media technologies, this book takes the experience of the spectator into account from the perspective of philosophical implications of the perceptual processes in relation to the cinema as an exemplary case-study. It takes an ontological approach, through a first hand reading of Bergson's philosophy in the context of the period of the emerging cinema and by applying some of his core conceptions to a contemporary meta-discourse of the perceptual processes of the experience of audio-visual media. In this way this book aims to reconstitute the agency of the spectator in the very experience of the perceptual processes, highlighting the aspects of memory, consciousness, and intuition, while dwelling on the intellectual framework of the late 19th century, early 20th century and its convergences of the arts, sciences and technology. In this, the reader may recognise an undercurrent and recurring theme in this study, which can be characterised by a reconsideration of the concept of 'spirit' as it relates to processes of the mind, rather than to a phenomenology of the image or certain connotations with 'magic' or the 'otherworldly'. This shift intrinsically proposes a

revised consideration of the so-called 'spiritual dimension' in the embedded cognitive processes of the perceiver.

The here proposed ontological approach to the cinema spectatorship remains of course necessarily always speculative, since it concerns a generalisation of a subjective and rather intimate event and
experience in a collective forum. However, such a treatment liberates
certain ideas concerning the relationship between matter and spirit that
reach beyond the object of study. In the past, textual and contextual
reception studies have oscillated between the extremes of an infinite
pluralism on the one hand and essentialism on the other, either drawing on empirical research of spectatorship situated in a specific socio-
economic context, or abstracting a subject-position constituted by the
techniques applied in the film. This book proposes a subject-position
of the spectator, which is not regarded as predominantly constituted
by the film (although clearly always in negotiation with it), but approached from an ontological/ anthropological perspective.[7] As a consequence the cinema *dispositif* will be discussed here with a focus on
what could be coined as the 'human perceptual apparatus', conceived
as crucial facilitator that accommodates the immaterial, imaginative
and spiritual dimensions of the cinema experience through cognitive
processes. In this way this book aims overall to restore the human faculty of consciousness, of agency and choice, as a significant intrinsic
dimension of the cinema *dispositif*, since it is identified as not merely
subservient to the ideological constraints of the cinematic apparatus
but as an empowering agency of the spectators' active engagement,
always in pro-active negotiation with the perceptual processes. This
model of the spectator will be defined as an embodied, immanent and
above all an actively participatory agent, and extends the concept of
the 'participant observer' to an 'observing participant' in the context
of the philosophical *dispositif* of the cinema.

The route that the following treatment takes straddles a variety of
different dimensions. It departs from the acknowledgement that the

---

[7] This is not to dismiss the function and importance of the narratological, structural,
compositional aspects of the film content and form, or reception studies; for a focus
on reception studies of ethnographic film see for example Crawford and Hafsteinsson
(1996), also see MacDougall (2005, 1999). The perspective taken here instead provides an approach to an understanding of the 'image' consistent with Bergson's philosophy, as well as Warburg's proposition that we need to look beyond the surface to
uncover underlying processes, which are intrinsic to the cinema experience during the
engagement with the content on the screen.

heterogeneity of the qualitative experiences during the perception of cinema inhibits empirical studies — at least this could be taken as a consequence rather than the grounding evidence, although having said this, of course any theory of cinema is in itself based on the very experience of the author of watching and processing the perceptions of movies. As an alternative route it takes Henri Bergson's philosophy as a steppingstone into some thoughts about the experience of the cinematic perception on a meta-discursive level. Bergson's philosophy offers an ontological approach that will be situated in the context of an interdisciplinary network of ideas through a convergence of cinema studies, philosophy and anthropology. This application invites a much wider treatment of audio-visual media (and) perception in general, by offering a starting point in that it takes the cinema experience as a paradigm; as an enhanced or amplified platform where certain ideas around perception, memory, consciousness, intuition, etc. become manifest and transparent, or at least call for a special treatment in an exemplary way.

Paradoxically, this qualitative perspective that seems to lie largely outside of reach of any tangible reality accessible to a scientific study, may appear as closer to our understanding when bound up with a philosophical approach that is embedded in the very experience itself. For this reason, this book offers what could be called a thought experiment interwoven with facts and an existing body of theories, situated in a historical context, to become alive and graspable through the experiential interconnection with its readers. This exercise is intended to broaden the study of the cinema and apply some of the expertise developed in related fields into a consideration of those processes of the mind that are accessible to our experience and observation, often referred to as 'consciousness'. While this is not a treatment of 'consciousness' per se and does not attempt to provide new insights or claims concerning this subject, it rather tackles some interdependent phenomena around the perceptual experience of audio-visual media to do with perception, memory, recognition, time, etc. in order to revisit some ideas around 'matter' and 'spirit' that might prove useful for contemporary research concerning the special conditions of the human mind in audio-visual environments.

Drawing on new-historicist research, the main intellectual focus of this book lies in the period of the public inception of the cinema from the 1890s until around 1907[8] when those constituting elements and imperatives that shaped the various heterogeneous forms of production, exhibition and reception of the emerging cinema were characterised by multiple interpretations. In this context the term 'emerging cinema'[9] has been chosen to keep reminding us that the cinema, as we know it today in its mainstream form, is rather different in many ways from the various projection practices during the first years of its inception. This also provides the main reason for the choice of this period since before a technology becomes standardised, these experimental stages offer a fresh way to untangle some of the very ideas that gave impetus to the emergence and development of its definite form, and most importantly, interpretations. The following treatment proceeds from the wider context of the emerging cinema in recent studies, for example with regard to the scientific interests in the production, the distribution and interventions in connection with conjuring practices. This provides the framework to remind us that the spectators were very well aware of the mechanisms of the technologies involved in the cinematic processes, through advertising and marketing strategies of new technologies such as popular scientific journals, or the narrator's explanations that accompanied most cinema performances. These characterise the historical significance of the intimate connections in the interactions between the various involved constituencies: science, conjuring, art and entertainment practices, technological innovations and popular culture with a particular focus on the interactions of the spectators with the cinema apparatus[10] and vice versa.

---

[8] This is commonly regarded as the period of the emerging cinema before certain production and distribution processes became standardised and industrialised, and the narrative structure and continuity editing became the dominant techniques applied to film form.

[9] This book avoids the terms 'early cinema' and 'pre-cinema' since they commonly refer to a teleological, determinist perspective that looks at the cinema as the presupposed outcome of a linear progressive development from hindsight.

[10] Stephen Heath (1980: 1) reminds us how a brief overview on the film titles followed on the programme of the Lumière brothers at their first screening in the *Grand Café* in Paris only after an explicit description of the workings of their Cinématographe: "This apparatus, invented by MM. Auguste and Louis Lumière, permits the recording, by series of photographs, of all the movements which have succeeded one another over a given period of time in front of the camera and the subsequent reproduction of these movements by the projection of their images, life size, on a screen before an entire audience".

By taking some of the wider intellectual concerns and reported interactions with these apparatuses at the late 19th century into account, this study proceeds from a first-hand reading of original texts by among others the scientist and philosopher Henri Bergson and the physiologist and inventor Étienne-Jules Marey. In this way it undertakes a philosophical journey to explore those qualities and aspects of the cinema *dispositif* that lie beyond the visible, the surface and the text of audio-visual media and establishes an ontological perspective focusing on the experiential dimensions of the spectators. In this context ideas around matter and spirit, time, memory, movement and consciousness will be highlighted, since they not only occupied some outstanding contemporary thinkers and were en vogue in the popular culture at the time, but still constitute a profound concern in contemporary discourses surrounding not only media technologies but also wider issues to do with the capacities and phenomena of the human mind. Although this may sound ambitious, the following should be considered as a first sketch, a thought experiment intended as an invitation to engage entangled minds into the broadened scope of its provided perspective.

Central to this book is Henri Bergson's philosophy, in particular his insights from his early work concerned with issues such as time, matter, spirit, memory, consciousness and intuition and especially how his studies of memory attempted to bridge the apparent dichotomy between 'matter' and 'spirit' *(l'esprit)*. It provides the matrix for the following engagement with the emerging cinema, especially in the way that his wide-reaching approach outlines the very scope of this investigation on a meta-level: while the majority of existing literature around the emerging cinema in terms of its *dispositif* embraces the technology, its scientific background, the institutions, socio-cultural and economic forces, popular culture, image phenomenology, etc., this study aims to extend the discourse around the spectators' active participation in the cognitive engagement during the cinematic experience with a particular focus on the qualities of an internalised perspective.[11] In a metaphorical way of speaking it could be said that this approach provides a method to hold juxtaposed elements in ten-

---

[11] Cinema perception here is taken to be a conscious human response of cognition in the presence of a particular apparatus and its setting, which is considered beyond textual or contextual theories such as the film content or the cultural or socio-economic perspectives of reception studies.

sion and in vibration to only momentarily put the flux of ever changing becomings in the very cinema experience at rest, through an intuitive encounter with an awareness of the spectators' own perceptual apparatus. In this sense, this book aims to liberate the underlying 'spirit' *(l'esprit)* as it manifests beyond the film text in the very processes at work during the perceptual experience as a first step to introduce this dimension for further considerations in the very core of film and cinema studies. Through this approach, the following is designed as a mnemonic encounter in a historical perspective to highlight an experience in the context of a critical conceptualisation from the vantage of the present. In this way it proposes an engagement with what could be coined as an 'anthropology of cinema' toward a recognition of a conception of a so-called 'spiritual dimension' in the context of an 'anthropology of mind' which reveals processes of 'shared consciousness' that could further be traced between various agencies from the entire production, distribution and exhibition processes to the multifold and multidimensional experiences of the spectator — central to this investigation.

The first chapter outlines some core aspects of Henri Bergson's ontological approach to the perceptual processes as he elaborated them in his early works,[12] which were developed concurrently with the emergence of the various projection technologies that led to the inception of the cinema. However, Bergson's philosophy is not taken into consideration for this immediately obvious reason. More significant is his recent reception in film and cinema theory especially as introduced by Gilles Deleuze through his *Bergsonism* (1991) and two cinema books (1986, 1989), as well as in the following scholarship. Moreover, Bergson's philosophy is particularly appropriate in this context since his ontological approach enables a treatment of 'spirit' as mind *(l'esprit)* in the embedded, immanent and embodied, cognitive experiences of the spectators beyond the dichotomy of realism and idealism and the ideological constraints of the cinema apparatus. Apart from Bergson's in-depth scientific knowledge into the contemporary scientific studies of psychophysiological phenomena such as the unconscious, hysteria, aphasia, etc. and the perceptual-cognitive processes

---

[12] *Essai Sur les Données Immédiates de la Conscience*, 1889 *(Time and Free Will*, 2001), *Matière et Mémoire*, 1896 *(Matter and Memory*, 1991), *Introduction à la Métaphysique*, 1903 *(An Introduction to Metaphysics*, 1912), *L'Évolution Créatrice*, 1907 *(Creative Evolution*, 1998).

of the human mind, his philosophy is especially significant here since it addresses some of the underlying aspects that drove the popular and prevailing fascination with the 'spiritual' or 'immaterial', concerning the conceptions of time as flux, synchronicity, simultaneity, movement, consciousness and intuition. A most crucial significance, however, derives from Bergson's treatment of the perception of *images* in terms of a relational model through his particular understanding of *images* as situated in between the realist notion of a 'thing' and the idealist notion of a 'representation'. He rather understood them as multi-sensorial perceptions and fully embodied relational networks through which during the perceptual processes, matter and spirit, outside and inside, meet through the faculty of memory — which Bergson chose not as the only, but exemplary and most accessible aspect for his thinking on the relationship between matter and spirit situated in the beholder's experience. The following re-reading of Bergson's work is informed mainly by a first hand study as well as secondary critical commentaries, and is designed as a virtual dialogue with Bergson's thinking.

Bergson's philosophy, especially his treatment of the aspects of movement, time as duration *(durée)*[13] and intuition are, in what follows, being applied to the discourse of the emerging cinema by looking at the intellectual, scientific and discursive precedents of cinema, especially some aspects of sophisticated commentaries and debates around the issues of movement and time in the fields of science, art and philosophy. Chapter one gives a brief introduction to this thinking in his early works with particular view on his understanding of 'spirit' in relation to 'matter' insofar it concerns the body-mind interconnectivity. Chapter two and three elaborate on some crucial aspects concerning the interventions by the physiologist Étienne-Jules Marey,

---

[13] F.C.T. Moore has proposed an alternative translation of *durée* through the old English term 'durance'. In this book, however, the term 'duration' is used according to the approved translation by Bergson, even though it may not exactly express the meaning of the French original (1996: 59). Suzanne Guerlac (2006: xiii) remarks in this regard that the different meaning in the English translation of 'duration' lies in its reference to: "… a period of elapsed time considered retrospectively and bounded by time limits of a beginning and an end". Bergson instead understood *durée* in his philosophy of time as a continuous flux of the whole of our internal states that are not spatially distinguished. See for example Bergson (2001: 100; 1996: 59) Where necessary the French original will be included in brackets in order to emphasise Bergson's definition.

especially at the threshold of their philosophical and artistic relevance. Whereas references to Marey's work in the context of cinema studies have mostly focused on his analysis of movement and technological innovations, his underlying research interest concerned foremost the principles of life in the way they are expressed and manifest through movement. These he attempted to capture by applying complex systems of recording techniques, which culminated in the recordings of invisible forces (in air or water) and a predominant concern with the issue of time as duration. While his search is commonly regarded within a strictly scientific context in which his work was situated at the time, this book suggests a fuller acknowledgement of the way that his interventions touched the so-called immaterial or ephemeral in various aspects.

Marey's investigations departed from the positivist assumption that the vital, often invisible, forces could be measured and explained by scientific methods; the physical body and its visible movement — the prevailing object in physiology — represented for Marey, however, merely the surface and symptom of these underlying forces. Most significant for his treatment of these dimensions is his recognition of the, at the time frequently acknowledged, insufficiency of the human sensory system — which conforms with Bergson's view — a lack that he, however, sought to resolve through scientific, technological instrumentation. In this respect Marey became a positivist foil for Bergson's critique of the scientific method, which Bergson exemplified through the analogy of the intellect with cinematographic method in reference to its basic principle of instantaneous photography. In addition to Marey's generally acknowledged body of work, chapter three emphasises some underexplored aspects of his interest in art by relating his concerns with aesthetic to some strands in the wider context of the 19th century convergence between art, science and technology, and a certain obsession with synchronicity, simultaneity and duration in the context of movement studies through photographic practice. For the purpose of this study, this chapter traces some selected aspects especially from the debates around instantaneous photography, commentaries on interpretations of Auguste Rodin's work relative to Bergson's philosophy, and the discourse surrounding the *persistence of vision* that signifies the threshold of the shift from a preoccupation with vision to that of the mind.

Subsequently chapter four introduces the late visual work by Aby Warburg, the *Mnemosyne Atlas,* into the nexus of a philosophical treatment of the cognitive implications of the emerging cinema. The interconnected moves through both the work of Marey and of Warburg in relation to Bergson's philosophy provide a foundation to shift the focus to an understanding of the emerging cinema as a pivot for investigations into the processes of the human mind, as it is suggested in this book. Of particular significance in this context is among other issues Bergson's recognition of the underlying processes of 'being' or 'life' as a continuous flux of change in duration *(durée),* a driving life-force, which he called *élan vital.* As mentioned earlier, Marey's work itself was imbued with the recognition of these underlying driving forces, although he only remotely touched upon the immaterial aspects of these issues explicitly. To emphasise the significance of Marey's 'diversions', or rather most profound concerns, the brief account of the art-historian Aby Warburg's intervention in respect of a new heuristic of art, is here considered as particularly valuable in relation to a further treatment of the processes of human cognition in audio-visual environments. Consequently this chapter places Marey's work alongside Warburg's insistence that art was primarily movement: an internal motion and dynamism that existed prior to the material form, from which it could be retrieved. This excursion highlights how both Marey's and Warburg's interventions straddled the dimensions beyond the visual and surface appearances, and in this way they intrinsically intersect with Bergson's innovative philosophical framework wherein the activity of the perceiver's mind is pivotal in interrelating the dimensions of matter and spirit.[14] The complexity of this triad with inherent overlaps, tensions, reiterations and speculative connections, can only be partially unravelled here for the scope of this study, and

---

[14] This dialogue is not about the emerging cinema per se, since in their work, the cinema features only marginally. Bergson merely related to it as an analogy in order to exemplify the tendency of the intellect and the scientific method, while Marey's work has historically been insufficiently or sometimes even incorrectly applied to the discourse around the so-called 'pre-cinema' technologies mostly from a teleological perspective, reducing his relevance to technological, materialist aspects. Recently the interconnection between Warburg's work and the emerging cinema has increasingly been addressed, most explicitly by Philippe-Alain Michaud (2004).

the main aim remains to ground a treatment of a so-called spiritual dimension in the intellectual context of the period.[15]

Through a re-reading of Bergson's early works against the background of some of these wider interdisciplinary intellectual concerns at the end of the 19th century (with a main focus here on France), it will become clear that Bergson understood the cinematic apparatus technologically, as it could be expected in the 1890s from somebody trained as a scientist.[16] This is similarly also evident in Marey's strict refusal to engage with the public projection of his work, as well as in the initial lack of interest by the Lumières to invest in their Cinématographe as an entertainment form before its popular reception was revealed. What emerges, however, from a close reading of Bergson's analysis in this wider intellectual context and from the vantage of the present understanding of the cinema *dispositif*, is that, when his insights are applied to a contemporary interpretation of the cinema spectators' cognitive processes, it allows us to more fully account for, what was called at the time, the psychical dimensions of the human condition. The key issue of time as quality becomes paramount, as it is experienced through conscious perceptual processes in the amplified cinema experience. In this way the cinema *dispositif* can be seen as an exemplification of Bergson's thinking and be reinterpreted as a pivot for an anthropological-philosophical study. Chapter five exemplifies this application of Bergson's philosophy by way of a thought experiment that takes a model-spectator on a meta-discursive level into its locus. The understanding of the human perceptual apparatus,

---

[15] Chapter two to four ask from the reader forbearance and some patience in order to undergo this intellectual journey; the route it undertakes is vital to the historical contextualisation of the interdisciplinary strands of this investigation.

[16] Bergson made continuously indirect references to chronophotography in his early works; however, it was not until *Creative Evolution* (1998), originally published in French in 1907 *(L'Évolution Créatrice),* that he explicitly referred to the cinematographic mechanism, which he compared to the processes of the intellect and the scientific method. In his view the cinematographical method exemplified the mechanisms of the intellect in its splitting of the whole into single instances, whereby time became compromised to a measurement in space. However, when reconsidering that not only the cinema as we know it today did not exist, but the manifold projection technologies initially were merely curiosities among many others, it becomes clear that a certain reception of Bergson through the Deleuzian film studies discourse, which accuses him to having ignored the relevance of the cinema in his ontological approach to perception, calls for a de-colonialisation of a hegemony that privileges the cinema in its historical treatment.

as an interface where spirit and matter meet, provides the basis to shift the focus from the technology and the screen as interface to the spectrum of the cinema spectators' processes of perception. This shift relocates the focus on the attention of the cinema as technological, socio-economical apparatus to an understanding of its philosophical implications, whereby the spiritual dimension of the cinema *dispositif* can be addressed as embedded within the spectators' cognitive processes.

The last chapter also attempts to rectify some of the current revision of Bergson's work, which has been distorted through an overemphasis on the 'virtual' in certain teleological histories of the 'moving image'.[17] A re-reading of Bergson's thinking in this context allows us to situate both the commonly perceived 'rational' and the 'irrational' and their diverging, contradictory forces, such that the cinema appears as a paradigm exemplifying the productivity of this nexus. Treated in a conceptual way but grounded in a historical context, the spectator in this vision appears in a fuller dimensionality that suggests an inclusion of a so-called spiritual dimension beyond the dichotomy of the material and immaterial, the body and the mind. It takes an approach that redefines the cinema spectators' agency, and suggests extending this to a wider treatment of the perception, uses and interpretations of contemporary media technologies, with a focus on choice and the political implications of approaches to distributed agency.

In summary this book brings together certain tendencies, intentions and philosophical aspects in Bergson's, Marey's and Warburg's interventions, treated in a conversational style. Rather than doing justice to their extensive individual bodies of work, it intends to draw attention to a specific dimension in relation to our understanding of the cinema, which proposes a wider treatment of conceptions of 'spirit' as a quality of mind, regarded as an underlying dynamic principle of life. Such interpretation necessarily remains speculative, however, a post-

---

[17] This has been addressed for example by Suzanne Guerlac (2004) who reminds us that the issue of experience has been ignored in the post-structuralist, French Bergsonism; and John Mullarkey (2004), who criticises the common bias in media studies for its emphasis on the 'virtual' in the contemporary reception of Bergson's philosophy. It could be suggested that this focus on the virtual may stem from a tendency toward the virtual in contemporary media studies pertinent to references of the conception of the so-called post-human and the popularity of cyborg culture throughout the 1990s, the period that characterises the belated reception of Deleuze in English speaking countries after the translation of Cinema 1 and 2 in 1986 and 1989.

Deleuzean understanding of cinema seems to have prepared and necessitated this move. An application of Bergson's philosophy to the
cinema experience opens a different and reconstructed way to address
the issue of 'spirit' not only in cinema studies, but also in a wider context of thematic interests. Through the focus on the perception of the
audiences, this approach suggests that the fascination and popularity
with the realm of the 'spirit' can be complemented, if not partially
resituated, in the very workings of the spectators' cognitive processes.
By applying Bergson's philosophy of perception to a meta-discourse
on the perception during the cinema experience, it further allows the
transfer of the obvious into a contextual, theoretical framework; that
no cinema spectator ever sees the same film in the same way, nor does
any group of spectators share identical experiences.

In the spirit of Aby Warburg this book suggests re-organising established discursive routines of thought according to new insights and
ideas, and proposes to proceed in this modus by drawing on historically informed research, rather than a mere refashioning of existing
concepts. As a consequence this investigation undertakes an intellectual journey by revisiting the historical context of the late 19th century
from the vantage of the 21st in order to liberate some of the highlighted dimensions and ideas for this investigation with the benefit of
the scholarship of the intervening period. This asks from the reader
some forbearance and it needs to be emphasised that this book does
not intend to make a contribution to cinema history itself. It instead
builds its argument on a very selective choice of historical accounts of
the period of the late-19th century, in order to draw an *image* that exemplifies certain aspects relating to the concepts of time, memory,
consciousness and movement, that may open a new way into how we
could embrace and approach the issue of the spirit in relation to the
cinema experience today. Bergson's thinking offers a clue, here suggested as a key, to ground an understanding of the experiential qualities of the cinema perception as situated within the domain of spirit,
the very creative processes of the human mind.

This book does not, however, claim to answer any unresolved
questions about the nature of the human spirit or the popularity and
persistence of this dimension in cinema but attempts to establish a
new perspective for investigations into the spiritual dimensions of the
human condition — here exemplified in respect of the cinema perception as immanent, experiential processes in an amplified arena. De-

parting from a critical view on the reductive connotations of technology and magic in the literature, it attempts to provide a more rigorous theoretical and methodological framework to study the spiritual implications as a mental domain in the context of the cinema experience with implications for other audio-visual or otherwise amplified environments. In addition to the in the literature established considerations of an ontology of the image, or a cultural (metaphorical) analysis of spirits, phantoms or spectres as immaterial manifestations — a well-established connection between the emerging cinema and 19th century spiritualism — this book proposes an ontology of the spectators' perception through which the spiritual dimension is sought within the perceptual processes of the mind. Here the spectator, treated in a conceptual way yet grounded in a historical context, is conceptualised in a fuller dimensionality with particular focus on the interrelation between thought and action and the interaction between memory and perception. In this way the so-called 'spiritual dimensions' of the cinema experience can be understood no longer in the sense of connotations with magic, transcendentalism or conditions of altered states, but rather as revealing an exemplary arena in the cinema *dispositif* to illuminate and enhance the workings of quotidian human cognitive processes. Through this approach the cinema *dispositif* is defined as a threshold where spirit and matter meet, a paradigm that exemplifies the productivity of a nexus of forces and provides a platform for further research into issues such as consciousness, precognition, intuition and psychic phenomena.

Prologue

Wings of Time: an Associative Prelude

Henri Bergson, Étienne-Jules Marey and Aby Warburg were vision-
aries and interdisciplinary pioneers, each trained in more than one discipline; Bergson in mathematics and philosophy, Marey in engineering and medicine, both with a substantial interest in art, Warburg in
art history and first hand experience in cultural anthropology. Although at the time the various disciplines in themselves were clearly
marked by institutions and in published outcomes, all three thinkers
and innovators embraced an interdisciplinary perspective in their
work. The opening of this book takes the liberty to start with an associative assemblage that might appear as a parallelism, however, one
that through what follows will reveal some intrinsic philosophical
interconnections at the convergence of certain aspects of science, art
and popular culture.

Bergson, Marey and Warburg all identified the perception of
movement at the fringes of the spectrum of the capacities of the human sensory perception. This is particularly evident in their preoccupation with time and space, and especially the (smallest) intervals,
(greatest) intensities and the significance of the dimensions beyond
the directly perceivable by the sensory apparatus. Bergson for example continued his elaboration on the distinction between time in space,
and time as duration in *Creative Evolution* (1998) in connection to his
concept of the *élan vital* and the evolution of consciousness. In this
context he treated the issue of instinct in polymorphic organisations of
species such as bees and other insects, in relation to the evolution of
consciousness and intuition. Marey studied and analysed the movements of insects' wings that are indistinguishable by human vision
and the movements they provoke in the air as a challenge to instrumental realism. Similarly, Warburg is reported to having been in-
trigued by the movement of butterflies, which for Michaud (2004)
symbolises the very meaning of images with reference to the term

imago that designates the last stage of the development of an insect in complete metamorphosis.

Marey's graphic notations of the movement of insects' wings revealed the transformation of the up-and-down movement by air resistance and wind influence, variously distorting the surface of the wing due to its unequal flexibility, which creates a double loop (lemniscate) describing irregular geometrical movements similar to the shape of the number eight. These movements over time are depicted in a watercolour drawing by E. Valton, with the title *'Aspect d'une guêpe volant captive'*, which Marey printed in his publication *Le Mouvement* in 1894 (*Movement*, 1895: 243), entitled 'Appearance of a wasp flying in the sun' — an image to which the *Musée Marey* ascribes the imaginative dimensions of Marey's work.[1] A very similar movement — it almost seems a direct translation — appears in the movements performed by the famous dancer and actress Loïe (Marie Louise) Fuller in her *Danse Serpentine,*[2] also captured in the astonishing hand-painted 1896 Lumières film with the same title, and in many other imitations around the world, such as those by Anabella, captured by W.K.L. Dickson 1894 entitled *Anabella Serpentine Dance* (I and II). In the Paris theatre *Folies-Bergère,* Fuller brought her extraordinary movements and innovative application of light and color to the attention of artists who had a particular interest in dynamism and movement over time, such as Toulouse-Lautrec, Jules Cheret and Auguste Rodin, in whose work she also featured as a model.

The associative collage of seeming coincidences described above can further be directed to Warburg's study of the serpentine ritual among the Hopi Indians. For him it revealed the ancient connection with the rhythm of time describing a zig-zag path between life and art, which he applied as a metaphor to the shift from the Dionysian to the Apollonian principle in Renaissance art. The movement of the figure eight in this associative collage turns into zig-zag lines, which for the Hopi Indians symbolised the untamed energies of lightening or the

---

[1] A reproduction of the water-color drawing can be found online at: http://www.musees-bourgogne.org/les_musees/musees_bourgogne_gallerie.php?id= 62&theme=&id_ville= (consulted 24.08.2008); and is also reprinted in Mannoni (2006: 21).
[2] For an extensive, interdisciplinary approach to Fuller's work see Albright (2007).

snake (Michaud 2004: 285-286).[3] It also draws us inevitably into Bergson's philosophy in which the zig-zag features as a metaphor for the improbabilities and contingencies of the mechanistic cause-and-effect principle when applied to the dimensions of life (1998: 57). Reminiscent of the reference to the zig-zag as a metaphor for his doctrine (Guerlac 2004: 45), there is an associative interconnection to be suggested from this thought experiment; a zig-zag pulse running from a mechanistic study of the movement of an insect's wing, via the artistic expressions of similar 'movements' or motions in their dynamisms, through a Warburgian transformation and anthropological inspiration into the very domains of spirit *(l'esprit)* in the oeuvre of Bergson. This is, rhetorically speaking, the very motion that the following chapters invite the reader to undertake.

---

[3] Michaud (2004) reminds us how among other existing symbolic interpretations and references against a film context, this conception of the snake symbolised for Sergei Eisenstein (1988: 138) the dynamic impetus of his concept of the montage-collision, as exemplified in 'Beyond the Shot'. In a scientific context of the 19th century it also can be related to the initially conceived 'untamed' force of electricity, which once domesticated was kept securely under human (technological) control. This evokes earlier scientific investigations into electricity and lighting such as by Nikolas Tesla (1993) and his wireless technologies. Warburg made an interesting remark in this respect, in his fieldnotes from his travel in North-America, on the perception of natural forces by North-American Indians and Western cultures: "The attempt at magical effects is thus first of all an attempt to appropriate a natural event in the living likeness of its form and contours: lightening is attracted through mimetic appropriation, unlike in modern culture, where it is drawn into the ground by an inorganic instrument and eliminated. What distinguishes such an attitude toward the environment from ours is that the mimetic image is supposed to bring about a relation by force, whereas we strive for spiritual and material distance" (Michaud 2004: 306).

Chapter 1

Bergson's Philosophy as Interdisciplinary Nexus with Catalytic Impact: Time, Memory, Consciousness and the Relation between 'Spirit' *(l'Esprit)*[1] and 'Matter' *(Matière)*

Ce professeur, paisible et de tempérament plutôt conservateur fut l'inventeur d'une philosophie explosive: celle-ci se présente comme une nouvelle vision du réel, imposant une rupture violente avec les systèmes d'idées et d'images quotidiennes.[2]
(Panéro, 2005)

The end of the 19th century can be characterised as a particularly dynamic milieu of competing cosmological paradigms and shifting concepts, especially as they related to the changing conceptions of time, to novel discoveries around the psychophysiological dimensions of the mind-body relationship, or to theories on evolution and the scientific as well as the widespread populist investigations into immaterial dimensions of existence. Against this background the philosopher Henri Bergson (1859-1941) became preoccupied with finding new ways for understanding some of these emerging ideas beyond a polemical, escapist or dialectical model. He wrote his early works in the late 1880s and 1890s, at the time when the impulse to investigate sub-

---

[1] *L'esprit* is translated in *Matter and Memory* (1991) as the 'mind' or 'spirit', a translation which Henri Bergson in 1908 approved. However, in its French meaning, it relates very strongly to the German meaning of *Geist*. Bergson also related the terms 'soul' and 'mind' with one another, in the original terms *ame* and *esprit* (1991: 11) The following elaborations in this book focus on the synonymous use of the terms 'spirit' and 'mind', as closely related to Bergson's use of the terms as possible.

[2] Panéro cites Henri Gouhier (1987: 11), which translates as follows: "This professor, peaceful and of a rather conservative character has created an explosive philosophy, one that presents itself like a new vision of the real, imposing a violent rupture onto the systems of ideas and the quotidian perception" (translation by the author).

jects such as time, movement and matter was vigorous and widespread and various cinematic technologies came into existence.

Bergson's innovative approach to the prevailing dualism of body and mind established a way to regard matter and spirit, along with consciousness and things, as contingent upon one another. His philosophy reveals both a heuristic and an epistemology in his approach, which is initially exemplified particularly through his study of memory that provided insights into the relationship between matter and spirit, and later in his conception of intuition, which opened his metaphysics for an application to, as well as an implication of, lived experience. Initially written mainly as a critique of Kant's extreme position of a transcendental philosophy, Bergson proposed to overcome the dichotomy of matter (body) and spirit (mind), without the necessity to establish a transcendental force or realm, or to consider consciousness as epiphenomenon. He reflected on the latter:

> We are thus led, sometimes to an "epiphenomenalism" that associates consciousness with certain particular vibrations and puts it here and there in the world in a sporadic state, and sometimes to a "monism" that scatters consciousness into as many tiny grains as there are atoms; but, in either case, it is to an incomplete Spinozism or to an incomplete Leibnizianism that we come back. (1998: 355-356)

As will be elaborated later, Bergson instead took an ontological approach to reality, which, in his view, in its lived experience he conceived as duration *(durée),* as an ever changing 'becoming' and not merely as a given. His intervention had as much to do with science as it had to do with philosophy, which was particularly expressed through his approach and writing style: he first meticulously studied the scientific facts of the latest discoveries on which he then built his hypothesis, continuously moving between fact, observation, experience and his innovative thinking.[3] Given his original training and early success as young mathematician,[4] it is not surprising that his

---

[3] For *Matter and Memory* (1991), for example, Bergson devoted five years to studying the contemporary and most recent literature available on scientific studies of memory, such as the psychological phenomenon of aphasia, characterised by a loss of the ability to use language.

[4] Bergson won the first prize in mathematics at the age of 17 for the prestigious *Concours Général*, which led to the publication of his solution to a problem by Pascal in

philosophical and metaphysical conclusions were grounded in scientific data that reflected some of the radical innovations of the epoch embracing a number of disciplines such as mathematics, psychology, physiology, biology, sociology, and anthropology.

Bergson's works from 1889 onwards were concerned with topics, which today are understood as germane to the study of consciousness.[5] At the time this led to numerous interventions not only within philosophy but also in the discipline of psychophysiology, what today would overlap with research in cognitive psychology and neuroscience. His oeuvre, even during his lifetime, extended the reach of the discipline of philosophy, which was also manifest in his widespread popularity that earned him the acclamation as the widest-read philosopher at the beginning of the 20th century.[6] The following brief introduction to his early works, which is in no way meant to be complete, is intended to make some influential vectors of his intervention transparent in order to outline the nexus of interdisciplinary thinking present and embedded in Bergson's philosophy. It will also highlight certain aspects that, even today, function as catalyst for related subject areas and ideas, which will also become relevant in the application of his philosophy to the cinema experience in the following chapters.

Bergson wrote his early works against the backdrop of a restructuring of temporality in the late 19th century, which manifested in the introduction of the worldwide twenty-four hour time-zones. The unification and rationalisation of measured time stood in contrast to an in-

---

1877, a problem that Pascal had claimed to have solved without leaving any publication or notation of the solution (Lawlor and Moulard 2004).

[5] Bergson's first major work was part of his doctorial thesis *Essai sur les Données Immédiates de la Conscience* from 1888, published in English in 1889 as *Time and Free Will*; preceded by his first scholarly publication, the article 'On Unconscious Simulation in States of Hypnosis', in the *Revue Philosophique*, 1886.

[6] After his appointment as Chair of Ancient Philosophy at the *Collège de France*, the international translation of his article *Introduction à la Métaphysique* ([1903] *Introduction to Metaphysics*, 1999), and particularly after the appearance of one of his most popular works *L'Évolution Créatrice* ([1907] *Creative Evolution*, 1998), for which he was awarded the Nobel Price in 1927, Bergson's popularity grew amongst the academic, literary and artistic circles, as well among the general public. A culmination of his popularity is reported from his lectures delivered at Columbia University in 1913 (entitled 'Spiritualité et Liberté' and 'The Method of Philosophy' — apparently causing the first traffic jam in the history of Broadway), and the Gifford Lecture at Edinburgh University in 1914 (on 'The Problem of Personality') (Lawlor and Mulard 2004).

creasing awareness of the experience of the subjectivity of psychological time and stimulated the enormous interest in and popularity of alternative ideas about time such as competing conceptions of simultaneity, synchronicity and duration.[7] It also informed the scientific endeavours in the context of the vigorous worldwide colonisation and the increasing interest in the study of intercultural phenomena in the late 19th century — a period when scientists, philosophers and the emerging disciplines of sociology and anthropology attempted to get some purchase on the debates concerning the supremacy of culture versus nature, or, in another range of categories, the mind versus the body.[8] The social re-interpretation of Charles Robert Darwin's (1809-1882) biology-based evolutionist theory in the Humanities fitted the 19th century imperialist politics promoting the supremacy of Western civilisation, which was closely intertwined with the preceding evolutionist approaches in anthropology, such as by Lewis Henry Morgan (1818-1881) or Edward Burnett Tylor (1832-1917). It was used to support the idea that traces of the ancestors of so-called Western society were still surviving in indigenous, at the time so-called 'primitive', cultures. Herbert Spencer (1820-1903) was one of Darwin's proponents and applied his evolutionist theory to the fields of Sociology and Associationist Psychology, drawing on mechanistic determinism and progress of culture, advocating positivist rationalism as the culmination of the evolution of intelligence.

Bergson studied Spencer's theories after his move from mathematics to philosophy, and set out to address and consolidate some weaknesses he saw in Spencer's work, later commenting that this was the

---

[7] Ernst Mach is frequently cited as an example for the scientific interest in alternative conceptions of time, particularly since in his work *The Science of Mechanics* from 1883 he refused Newton's views on absolute time and absolute motion and dismissed absolute time as an "idle metaphysical conception" (Kern 1983: 18). The popular concept of the flux of time for example exceeded any form of representation and became wide-spread following William James' introduction to the concept of the 'stream of consciousness' (24-26), which bears similarities with Bergson's (1991) articulation of time as duration *(durée)*.

[8] Émile Durkheim for example (who also occupied a chair at the *Collège de France*, alongside Bergson and Marey), discussed the issue of time in relation to social organisation and distinguished between private time and 'time in general', conceiving of time as the 'rhythm of social life' (Kern 1983: 19). Unlike Bergson, Durkheim located the variability of perceptual categories not in the domain of subjective experience, but in differences among various forms of social organisation (Olick 2006). In his view, different societies produce different conceptions and perceptions of time.

catalyst that drew him into the consideration of a critical reflection on time, particularly with regard to Spencer's assertion that: "... time served no purpose, did nothing" (1992: 93).[9] Whereas Bergson (11-12) appreciated in Spencer's work the traits of a philosopher who tried to use precision and facts in a scientific and disciplined way, he took the counter-position that time acts, since in his view it: "... hinders everything from being given at once" (93). He speculated: "... how real time, which plays the leading part in any philosophy of evolution, eludes mathematical treatment..." and considered that: "... this duration which science eliminates, and which is so difficult to conceive and express, is what one feels and lives" (12-13). Bergson consequently directed his critique of the reduction of internal psychological states and life in general against mechanistic and determinist laws of classical physics and radically claimed indeterminism as a principle of psychic life. He asserted free will as a profound modus of human agency, and an open and dynamic morality as ethics beyond institutionalised dogmas.

From a contemporary perspective, his position, especially in his treatment of *l'esprit* and the issue of consciousness, as developed in *L'Évolution Créatrice* in 1907 (*Creative Evolution*, 1998), can be regarded as an intrinsic critique against the postulates of evolutionist theory as propagated among others by the discipline of anthropology during the 19th century. Cultural anthropology was at the time emerging as a positivist science and in this way contributed to the deprivation, or at least degeneration of the studies of the faculty of 'spirit', by shifting the discourse of 'spirit' almost entirely to investigations of so-called 'primitive magic' in human culture, mostly non-Western societies. Anthropologists such as Edward Burnett Tylor (1865, 1871), Johann Jakob Bachofen (1861), James Frazer ([1890] 1981), Émile Durkheim ([1912] 1965) or Lewis Henry Morgan (1877), investigated 'primitive forms of religion' from a historical, unilinear evolutionary perspective — this, from hindsight remarkably with hardly any or

---

[9] According to Bergson (1998: 364-365), Spencer: "... takes reality in its present form; he breaks it to pieces, he scatters it in fragments which he throws to the winds; then he "integrates" these fragments and "dissipates their movement". Having imitated the Whole by a work of mosaic, he imagines he has retraced the design of it, and made the genesis".

very scarce attention to the emerging and expanding contemporary spiritualist practices in their own societies.[10]

Whereas Bergson's own evolutionary theory, *L'Évolution Créatrice,* published in 1907 (*Creative Evolution,* 1998) confirmed Darwin's and Lamarck's theories on the progressive generation of species, it, however, emphasised that the intrinsic impulse that furthered the movement into ever new forms, the *élan vital,* manifested in multiple forms:

> Even a cursory survey of the evolution of life gives us the feeling that this impulse is a reality. Yet we must not think that it has driven living matter in one single direction, nor that the different species represent so many stages along a single route, nor that the course has been accomplished without obstacle. It is clear that the effort has met with resistance in the matter which it has had to make use of; it has needed to split itself up, to distribute along different lines of evolution the tendencies it bore within it; it has turned aside, it has retrograded; at times it has stopped short. (1920: 19)

In this lies one of the aspects for what, today, can be read as argument against the prevailing linearity of evolutionist determinism and the development of a predominantly materialist anthropology at the time, as it was most explicitly expressed in the new discipline of physical anthropology. Bergson's wholehearted acknowledgement of contingency also indicates that his philosophy could be further regarded as a rigorous attempt to situate the spiritual *(l'esprit)* within contemporary science and as an approach towards an understanding of human as well as non-human consciousness. With regard to the so-called spiritual dimension, Bergson's philosophy eschewed institutionalised belief. He rather put the emphasis on experience,[11] which added an intrinsic empirical dimension to the scientific evidence on which he

---

[10] Edward B. Tylor, for example, who wrote *Primitive Culture* in 1871, regarded psychic phenomena in the Western civilisation as degeneration, and James Frazer ([1890] 1981) more explicitly denounced "magic practice" as a "spurious system of natural law as well as a fallacious guide of conduct", in his view: "... it is a false science as well as an abortive art" (Inglis 1992: 400).

[11] Suzanne Guerlac (2004) emphasises the underexplored significance of the concept of experience in the reception of Bergson's work, which in her view has also been undervalued in Deleuze's Bergsonism in order to distinguish his approach from phenomenology during the 1960s.

built his claims. This liberating approach and perspective restored a fuller account of agency in the subject, which accommodated both, multiplicity and difference (the very characteristic of *durée*), and reached beyond the externalised phenomena of cultural and material manifestations — and in this way especially appears to be current and contemporary.[12]

It is not the purpose here to resituate Bergson's philosophy in a contemporary context, however, the recent reception and revitalisation of his works shows that his wide reception in film and cinema theory is only a small part in a spectrum of discourses where his philosophy has been reconsidered of significant influence.[13] His oeuvre has been re-introduced extensively by various scholars and extends the existing philosophical discussions to a wide range of disciplines. The renewed attention to Bergson's thinking specifically in the fields of cinema- and media studies and the recent engagement with media philosophy, can be said to be largely due to Gilles Deleuze's (1991) initial re-introduction to Bergsonism since the 1960s, particularly in his film philosophy (Deleuze 1986, 1989). In this way Bergson's understanding of time as duration has been taken up as a support for the challenge of the materialist treatment of the cinema as a technology of 'moving images' or of a 'representation of realism' and redirects the attention to the cinema as time-machine[14] — not on a fictional but ra-

---

[12] Bergson's work, it seems, has lost none of its novelty and originality even today and it bears particular relevance to some of the unresolved questions around consciousness and the relation between internal and external states; for example discussions around the so-called 'hard problem' in consciousness studies and neuroscience. — The hard problem concerns the common scientific conception of the world as consisting of pure matter and the difficulty to reconcile this perspective with the issue of consciousness. See for example discussions around the works by David Chalmers (1995, 1996).

[13] See for example Gallois (1997), Guerlac (2006), Mullarkey (2004), Pearson (2002) etc. Gallois (1997) discusses Bergson's philosophy in relation to contemporary neuroscience, Guerlac (2006) introduces Bergson's thinking in his early works and contextualises its relevance for contemporary science, Mullarkey (2004, 1999) situates Bergson's central concepts within a spectrum of disciplines such as sociobiology, cognitive science, ethics and metaphysics, and Pearson (2002) explores major aspects of Bergson's oeuvre against the backdrop of the reception of Deleuze's oeuvre.

[14] An explicit early conceptualisation of the cinema as time-machine can be found in Robert Paul's plans to develop a unique platform to transport the audiences into a spectrum of a fully immersive time-experience oscillating between the past, the future and the present. Informed by H.G.Wells' novel *The Time-Machine: An Invention* (1895), and a reported exchange with the author, Paul's idea resulted in a patent de-

ther based on an experiential level of a reconstructed, relational subject position.

However, Deleuze applied Bergson's philosophy to film content
from a perspective prior to new film history, that is, before a theorisation of the so-called 'early cinema' underwent its crucial revision in
the late 1970s, 1980s. Although he championed the idea of the spiritual life *(la vie spirituelle)* of cinema, he only marginally touched
upon the dimension on which he explicitly commented in an interview
in *Cahiers du Cinéma* in 1986[15] by describing his initial fascination
with cinema as: "... its unexpected ability to show not only behaviour
but spiritual life as well" (Flaxman 2000: 366). It is, however, an aspect that Deleuze did not emphasise in his Bergsonism and to which
scholars rather rarely direct their attention explicitly.[16] Suzanne Guerlac (2006:179) highlights this in her comment that: "Deleuze had carefully edited out all those features of Bergson's thought that might appear 'metaphysical'", which she regards as pertinent to the context of
structuralism, post-structuralism and the anti-Hegel-project that
Deleuze initially pursued with his revival of Bergson's thinking from
1966 onwards. In the recent reception of Bergson's philosophy, the
implications of his work for a treatment of 'spirit' or consciousness
have been approached with reticence, similar to the way in which
these dimensions remain underexplored in film and cinema studies,
while, as new historicist approaches show, they persist as significant
forces in the way that cinema and related media technologies have
been shaped and perceived. As a consequence there is a general
understanding of a need to return to Bergson's original work, which
the following intends to contribute to by a first-hand re-reading of his
philosophy in the context of the emerging cinema.

Two of Bergson's earliest works, *Essai Sur les Données Immédiates de la Conscience,*[17] 1889 (*Time and Free Will,* 2001) and *Matière
et Mémoire,* 1896 (*Matter and Memory,* 1991), written during the time
of the emerging cinema, established his main thesis regarding his concept of time and space, and the relationship between matter and spirit.

---

scription in 1895, which is referenced in excerpts by Ramsaye (1926: 147-162). See
also Williams (2007).

[15] *Cahiers du Cinema:* Issue 380: 25-32.

[16] See for example Pisters (2006).

[17] This work was part of his doctorial thesis, the second part consisted of a then required Latin thesis, *Quid Aristoteles de loco senserit* (Aristotle's Conception of Place).

Bergson remained committed to his early works while he moved on with his thinking and refined his philosophy within the context of modern science and his political engagement on an international level. He developed his works grounded in a familiarity with innovative theoretical models that challenged existing orthodoxies, which included in his early work innovative scientific research into, for example experimental psychophysiology (Wundt 1874), hysteria and hypnotism (Pierre Janet 1894, 1898, 1903), and the unconscious and psychic conditions (James 1950, 1986; Freud 1891).[18] William James (1842-1910), whose work Bergson appreciated, and which he referred to occasionally,[19] had already made significant interventions into the study of consciousness (preceded by Gustav Theodor Fechner's psychophysiological studies) in the fields of cognitive science, transpersonal psychology (investigations into spiritual and religious experience), and psychical research. James's understanding of consciousness as a stream or flux gained him widespread popularity, and it comes as no surprise that he was outspokenly equally fascinated by Bergson's work, which is sometimes assigned to Bergson's influence on American pragmatism.

As a trained scientist Bergson was familiar with the seismic ruptures in the fields of classical physics whose scientific community got deeply shattered at the end of the 19th century by the so-called second scientific revolution. The first and second law of thermodynamics, which built on Newton's law of causal relations, had previously provided classical physics the foundation of certainty. These were questioned from several sides, when science moved to consider the subatomic level and at more or less the same time began exploring spectral analysis.[20] These theoretical and experimental innovations intro-

---

[18] Bergson is sometimes regarded as having foreshadowed the mapping of the unconscious; he cited among other things Freud's early research into aphasia in *Matter and Memory* (1991: 124).

[19] See for example Bergson (1991: 100). Even though Bergson has expressed certain differences in his own thought in regard to the intellectual work of James, they both expressed in their correspondence up to their first meeting in 1905 their mutual agreement on certain ideas (Guerlac 2006: 28). For a contemporary critical account on James' appropriation of Bergsonism for his anti-intellectualism see Pitkin (1910).

[20] Guerlac (14-41) contextualises Bergson's oeuvre and provides an overview on the scientific innovations around the turn of the century in the chapter 'From Certainties to the Anxieties of Indeterminism'. Some key developments included Boltzmann's mathematical demonstration of entropy in 1872, Lorentz' electron theory of electri-

duced an irrefutable indeterminism into science, not only in regard to what is measurable but also to what actually may be knowable. Some claim that Bergson anticipated the direction modern science would take, in the way his intervention asserted the contemporary view of the relativity of knowledge.[21] Guerlac (2006: 41) is more cautious in expressing Bergson's anticipation and gives a detailed outline of the scientific developments of the time, which, in her words: "... would have enabled him to grasp the direction in which modern physics was heading".[22] What is clear is that Bergson was both profoundly and widely informed and had considerable impact in several disciplines, particularly in the way that he reconceptualised the understanding of time within the discipline of philosophy.

In *Essai Sur les Données Immédiates de la Conscience,* 1889 (*Time and Free Will,* 2001), his doctoral thesis, Bergson has laid out the foundation for his critique of binary oppositions and of the prevailing dualism of subject and object, quality and quantity, matter and spirit through a close analysis of the concepts of time and space, which led to his proclamation of the agency of free will. Whereas in science the investigations into psychical states were still closely entwined with certain phenomena of the occult during the 19th century, this dualism appeared at the root of the barrier that largely excluded the spiritual dimension in the following research context during the 20th century in light of the prevailing scientific positivism. Bergson (2001: 238) instead offered a 'third course', which opened a way to approach the so-called spiritual dimension beyond the polemical approaches to dualism.

---

fied matter in 1892, Röntgen's discovery of X-Ray in 1895, Bequerel's discovery of radiation in 1896, Kelvin's experimental engagement of physics with subatomic particles by 1897, Curie's discovery of radioactive emissions from the newly discovered elements polonium and radium, Planck's theory of energy quanta and the Planck Constant in 1900, and Einstein's discovery of the photon in 1905.

[21] Canales (2005: 1176) reminds us that the issue of relativity was already known since at least 1795 and that it concerned a rediscovery of a knowledge for which Einstein eventually provided the mathematical proof (introduced in his 1905 paper 'On the Electrodynamics of Moving Bodies').

[22] Guerlac (2006: 41) quotes Milič Capek (1971) with a statement that recalls Henri Gouhier's citation at the beginning of this chapter: "... hardly anyone could then guess even remotely the extent of the coming scientific revolution", a vision that: "... loom[ed] on a very distant horizon... only in a few and heretically daring minds. Bergson was one of these".

One of his main premises was that internal conscious states are qualitative, interpenetrating multiplicities, enduring in an unquantifiable time quality and intensity, which he called *durée*. This follows his distinction between time that is quantified and measured in space (thus externalised) and time as duration *(durée)* i.e. that lacks any externality. In Bergson's view there is a great deal at stake in the conflation of these two concepts of time, particularly in relation to the resulting denial or disavowal of free will. Bergson (2001: 229) described this inner *durée* more fully as: "... the continuous evolution of a free person", since he regarded freedom as constituted by a constant interpenetrating process of "becoming" (231), executed in: "... the relation of the concrete self to the act which it performs" (219). According to Bergson, we are able to grasp this "concrete self" by deep introspection (what he later called "intuition"), which happens rather rarely since we are mostly concerned with the outwardly focused self and its social representations. In Bergson's view it is indeed a necessity of the intellect to support the external requirements relating to the 'social self' within space, such as the construction of language, but it is intuition that places the self *in* time through the experience of its own becoming. This act of introspection requires, what Bergson (2001: 233) called, a "strenuous effort of reflection", through which we rest our attention within ourselves. He suggested:

> Hence there are finally two different selves, one of which is, as it were, the external projection of the other, its spatial and, so to speak, social representation. We reach the former by deep introspection, which leads us to grasp our inner states as living things, constantly *becoming*, as states not amenable to measure, which permeate one another and of which the succession in duration has nothing in common with juxtaposition in homogeneous space. (2001: 231 — emphasis in the original)

As a consequence, *durée* for Bergson escapes the paradigms of science and mathematics, and he regarded metaphysics (philosophy) as a necessary parallel component together with science in order to avoid a reductionism to the external, measurable phenomena in space, and to retain a grasp of time as it is lived and experienced internally. From this perspective Bergson addressed in his second major work, *Matière et Mémoire*, 1896 (*Matter and Memory,* 1991) the issues of metaphysics of matter, the psychology of perception and the problem of the relation of consciousness with matter. He established his hypothesis by using clinical data from pathology and psychophysiology, such as memory disorders of aphasia and amnesia. This data constituted a crucial dimension for the development of his thesis through which he critiqued the theory of psychophysiological parallelism, which held that for every psychological fact there was a corresponding physiological fact that strictly determined it. The data that Bergson used from the study of aphasia showed, for example, that language memories were not lost, only the motor-sensor mechanisms to retrieve those memories in speech were broken. Based on these scientific insights, Bergson developed his argument that memory, and consequently the mind, acts upon the body but is not predetermined by it and hence has to be regarded as independent.

Contextual reading into consciousness studies and neuroscience today suggests that the canon of the sciences still proceeds much in the way that Bergson had anticipated with regard to certain tendencies at the end of the 19th century in relation to the complex processes of perception. Already at the time Bergson had observed a tendency to localise sensations and movements in the physiology of the brain rather than treating the issue at its roots, for example to investigate into the question how ideas come about. He maintained that: "… the theory grew more and more complicated, yet without ever being able to grasp the full complexity of reality" (1991: 124). He suggested that the scientific method in this way restricted the range and value of the senses as well as the development of an epistemology that could more fully accommodate the dimension of personal experiences and common sense. What for Bergson (1991) had initially started as an analytical study of the subject of memory, as he commented, ended up as a critique of materialism and idealism by showing, through a hypothetical thesis situated in metaphysics, how matter (the body) and *l'esprit* (the mind) relate to one another through the activity of memory.

In the introduction of *Matter and Memory* (1991) he emphasised that although the subject of the 'spirit' (the mind, the soul) had been treated extensively throughout the history of philosophy, in his view, it had been studied in a very limited manner, if considering it in terms of a psychophysiological relation beyond mere parallelism or epiphenomenalism. Bergson instead established a conceptualisation of 'spirit' beyond epiphenomenalism, theology or philosophical heuristics that needed the faculty of an 'absolute' to sustain their system when it came to the relation between 'matter' and 'mind'.[23] He thereby eliminated the conception of hidden powers, mysteries and epiphenomena from matter (as for example applied in Platonean or neo-Platonean philosophy, or the treatment of consciousness as epiphenomenon in certain approaches within scientific materialism), and established the faculty of 'spirit' *(l'esprit)* as an independent reality. In doing so Bergson (1991: 65) defined memory as the: "... point of contact between consciousness and things, between the body and the spirit". In this way Bergson's philosophy provided a new pathway to bridge the dualism between body and mind, for which he saw the cause in the two extreme conceptions of matter: realism and idealism. According to his view, dualism regarded matter as essentially divisible into separate objects and the states of the mind as rigorously inextensive, while the interaction between the two remained obscure (220). It is important to emphasise that Bergson treated matter in this book merely with regard to the relation between body and mind, and considered it conceptually as being placed: "... before the dissociation which idealism and realism have brought about between its existence and its appearance" (10). In this sense, he situated the appropriate understanding of matter midway between René Descartes' and George Berkeley's conceptions, and critiqued Descartes' understanding of matter as a mathematical, geometrical extensity, and Berkeley's idealist conception of matter as pure idea (10-11). This middle way, according to Bergson, concurs with the understanding that common sense also assigns to it and he continuously, throughout *Matter and Memory*, referred to common sense as an agency that intuitively often seemed to get it right.[24] His strategy brought his theory of perception

---

[23] Not least because of his alliance with evolutionary theory and the extermination of the faculty of 'god' as a superior, transcendent being in his philosophy, Bergson's work had been put on the Index by the Roman Catholic Church following the publication of *L'Évolution Créatrice* in 1907 (*Creative Evolution*, 1998; first published in English as *Creative Evolution* in 1911) (Lawlor and Mulard 2004).

[24] The relevance of common sense to him was something of a virtue, but some of his opponents took this up as an issue, especially that, according to Bergson, every philosophical system should be possible to be expressed in 'ordinary' language. Not surprisingly, his radical approach to matter and his literary style in his philosophy had a great appeal to the general public (his lectures at the *Collège de France* very enormously popular) and made him a cult-figure after the publication of *L'Évolution Créatrice* in 1907.

into harmony with both, common sense — the experience of *l'esprit* (spirit) — and with science, in the way it accommodated the heterogeneity of matter as a whole, and escaped the relativism of idealism and the inexplicable gap between the realist notion of matter and its internal unextended perception.

The particular significance of Bergson's philosophy in the context of this book, can be regarded in the way his insights into the processes of perception and recognition in relation to affect and action, were conceived within a spectrum of innumerable, multiple states of consciousness, or, as he called them, "planes of consciousness" that act upon each other (1991: 241). As we shall see later, this spectrum seems to allow us to enfold a great variety of theoretical perspectives around the issue of the cinema perception, such as approaches to the cinema as illusion, dream- and personality-factory, mirror-phase, the double, the signifier of the imaginary, etc., and provides for a heterogeneous, multiple reading of the cinema experiences in terms of the potentiality that lies within the spectrum of ordinary cognition. Bergson (241) proposed:

> Between the plane of action — the plane in which our body has condensed its past into motor habits — and the plane of pure memory, where our mind retains in all its details the picture of our past life, we believe that we can discover thousands of different planes of consciousness, a thousand integral and yet diverse repetitions of the whole of the experience through which we have lived.

The crucial foundation that Bergson established in his treatment of consciousness is the hypothesis that matter and 'spirit' are independent entities. He regarded the body as a mere instrument of action; in this sense: "… matter is here as elsewhere the vehicle of an action and not the substratum of a knowledge" (74). He posited further that our psychic life is independent from matter but interacts with it in the present moment of perception. Bergson defined 'matter' as an aggregate of *images*[25] that react to each other in the form of movements: *"I call matter the aggregate of images, and* perception of *matter these same images referred to the eventual action of one particular image,*

---

[25] Whenever throughout this book the term 'image' is used in a Bergsonian sense it will be emphasised in Italic.

my body" (22 — emphasis in the original) By *image* Bergson (9-10) understood:

> ... a certain existence which is more than that which the idealist calls a representation, but less than that which the realist calls a thing — an existence placed halfway between the "thing" and the "representation." This conception of matter is simply that of common sense.

Bergson asked the readers to step out of their common frameworks of thinking, which seems notable in a re-reading of his philosophy today, especially with regard to the long history of numerous connotations with the term 'image', from phenomenological, materialist-realist, cognitive to post-structuralist conceptions. Therefore it is necessary to elaborate that the perceived *images* for Bergson did not merely refer to the sense of vision and they were not 'representations' of objects and things, but were formed by states of the mind perceived through the filter of our sensory apparatus —including the senses of touch, sound, smell, taste, etc. For Bergson every reality has a relation with consciousness; to this extent he concurred with idealism, but he critiqued the idealist point of view that all reality is confined to psychic states. He asserted:

> ... positing my body, I posit a certain image, but with it also the aggregate of the other images, since there is no material image which does not owe its qualities, its determinations, in short, its existence, to the place which it occupies in the totality of the universe. My perception can, then, only be some part of these objects themselves; it is in them rather than they in it. (1991: 228-229)

A materialist perspective, which understands objects in the universe reacting to one another in relation to the mere cause of an action — according to Newton's law of cause and effect — executed through physical movement, for Bergson, did not satisfactorily explain the relation of things in the world with consciousness. Through a thought experiment Bergson raised the question that if the body was merely understood as matter, how could it produce new *images* beyond reflecting its own *image* onto the world (which we perceive from within, through affections). By accommodating change and process,

Bergson (25) did not make a distinction between *images* inside or outside of perception: "Every image is within certain images and without others...". He emphasised, however, that the *image* of our body is the only one that can bring forth conscious changes by choice; it is a privileged *image* in this sense. The *image* of the body is like the part of the whole, an *image* amidst all other *images* — hence the internal is part of the external and vice-versa. It is in this sense that Bergson (47) regarded the body as a: "... center of action from which the interesting images appear to be reflected". During the perceptual processes, therefore, other objects are being analysed according to various plausible actions that the body can exercise upon them. He proposed:

> Perception, therefore, consists in detaching, from the totality of objects, the possible action of my body upon them. Perception appears, then, as only a choice. It creates nothing; its office, on the contrary, is to eliminate from the totality of images all those on which I can have no hold, and then from each of those which I retain, all that does not concern the needs of the image which I call my body. (1991: 229)

It follows that what we perceive is determined by the interest of consciousness in regard to the decisions we take to act upon our environment; according to Bergson (40): "What you have to explain, then is not how perception arises, but how it is limited, since it should be the image of the whole, and is in fact reduced to the image of that which interests you". It follows that *images* are limited with regard to the fullness of the objects' materialised existence and inherent qualities. Bergson (229) exemplified: "... if we could assemble all the states of consciousness, past, present and possible, of all conscious beings, we should still only have gathered a very small part of material reality because images outrun perception on every side". In this sense, perception is partial but, according to Bergson (230), does not distinguish the *images* from matter in kind, only in degree:

> My consciousness of matter is then no longer either subjective, as it is for English idealism, or relative, as it is for the Kantian idealism. It is not subjective, for it is in things rather than in me. It is not relative, because the relation between the "phenomenon" and the "thing" is not that of appearance to reality, but merely that of the part to the whole.

Consequently, realism needed a kind of *Deus Ex Machina* to bridge the gap between distinct objects in space and internal states of consciousness without falling pray to determinism or extreme behaviourism. In Bergson's (71) view, however, the brain: "... cannot exercise powers of any kind other than those which we perceive"; it neither creates mental images nor stores them, but merely "... limits them, so as to make them effective" (1935: 315). In this regard, he countered the opinion that perception might arise from or originate in brain states; he claimed: "... its office is to allow communication or to delay it. It adds nothing to what it receives" (1991: 30). He saw the brain as an instrument to analyse movement, and an instrument to select movements that are executed, and also compared it to the gestures of the conductor, which merely mark the motor articulations, but don't produce the music (1920: 74).[26] In a lecture in 1911 Bergson (1920: 9) defined the brain as: "... a crossway, where the nervous impulse arriving by any sensory path can be directed into any motor path". He regarded it therefore as an instrument of action and not one of representation (1991: 74): "... in order that it may set in action a motor mechanism which has been chosen, instead of one which is automatic" (1920: 9), to ensure it executes the most effective action on the object or situation we perceive. By taking the agency of free will into account, Bergson (9) consequently concluded that: "... the brain is an organ of choice" by which he treated invention and freedom in relation to the interconnection between brain and consciousness. He suggested:

> In reality, consciousness does not spring from the brain; but brain and consciousness correspond because equally they measure, the one by the complexity of its structure and the other by the intensity of its awareness, the quantity of choice that the living being has at its disposal. It is precisely because a cerebral state expresses simply what there is of nascent action

---

[26] Bergson referred here clearly to the instrumental enactment of music in terms of the "making". This issue could, however, be opened up further and lead to an interesting discussion as to how Bergson's thinking on duration could moreover be reflected in the act of conducting, in that the instrumental expression is preceded by an intuitive act of "being" or "becoming" the music by the conductor, as it was for example very visually embodied and explicitly expressed in the conducting style of Carlos Kleiber (1930-2004).

in the corresponding psychical state, that the psychical state tells us more than the cerebral state. (1998: 262)

Bergson situated perception amidst the aggregate of *images* where centres of indetermination for possible actions are filtered and selected, according to the interests of the mind-body correlate, that lead to affection of one particular *image*, which our body is subjected to (1991: 64). As a consequence he asserted: "Conscious perception signifies choice, and consciousness mainly consists in this practical discernment" (49). He further proposed that, what he called, "our zones of indetermination" play in some ways the part of a screen (39): "... the brain is an image like others, enveloped in the mass of other images, and it would be absurd that the container should issue from the content" (41).[27] Bergson regarded the body, as we perceive it, as an internal *image*, not any different from all the other (externally perceived) *images*. This is why for him the body cannot function as storage for *images*, since it is a part of these same *images*. The *images* are not *in* the brain, but, according to Bergson (151): "... it is the brain that is in them". He further claimed that the fact that often misleads us to see the brain as a source of *images*, is that the cerebral movements of the brain are synchronous with perception. However, perception is directed by choice and this ultimately determines the correspondence with those brain mechanisms that enable the body to act. Bergson (56) proposed: "The greater the body's power of action (symbolised by a higher degree of complexity in the nervous system), the wider is the field that perception embraces".

In Bergson's (61) view the body reacts according to the sensorimotor power of a certain *image* (our body) that is privileged among other *images* (limiting itself as the centre of the aggregate of *images*) by conceiving affections and performing actions. In this context Bergson (70) critiqued the common notion that sensation is unextended and perception is composed by an aggregate of sensations, through which scientific positivism conceived matter as: "... homoge-

---

[27] It is this concept that informs Deleuze's (1995: 149) frequently discussed notion 'the brain is the screen': "Something that's interested me in cinema is the way the screen can work as a brain...". By returning to Bergson's original suggestions, the cinema can be regarded as a paradigm for the processes of consciousness, which this study has identified in a focus on the spectators' perception as an ontological enquiry, rather than the direction that Deleuze took with his focus on a matrix for an analysis of specific film contents.

neous changes in space, while it contracts perceptions into unextended sensations within consciousness...". He elaborated further:

> Realists and idealists are agreed in this method of reasoning. The latter see in the material universe nothing but a synthesis of subjective and unextended states; the former add that, behind this synthesis, there is an independent reality corresponding to it, but both conclude, from the gradual passage of affection to representation, that our representation of the material universe is relative and subjective and that it has, so to speak, emerged from us, rather than that we have emerged from it. (1991: 54)

As this citation exemplifies, Bergson attempted to bridge the dualism between external and internal states through the notion of extensity — the extension of consciousness placing itself into the things to be perceived. In this activity memories overlap with the process of perception and shift from virtual into actual qualities. He proposed:

> We have said that the material world is made up of objects, or, if you prefer, images, of which all the parts act and react upon each other by movements. And that which constitutes our pure perception, is our dawning action, in so far as it is prefigured in those images. The *actuality* of our perception thus lies in its *activity*, in the movements which prolong it, and not in its greater intensity: the past is only idea, the present is ideo-motor. (1991: 68 — emphasis in the original)

Given that *images* are external to the body (in the sense that the body cannot be considered as storage space for *images*), Bergson continued, they subsist even when the body disappears, and sensations, because they are internal and intrinsically linked with the sensory system vanish together with the existence of the body.[28] In order to distinguish *image* from sensation, for Bergson (1991: 57), perception (hence the *image*) is situated outside the body (in the object to be perceived), and the affection arises within the body, which is "its actual effort upon

---

[28] This conception of consciousness led Bergson (1920: 29-59) to hypothetically assume the survival of consciousness, the mind or the soul after death, as he discussed in a lecture in 1912.

itself". Hence affection consists of interior sensations relating to our body, as he suggested:

> Between the affection felt and the image perceived there is this difference, that the affection is within our body, the image outside our body. And that is why the surface of our body, the common limit of this and of other bodies, is given to us in the form both of sensations and of an image. (1991: 234)

The important step Bergson subsequently took is to affirm that usually perception is always accompanied with affection, since virtual actions overlap with real actions; consequently perception consists of a virtual action of things upon our body and vice versa (232). He explained: "Affection is, then, that part or aspect of the inside of our body which we mix with the image of external bodies; it is what we must first of all subtract from perception to get the image in its purity" (58). Bergson (1991: 233) defined perceptions as our virtual action, as the "cerebral state our action already begun". He asserted that:

> Our sensations are, then to our perceptions that which the real action of our body is to its possible, or virtual, action. Its virtual action concerns other objects and is manifested within those objects; its real action concerns itself, and is manifested within its own substance. (1991: 57)

It is in this sense that Bergson considered a difference in kind, and not in degree, between perception and affection. Sensations for Bergson (235): "... far from being the materials from which the image is wrought, will then appear as the impurity which is introduced into it, being that part of our own body which we project into all others". Therefore affection does not constitute perception, but Bergson saw it rather as the impurity that becomes compounded with perception.

For the sake of analysis, Bergson (75) introduced the concept of "pure perception", which concerns the momentum of perception before memories join up and overlap this immediate perception; it is conceptually a state in which we are placed outside ourselves and touch the reality of the object in an immediate intuition. He defined this "pure perception" as follows:

> By this I mean a perception which exists in theory rather than
> in fact and would be possessed by a being placed where I am,
> living as I live, but absorbed in the present and capable, by giv-
> ing up every form of memory, of obtaining a vision of matter
> both immediate and instantaneous. (1991: 34)

Pure perception for Bergson constitutes the foundation of our perceptual process — it is the grasping of an essential being of things prior
to the attribution of 'accidents' (used in an Aristotelian sense of internalised qualities). Bergson positioned his thinking here against theories that saw perception as mere projections of internal states, and emphasised the partial coincidence of the moment of pure perception in
the object to be perceived as an externalised perceptual process of extended consciousness, while simultaneously memories from the past
impinge on the present moment. He explained: "These two acts, perception and recollection, always interpenetrate each other, are always
exchanging something of their substance as by a process of endosmosis" (67). These two states, according to Bergson, are commonly
mixed up and undifferentiated, regarded as a difference in intensity
and not in kind. Bergson attempted to illuminate this difference by
assigning to pure perception a specific time quality called *durée*. He
proposed:

> Pure perception, in fact, however rapid we suppose it to be, oc-
> cupies a certain depth of duration, so that our successive per-
> ceptions are never the real moments of things, as we have hi-
> therto supposed, but are moments of our consciousness. Theo-
> retically, we said, the part played by consciousness in external
> perception would be to join together, by the continuous thread
> of memory, instantaneous visions of the real. But, in fact, there
> is for us nothing that is instantaneous. In all that goes by that
> name there is already some work of our memory, and conse-
> quently, of our consciousness, which prolongs into each other,
> so as to grasp them in one relatively simple intuition, an end-
> less number of moments of an endlessly divisible time. (1991:
> 69-70)

Memory, according to Bergson, covers up and submerges, replacing
continuously the present moment of perception. For the sake of analysis he corroborated an extreme view on this activity of recollection
when he suggested that:

> Your perception, however instantaneous, consists then in an incalculable multitude of remembered elements; in truth, every perception is already memory. *Practically, we perceive only the past,* the pure present being the invisible progress of the past gnawing into the future. (1991: 150 — emphasis in the original)

Therefore the moment of "pure perception" in which intuitively a present moment, or thing, is grasped by placing ourselves in the very heart of things, is always already supplanted by memories and recollections, driven by utility overruling the perceptions of the present moment. As a consequence, memory constitutes for Bergson the faculty that colours (external) perception with subjective qualities; it forms the "subjective side of the knowledge of things" (34). Hence perception is never "pure", but always overlaps with memory-*images* that root in "pure memory" with the tendency to actualise and materialise in the present moment. Bergson (130) explained:

> Pure memory, as they become actual, tend to bring about, within the body, all the corresponding sensations. But these virtual sensations themselves, in order to become real, must tend to urge the body to action and to impress upon it those movements and attitudes of which they are the habitual antecedent.

"Pure memory", which for Bergson constitutes the deepest layer of our virtual aggregate, has no link with sensations or any interests in the body in the present. Only when it coincides with the interest of the present moment does it turn into a memory-*image* in preparation for possible sensori-motor actions. For Bergson it was most significant to consider that memory does not consist in a regression from the present to the past, but on the contrary, in a progression from the past into the present. The past, in this sense, is a potentiality, which might actualise again and turn recollections into perceptions once more. Bergson (239-240) described this movement as follows:

> We start from a "virtual state" which we lead onwards, step-by-step, through a series of different *planes of consciousness,* up to the goal where it is materialised in an actual perception; that is to say, up to the point where it becomes a present, active

state — up to that extreme plane of our consciousness against
which our body stands out. (Emphasis in the original)

In Bergson's view, the past is no less intense than the present, since
the idea does not derive from a perception, but on the contrary, our
perception derives from our ideas; in this sense: "...the essential process of recognition is not centripetal, but centrifugal" (130). He even
maintained that memory does not emerge from matter, but quite the
contrary, as he proposed: "... matter, as grasped in concrete perception which always occupies a certain duration, is in great part the work
of memory" (182). This radical perspective supported Bergson's criticism of ancient and modern science in that it deprived matter of those
qualities by which we perceive it;[29] in his view, science regarded it as
an "accidental garb of space" (72), and therefore, he posited, it paradoxically created room for connoting it with mystical powers and
'representations of spirit'. The mistake, in his view, lies in the fact that
perception is regarded as being placed within our consciousness, instead of the recognition that perception takes place in the thing we
perceive, hence we perceive 'matter within matter.' By separating the
processes of "pure perception" in the thing we perceive and the continuous flow of memory importing the past into the present moment
(which colours perception with personal attributes), matter can be regarded as independent from spirit (*esprit*). According to Bergson,
'spirit' manifests in its most tangible form as memory (which he also
referred to as the virtual, which is as 'real' as the actualisations of
memories are in the present moment of perception and action).
Bergson (73) maintained: "If, then, spirit is a reality, it is here, in the
phenomenon of memory, that we may come into touch with it experi-
mentally". He summarised:

> We maintain that matter has no occult or unknowable power
> and that it coincides, in essentials, with pure perception. There-
> fore we conclude that the living body in general, and the nerv-
> ous system in particular, are only channels for the transmission
> of movements, which, received in the form of stimulation, are
> transmitted in the form of action, reflex or voluntary. That is to

---

[29] Bergson (1998: 342-343) differentiated modern from ancient science in that it: "...
considers any moment of time whatever, it rests altogether on a substitution of time-
length for time-invention", while for the ancients, time was theoretically negligible.

say, it is vain to attribute to the cerebral substance the property of engendering representations. Now the phenomena of memory, in which we believe that we can grasp spirit in its most tangible form, are precisely those of which a superficial psychology is most ready to find the origin in cerebral activity alone; just because they are at the point of contact between consciousness and matter, and because even the adversaries of materialism have no objection to treating the brain as a storehouse of memories. (1991: 73-74)

This distinction that Bergson made between the personal interior perceptive processes relating to memory and the notion of a pure perception at the foundation of our relationship with the external world, constitutes the threshold where matter and spirit meet: "It is in very truth within matter that pure perception places us, and it is really into spirit that we penetrate by means of memory" (180). He suggested further:

Essentially fugitive, they [personal recollections, pure memory] become materialised only by chance, either when an accidentally precise determination of our bodily attitude attracts them or when the very indetermination of that attitude leaves a clear field to the caprices of their manifestation. (1991: 106 — Insert by the author)

In his argument against the misconception that the brain acts as a 'container' of images, of memory,[30] Bergson saw the origin for this misunderstanding in a confusion of two kinds of memory — one of his widely recognised crucial contributions to psychophysiological studies: on the one hand "pure memory" that constitutes an independent faculty (not locally defined) comprising all details of our psychical

---

[30] When it comes to the question of where pure memory should be localised, Bergson (1991: 129-130) suggested: "The centers of images, if these exist, can only be the organs that are exactly symmetrical with the organs of the senses in reference to the sensory centers. They are no more the depositories of pure memories, that is, of virtual objects, than the organs of the senses are depositories of real objects". He concluded: "Hence the only one plausible hypothesis remains, namely, that this region occupies with regard to the center of hearing itself the place that is exactly symmetrical with the organ of sense. It is, in this case, a mental ear" (129). This recalls philosophical and metaphyscial systems of thought that account for an 'ethereal body' as a double layer integrated with the physical body, which relates to similar conceptions in alternative medicine and spiritual practices. See for example the elaborations on the ethereal body by Leadbeater (1920).

life qualified by intensities, and on the other hand "body-memory", constituted by the body's motor mechanisms and habits (152). According to Bergson, body-memory is determined by utility, which is understood as an instantaneous action, while, in contrast, pure memory constitutes conscious states by an association with explicit memory-*images* (88-95). He suggested: "… it is from the present that the appeal to which memory responds comes, and it is from the sensorimotor elements of the present action that a memory borrows the warmth which gives it life" (153). Through a rupture between incoming impression and a defined movement, the memory-*images* most similar to this stimulus slip in and allow recollection and recognition by adapting themselves to the present situation for which the sensorimotor movements have prepared. If this action is performed consciously through attention, which Bergson (102) described as the "power of analysis", an effort is needed in order to go backwards by selective memory retrieval (recollection), while the movement of perception is driving us continuously into the future (95). He proposed: "Memory thus creates anew the present perception, or rather it doubles this perception by reflecting upon it either its own image or some other memory-image of the same kind" (101). This, Bergson suggested, can happen to the extent that perception and memory are no longer distinguishable, especially when the memory-*images* follow the movements of the body (106).[31] He explained:

> The progress by which the virtual image realises itself is nothing else than the series of stages by which this image gradually obtains from the body useful actions or useful attitudes. The stimulation of the so-called sensory centers is the last of these stages: it is the prelude to a motor reaction, the beginning of an action in space. In other words, the virtual image evolves toward the virtual sensation and the virtual sensation toward real movement… (1991: 131)

In Bergson's view, the virtual — understood as the realm of *l'esprit* in the context of his study of memory referring to the so-called 'past' — tends to reconquer the influence it has lost by actualising itself in the

---

[31] Bergson (1991: 103) cited in this regard the studies by Münsterberg (Beiträge zur Experimentellen Psychologie, vol. IV) and Külpe (Grundriss der Psychologie, Leipzig 1893).

present (131). He suggested further: "Consciousness, then, illumines, at each moment of time, that immediate part of the past which, impending over the future, seeks to realise and to associate with it" (150). Bergson referred to this process of recollection as a continuous recirculation of memory-*images* in order to strengthen, enrich and complement perception with ever-greater details, a constant process of recreation and reconstruction. He maintained that:

> ... every *attentive* perception truly involves a *reflection*, in the etymological sense of the word, that is to say the projection, outside ourselves, of an actively created image, identical with, or similar to, the object on which it comes to mold itself. [...] ... reflective perception is a *circuit*, in which all the elements, including the perceived object itself, hold each other in a state of mutual tension as in an electric circuit, so that no disturbance starting from the object can stop on its way and remain in the depths of the mind: it must always find its way back to the object from where it proceeds. (1991: 102-104 — emphasis in the original)

The selection of memory-*images*, according to Bergson, is facilitated by two movements: one by rotation upon itself, revealing the closest recognition of contiguity or similarity in the pure memory; the other, more disposed towards the immediate response of action, through which the memory-*image* is translated into the present situation (169). Memory in Bergson's view is not organised as a series of atoms side by side, but it constitutes a whole in which some memories may be dominant through their intensity. It follows that it is not our memory that is selective in terms of dissociation, but our processes of reflection and recollection are selective instead, in that only those parts of the whole of memory are chosen that are characterised by usefulness and contiguity with the present situation. In the way Bergson described the processes of recollection, this whole of pure memory appears like a living entity, not like a database with categorical, fixed segments. It is rather seen like a kind of 'breathing' entity[32] that expands and contracts continuously reacting to the needs of the present moment. He suggested:

---

[32] See also the definition of 'spirit' as 'breath' at the beginning of this chapter.

> The work of localisation consists, in reality, in a growing effort
> of expansion, by which the memory, always present in its en-
> tirety to itself, spreads out its recollections over an ever wider
> surface and so ends by distinguishing, in what was till then a
> confused mass, the remembrance which could not find its
> proper place. (1991: 171)

One of the important conclusions that Bergson drew from his study of memory suggests that our memory is always complete and whole, consisting of all details of our previously lived experiences. These deep-seated, privileged *images* of affections define our personality; hence our character, so Bergson (146) proposed, is the actual synthesis of all our past states: "In this epitomised form our previous psychical life exists for us even more than the external world, of which we never perceive more than a very small part, whereas, on the contrary, we use the whole of our lived experience".

At this point in Bergson's analysis it becomes evident that the factor 'time' is most crucial for the way consciousness interacts with matter. In his view, perception occupies a certain duration, however short it may seem, and involves: "… an effort of memory which prolongs, one into another, a plurality of moments" (34). Bergson further reminded us that what we actually perceive is infinitely more than we are able to consciously conceive, however, even the: "…"subjectivity" of sensible qualities consists above all else in a kind of contraction of the real, effected by our memory" (34). He concluded:

> The qualitative heterogeneity of our successive perceptions of
> the universe results from the fact that each, in itself, extends
> over a certain depth of duration and that memory condenses in
> each an enormous multiplicity of vibrations which appear to us
> all at once. (1991: 70)

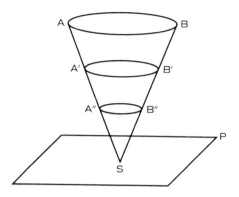

With the diagram of the inverted cone (above), Bergson indicated a schematic illustration for the purpose of analysis of the two constant movements of mental life; between the present moment (S) where we focus our attention to the action to be undertaken — indicating the present perception of our body, which he also called "sensori-motor equilibrium" (161) — and the other extreme the unconscious past of pure memory, the totality of recollections (in the schematic the plane A, B). According to Bergson, these mental states — pure memory — have affinity to one another, as all *images* do. In this way they are attracted, through either continuity or resemblance, to the present moment of perception in order to facilitate the proceeding action. In this process — which he also referred to as "becoming" — from the base A and B memory-*images* are drawn in various intensities and through various layers of consciousness (A', B', A'', B''). This happens the more we allow our attention to dwell momentarily beyond the focus in the present moment (point S). Bergson described our mental life as a continuous fluctuation between the actual moment of the present (S) and the totality of memory (A, B), through which uncountable variations and repetitions of our virtual lives were possible (161ff). If we attempt to trace a general idea, as Bergson (162) suggested, we need to recognise this double current: "… which goes from the one to the other — always ready either to crystallize into uttered words or to evaporate into memories".

On the one extreme Bergson schematised the "man of instinct", an automaton mainly acting according to sensori-motor schemata in the present moment, and on the other extreme the "dreamer", for whom recollections emerge with no advantage in the present situation. In his view: "… the mind travels unceasingly over the interval comprised between its two extreme limits, the plane of action and the plane of dream" (172). When an equilibrium is reached between these two extreme positions — Bergson (153) spoke about "good sense", "practical sense" — which concerns the: "… happy disposition of memory docile enough to follow with precision all the outlines of the present situation, but energetic enough to resist all other appeal". The sensori-motor states in Bergson's view constitute intelligently constructed mechanisms, so-called "body memory" (152); they delineate the present direction of memory and, in this sense, form the acting and actual extremities of our memories (168). Memory-*images* are continually forcing themselves into the present in order to modulate habit, and, especially when directed by free will and choice, a greater variety of past experiences can shape every idea in the actualisation of our becoming. Of course in reality, as he added, there is never a "purely sensori-motor state" or "imaginative life without some slight activity beneath" it (168). In this way the cone and his analysis, as he made explicit, are merely schematic tools to separate what normally appears indistinguishable, which indicate signposts for Bergson's process-related philosophy. Bergson (241) summarised this oscillating movement of our mind as follows:

> Between the plane of action — the plane in which our body has condensed its past into motor habits — and the plane of pure memory, where our mind retains in all its details the picture of our past life, we believe that we can discover thousands of different planes of consciousness, a thousand integral and yet diverse repetitions of the whole of the experience through which we have lived. To complete a recollection by more personal detail does not at all consist in mechanically juxtaposing other recollections to this, but in transporting ourselves to a wider plane of consciousness, in going away from action in the direction of dream.

These "planes of consciousness", according to Bergson (242), exist virtually: "… with that existence which is proper to things of the spirit". We can conclude from this review, that for Bergson, a spiritual dimension is then active, when we creatively interact and act upon the world involving as many "planes of consciousness" as possible within a healthy equilibrium of sensori-motor activity, the very creative process of becoming. He asserted that:

> ... to touch the reality of spirit we must place ourselves at the point where an individual consciousness, continuing and retaining the past in a present enriched by it, thus escapes the law of necessity, the law which ordains that the past shall ever follow itself in a present which merely repeats it in another form and that all things shall ever be flowing away. We then pass from pure perception to memory, we definitely abandon matter for spirit. (1991: 235)

Bergson referred to this very action as a manifestation of a difference, an expression of free will within our sensori-motor driven actions, which consequently supersedes the mere motor mechanisms or habitual body-memories. The spiritual dimension in his view lies in the domain of pure memory, in those virtual psychic states that can actualise any moment in the present in ever new forms and modulations. For Bergson (1991: 240) this virtual, consisting of pure memory, is a spiritual manifestation: "With memory we are, in truth, in the domain of spirit". This most tangible constituent of *l'esprit* (mind, or soul) — the whole of our lived experience — has a greater intensity than the parts we perceive from the external world that never remain in their purity since our psychic states continuously overlap with them. In these two distinct yet converging processes of consciousness, the links that are being established with memory-*images,* are not as close and stable as those we establish with material objects in our perception. Yet the content of the past, our memories, when actualised in the present moment, reveals its full potential, whereas in our perception of external objects, Bergson (147) suggested that:

> ... it is the connection which is perfect, since these objects obey necessary laws; but the other condition, presentation in consciousness, is never more than partially fulfilled, for the material object, just because of the multitude of unperceived elements by which it is linked with all other objects, appears to enfold within itself and to hide behind it infinitely more than it allows to be seen. We ought to say, then, that existence, in the

empirical sense of the word, always implies conscious appre-
hension and regular connection; both at the same time, although in different degrees.

By including Bergson's notion of the *élan vital,* as developed in his
Creative Evolution (1998), it follows that memory-*images* are not
fixed or motionless but constantly push into the future and manifest in
the present moment with their potential of intensity — hence to engage with the virtual in a Bergsonian sense is not a dwelling in the
past, but rather an actualising of our becoming by making the past
useful and work in the here and now. This present is a concrete, lived
'real' in which the body serves as an instrument of action, and it necessarily occupies a certain duration of time. It is characterised by
sensation and movement directed towards the future, what Bergson
(1991: 138) called the: "... actual state of my becoming, that part of
my duration which is in process of growth". The brain, as our body,
always only occupies the duration of the present moment, while our
psychological states endure.[33] The present, in this sense, is not "that
which is", but: "... that which is being made" (150).

The degree to which an existence in Bergson's view can be called
'spiritual' is related to the intensity by which we allow an ever richer
and fuller access of our psychic life to connect with the present moment of interaction within the world, which in itself is composed of
the same virtual forces as our bodies. He described this motion as a:
"... more or less high degree of tension in consciousness, which goes
to fetch pure recollections in pure memory in order to materialise
them progressively by contact with the present perception" (238). In
other words; it depends on our degree of choice and creative activity
of our will, as well as on the extent of our awareness by which we enable our experiences to grasp the needs of the present moment beyond
the mere needs of the body, which include affections and sensations.[34]
Bergson (1998: 301-302) suggested:

---

[33] Here it becomes clear what problem the attempt to localise the 'containing' of the
virtual poses, in that it imposes a spatial quality to purely psychological states, which
for Bergson only endure as a non-measurable time quality.

[34] At this point altruism could be situated in Bergson's approach to perception, which
he elaborated in *The Two Sources of Morality and Religion* (1935), see for example
on pages 36-37.

> A man is so much the more a 'man of action' as he can em-
> brace in a glance a greater number of events: he who perceives
> successive events one by one will allow himself to be led by
> them; he who grasps them as a whole will dominate them.

The 'spiritual' dimension in Bergson is consequently not simply
determined by the realm of the 'virtual', but constituted by its actualisation through embodied action in the present and by its degree of
creative potential which sets out to mould matter. Spirituality, in this
sense, is characterised by action and by choice. One of the more advanced developments that Bergson saw in the process of evolution, is,
for example, the ability to wait before reacting, of: "... putting the
excitation received into relation with an ever richer variety of motor
mechanisms" (1991: 222). It follows that for Bergson (222), the nervous system is:

> ... only the symbol of the inner energy which allows the being
> to free itself from the rhythm of the flow of things and to retain
> in an ever higher degree the past in order to influence ever
> more deeply the future — the symbol, in the special sense
> which we give to the work, of its memory. Thus between brute
> matter and the mind most capable of reflection there are all
> possible intensities of memory or, what comes to the same
> thing, all the degrees of freedom.

In Bergson's view, more generally speaking then, any vital organism
endures. Matter is not inert but part of an undivided whole, and life is
considered as a flux rather than a succession of instances (1998: 186).
What has mostly been overlooked, according to Bergson (1991: 248)
— and here lies one of his most original interventions — is the "growing and accompanying tension of consciousness in time". He suggested:

> Not only by its memory of former experience, does this con-
> sciousness retain the past better and better, so as to organise it
> with the present in a newer and richer decision; but, living with
> an intenser life, contracting, by its memory of the immediate
> experience, a growing number of external moments in its pres-
> ent duration, it becomes more capable of creating acts of which
> the inner indetermination, spread over as large a multiplicity of

the moments of matter as you please, will pass the more easily through the meshes of necessity. (1991: 238-239)

This citation most explicitly shows how spirit can manifest through a conscious engagement with matter by allowing memory-*images* to pass through the restraints of necessities in order to achieve a fuller perception and interaction beyond a mere automatic response in the requirements of the body preparing to act. In Bergson's (180) elaboration on the function of the body in the life of the spirit, he proposed that: "It is in very truth within matter that pure perception places us, and it is really into spirit that we penetrate by means of memory".[35] According to Bergson (220), spirit can:

> ... rest upon matter and, consequently, unite with it in the act of pure perception, yet nevertheless be radically distinct from it. It is distinct from matter in that it is, even then, memory, that is to say, a synthesis of past and present with a view to the future, in that it contracts the moments of this matter in order to use them and to manifest itself by actions which are the final aim of its union with the body.

Bergson's view on perception insists that it remains always partial in the way that it captures matter through the sensory apparatus, a condition to which his philosophy offers a pathway by which a fuller *image* can be perceived through an introspective movement of the intellect; a process that he called "intuition". Intuition for Bergson is the gesture of the intellect, an immediate grasping of pure perceptions (multiple moments of duration), as a reflection of "mind" upon itself — an endosmosis or reciprocal penetration of minds. It is that through which we enter into contact with others within our selves. This thrust contracts a wide range of memory-*images* into the present moment of perception and recollection, in preparation for an outgoing action, and in its extension of consciousness constitutes the perception of pure movement. In this way intuition reinforces the influence of spirit on our action upon matter, as Bergson (228) said:

---

[35] John Durham Peters (1999: 22), who called the profound irreducible qualities of communication 'touch' and 'time', seems to have tapped into a Bergsonian approach of perception in the way he attempted to dismantle spiritist connections with technology from their mysticism and invested matter with subjectivity in order to identify a middle position "... with a pragmatism open to both the uncanny and the practical".

> By allowing us to grasp in a single intuition multiple moments
> of duration, it frees us from the movement of the flow of
> things, that is to say, from the rhythm of necessity. The more of
> these moments memory can contract into one, the firmer is the
> hold which it gives to us on matter: so the memory of a living
> being appears indeed to measure, above all, its powers of ac-
> tion upon things and to be only the intellectual reverberation of
> this power.

The more sophisticated these processes are developed in a conscious
being, the more differentiation in this function and the more complex
the nervous system and its sensori-motor path: for Bergson (221), a:
"... growing intensity of life, corresponds to a higher tension of duration and is made manifest externally by a greater development of the
sensori-motor system". Hence the spiritual dimension is expressed by
the degree to which an action is being fed by memory-*images* steered
by conscious choice and the liberty the will takes in these processes.
Bergson understood this as a domain that rests on experience and activity, and, in this sense, transforms Kardec's definition of 'spiritualism', cited at the beginning of this chapter, by replacing the reference to 'belief' with experience.

From this brief exposition it should become obvious how the relevance of Bergson's thinking extends into many disciplines and areas
even of contemporary research. The increasing return to his work and
commentaries along with a renewed interest in the issues of the spiritual and consciousness is timely in the light of a burgeoning relativism
and a lurking biological determinism in both the Sciences and Humanities, which already was reflected in contemporary developments
in the Sciences at the turn of the 19th century.

Chapter 2

The Analysis and Synthesis of Movement in Relation to Time: Revisiting Étienne-Jules Marey's Work in a Virtual Dialogue with the Philosophy of Henri Bergson

Étienne-Jules Marey's (1830-1904) oeuvre and writings, in particular his challenge to instrumental realism, reveal his pioneering and innovative engagement with the thresholds of the unknown in a convergence between, what today would be distinguished as, science, technology and the arts. His work, seen in a more profound dimensionality in this complexity of vectors, can be regarded as a paradigm that provides insight into a constituent part of the critical mass from which the cinema emerged. However, the way the cinema finally took shape had no direct relevance to his work except for the major impact of some of his acclaimed technological innovations that became incorporated in most commercialised recording and projection devices of the time. Marey was not an exceptional case in this regard, as many scientists' intentions in respect of their innovative technologies did not always match with the way their inventions were perceived and reinterpreted. This was especially the case in the context of the early technological innovations from which the cinema emerged, as Michael Punt (2000: 147) reminds us:

> ... not only did many of them [scientists, entrepreneurs, etc.] use moving pictures to represent different mental models, but they also functioned publicly in a prevailing cult of personality which placed a burden of representation on their patents that had little to do with making pictures move. (Insert by the author)

This chapter looks at some of the philosophical implications of Marey's work in relation to the widespread, contemporary interest in

the sciences and the arts in the study of locomotion and force in relation to the representability and inscription of movement through time.[1]
Marey's background in engineering at the *École Polytechnique* in
Paris and a degree in medicine, which he received from the *Faculté de
Médecine de Paris* in 1859, provided him with a unique interdisciplinary framework for his scientific and technological innovations in the
emerging discipline of physiology.[2] When he established himself as a
physiologiste en chambre,[3] his innovative graphical recording devices
and technophile methods for the scientific study of diverse forms of
movement in the vital functions, initially aroused suspicion in the field
of physiology. The famous physiologist Claude Bernard, the authority
in the discipline in France, was at first highly critical of Marey's dependence on and fidelity to instrumentation and considered him a con-

---

[1] The following sections on Marey are selective and draw foremost on his own account of his scientific research into movement in the context of the contemporary
technological developments (around the 1880s and 1890s) in his 1894 publication *Le
Mouvement* (*Movement*, 1895). The wider context builds on Marta Braun's research
on Marey (2006, 1992, 1983), which is taken up as the most extensive source, particularly since it includes many first-hand archival references, as well as Rabinbach's
(1990) insightful recovery of Marey's work in the context of French scientific studies
of the body in its energetic, ergonomic capacities. Some crucial aspects are also
drawn from Font-Réaulx's (et al.), not yet translated into English, *E.J. Marey: Actes
du Colloque du Centenaire* (2006), published for the centenary of Marey's death following an exhibition by the Musée d'Orsay and the Cinématèque Française, which
comprises a DVD with 400 chronophotographic sequences.

[2] Marey completed a thesis on the dicrotic pulse, entitled *Recherches sur la circulation du sang à l'état sain et dans les maladies* (Research on blood circulation in the
physiological state and in diseases) which followed on his discovery of the influence
of vascular elasticity on the circulation of blood. For Marey's medical background see
Braun (1992), Debru (2004), Rabinbach (1990). Braun emphasises the perfect convergence of Marey's mechanical gifts and engineering skills in the field of cardiology
where his command on mechanical principles such as hydraulics and hydrodynamics
provided an invaluable application. (1992: 3; for Marey's graphic methods see 8-41)
Rabinbach (1990: 88) points to the shift in French medicine in the 1850's from an
empirical medicine founded on clinical observation to collaborations between clinical
practice and experimental biology and physiology.

[3] After his doctorate Marey first worked in his private laboratory and later on in the
laboratories of the *Collège de France,* however, mostly restricted to an indoor space,
which made certain set-ups for his movement studies very difficult. It was only later
from 1881 onward that Marey was granted funding from the City of Paris for a *Station Physiologique* in the outskirts of Paris. Rabinbach (89) contextualises the slow
introduction of the German model of independent physiological laboratories in France
and refers to Marey's own commentaries on the inadequate technical support in
France in contrast to the German "riches of instruments".

tentious figure.[4] This characterised a wider dispute that throughout the 1860s and 1870s exemplified the struggle in science between the vitalists and the rationalism of the mechanists; however, Marey distanced himself from the vitalist doctrines and incorporated the study of energy and force within a positivist framework (Braun 1992: 37-38; Rabinbach 1990: 91).

Drawing on the new German school of physiology pioneered by the physicist and physiologist Hermann von Helmholtz, Marey converged insights from older medical traditions and their study of the ether, magnetism[5] or electricity[6] as fundamental forces in both the animal and human body. He combined these with a visionary integration of novel technological innovations (to which he contributed substantially) into the scientific research practice. This is evident in the way he merged complex systems and dynamics, combining the measurement of invisible movements within the body, such as contractions, rhythms, pulses and forces (of the heart, muscles, blood flow, etc.), and his specialisation in the recording and measurements of forces at work in their execution, such as the shift in gravity, forces of pressure, mass, in different body parts within a framework of a Lamarckian anatomical adaptation.[7] His unique approach reflects the shift in the

---

[4] Rabinbach (91) reports how still in the mid 1860s, Bernard argued in an official government-sponsored report against the convergence between the studies of the physicist and the physiologist, and insisted on a separation of organic and inorganic nature in scientific studies.

[5] See for example the measurements of electro-magnetic forces by Michael Faraday and also the application of electro-magnetism, so-called *animal magnetism,* by the physician Franz Anton Mesmer in his medical practice through telepathic healing methods (popularly referred to as *mesmerism)* (Inglis 1992: 141-151).

[6] David Nye (1990: 153) reminds us how the very nature of electricity and its ephemeral and ambiguous characteristics led to speculation and confusion. In this respect he elaborates on examples of electrotherapeutic devices such as McLaughlin's electric belt and Dr. Scott's electric corset. Iwan Rhys Morus (1998) provides a historical overview on electrical science in England and also points to the homology between the electric telegraph (and electricity in general) and the nervous system. In this regard Jonathan Crary (1990: 93), who discusses the shifts from 18th to 19th century epistemologies on the sensory processes of the body with regard to vision, refers to Helmholtz' comparison of the functionality of nerves with telegraph wires.

[7] Marey made this convergence explicit for example in the article *Des Lois de la Mécanique en Biologie* (1886), with particular emphasis on the interconnection between thermo-dynamic and electro-dynamic occurrences in muscles in mechanistic body function during physical labour with reference to thermometrical and calorimetrical studies.

scientific pursuit in the study of life-forces from a vitalist consideration of fluids and chemistry in the 18th century to mechanics and physics in light of the thermodynamic principles in the 19th century. These developments led to a consideration of the body as a thermodynamic machine, following the significant contribution by Helmholtz with his elaboration on the universal law of the conservation of energy in 1847.[8]

During Marey's career from the mid 19th century onwards, especially in the discipline of physiology, the focus in the scientific canon lay on mechanistic occurrences in the body (the optical apparatus of the human eye, the electrical apparatus of the nervous system, and the rhythmic apparatus of the heart pumping the bloodstream, etc.).[9] This focus led in the following to a great variety of mechanistic extensions and apparatuses for technological measurement. The previous metaphor of the body as a machine in terms of a clockwork changed into that of a motor, which was modelled on the steam engine, or electric powered technology (Rabinbach 1990: 66). Founded on the research by Helmholtz, the perceiving subject was understood as: "… a neutral conduit, one kind of relay among others allowing optimum conditions of circulation and exchangeability, whether it be of commodities, energy, capital, images, or information" (Crary 1990: 94). According to Crary, these developments reinforced new forms of control and standardisation, which was especially evident in Marey's ambition to establish a uniformity of instrumentation within the discipline of, what he called, "dynamic" physiology (Rabinbach 1990: 97).[10]

Against the background of this understanding of the body as a physiochemical apparatus — a convergence between matter and en-

---

[8] For an extensive overview on these developments in central Europe from a broad perspective on scientific, philosophical, social and cultural developments see Rabinbach (1990).

[9] This conception is still present in one of Marey's early publications in 1874 entitled 'Animal Mechanism', a title that is reminiscent of Franz Anton Mesmer's term 'Animal magnetism', by which Mesmer understood a kind of universal magnetism both referring to physical attraction (gravity) and social attraction (love), and which differed from physical magnetism in its reference to the Latin term *animus* or spirit (Peters 1999: 90).

[10] As Crary (1990: 81) points out, the collective achievement of European physiology in the first half of the 19th century produced a knowledge base that served: "…the formation of an individual adequate to the productive requirements of economic modernity and for emerging technologies of control and subjection". See also Braun (1992: 224).

ergy, which followed laws that could be explained by science — Marey emerged as a pioneer in a young discipline[11] and positioned himself from the initial fringes to what was later established as the canon of physiology. As Rabinbach (90) reminds us, Marey was among the first physiologists in France who used the new metaphor for the body as thermodynamic machine in his redefinition of the life sciences through technological, engineering solutions. His rigour, dedication, inventive spirit and significant scientific interventions, earned him the 'Chair of Natural History of Organized Bodies' at the *Collège de France* in 1869,[12] he became director of Duruy's experimental physiology laboratory at the *École Pratique des Hautes Études* and was admitted to the *Académie de Médecine* in 1872. By that time he was a key figure and established scientist in the intellectual context of French academia and had befriended key scientific innovators of the time, such as Gabriel Jonas Lippmann,[13] the electro-physiologist Jacques-Arsène d'Arsonval, Pierre and Marie Curie, and the Lumières (who provided his *Station Physiologique* with photographic plates).

Marey regarded movement as the effect of those forces that constituted the primary functions of life and, in this sense, his interest can primarily be located in the relationship between duration and energy expenditure of the body's economy, which concerned those forces that drove movement. He considered the discipline of physiology as intrinsically linked to all other sciences in relation to both their methods and laws, with a particular extension to the fringes of the so-called natural sciences. In his contribution on the 'Natural History of Organized Bodies' for the *Annual Report of the Board of Regents of the Smithsonian Institution for 1867, 1868,* Marey emphasised how the new scientific methods advanced the study of natural forms to the very principles of life: "The naturalist who is not content with observing the forms, however varied, of organization in animals and plants, must proceed like the physicist and chemist, if he desires to discover

---

[11] Crary (79) reminds us that between 1820 and 1840 physiology: "... had then no formal institutional identity and came into being as the accumulated work of disconnected individuals from diverse branches of learning".

[12] Marey was successor to the eminent neurophysiologist Pierre Flourens (Rabinbach 1990: 89).

[13] Marey (1895: 49) referred to Lippmann as his colleague and friend from whom he took over the Electrometer in 1877 to connect it to a photographic camera in order to study slightest electrical variation in living tissues.

the conditions of life" (Braun 1992: 15).[14] He later noted the interdisciplinary scope of his work in the preface of *Movement* (1895), in which he addressed its particular value (especially that of chronophotography) for a broad constituency, such as geometricians, hydraulic engineers, naval and military men as well as artists and naturalists:

> It is more especially to this latter class that we dedicate our work, since it appeals to their particular ambition, namely that of discovering among the phenomena of life something that has hitherto escaped the most attentive observation. (Marey 1895: viii)

In this spirit Marey was convinced that technology offered a more perfect and capable extension of the sensory system, which led him to postulate the superiority of 'technological perception' over human observation. Through his technophilia he concurred with contemporary studies concerning the limits of human vision and sensory perception that were recognised as being subject to error and deception. He believed that technology would be able to equip humans with a more advanced eye and sensors in order to enable a more detailed and quicker perception of *kinema* (Greek for 'movement'). Marey proposed in *Méthode Graphique* (1878):

> Not only are these instruments sometimes destined to replace the observer, and in such circumstances to carry out their role with an incontestable superiority, but they also have their own domain where nothing can replace them. When the eye ceases to see, the ear to hear, touch to feel, or indeed when our senses give deceptive appearances, these instruments are like new senses of astonishing precision. (Braun 1992: 40)[15]

---

[14] Rabinbach (1990: 65) mentions a letter by the physiologist Carl Friedrich Wilhelm Ludwig from 1848 to Du Bois-Reymond where he asserts that physiology "had to be founded on the physics and chemistry of the organism".

[15] In this context it could be said that from a conceptual point of view of technology as extension of the body, Marey anticipated Vertov's kino-eye and kino-ear as expressed by the *kinoki* movement in the 1920s. For a related discussion on experimental films with regard to Marey's oeuvre, see Nicole Brenez (2006: 121-138).

In his response to this imperative Marey deployed technological mechanisms for observation and for the analysis of movement, as well as devices for movement synthesis which replicated the phenomena under investigation, for example artificial mechanisms (organs such as hearts and lungs), or ornithopters: mechanical insects and birds (22).[16] Key in his application of the laws of the conservation of energy was his particular understanding of motion not only in terms of the amount of energy used, but in terms of its deployment in time and space. Marey's occupation with the analysis of movement especially within the body (such as muscles and organs) and those of great speed (such as the wing's movements of birds or insects) required the recording of very small time intervals of movements often invisible to the observer. The method of chronography, from the Greek *chronos* ('time') and *grapho* ('I write'), as it has been applied earlier in 18th century meteorology, demography or the social sciences, provided him the basis for numerous innovative graphing instruments. He addressed the issue of time measurement and the shift from mathematical statistics to geometry in graphing methods for recording purposes in the preface to his publication *Le Mouvement* in 1894 (*Movement,* 1895):

> Laborious statistics have been replaced by diagrams in which the variations of a curve express in a most striking manner the several phases of a patiently observed phenomenon, and, further, a recording apparatus which works automatically can trace the curve of a physical or physiological event, which by reason of its slowness, its feebleness, or its rapidity, is otherwise inaccessible to observation. (1895: vii)

Coextensive with the contemporary interest of science in the so-called 'infinitely small',[17] Marey constantly pushed the boundaries of the

---

[16] From Greek *ornithos* ('bird') and *pteron* ('wing'): they were complex apparatus comprising wings, drums, levers, flexible sails, air pumps, etc. For illustrations see Braun (1992: 33-34, 36, 38). Marey's studies of the flight of birds and insects, as well as the dynamics of air movements, had a major impact on research into aerodynamics. This led to his function as vice-president of the *Société de Navigation Aérienne* in 1874 and is reported to have inspired the Wright brothers in their aeronautic investigations (51, 222). In 1879 Marey advised his assistant Tatin — who took over the aeronautic research — to construct a model aircraft, which they tested at the military aerostation at Chalais-Meudon (Braun 1992: 50).

[17] This constituted a threshold that during the 19th century was increasingly approached through optical technologies such as microscopy, micro-chronophotography

recordability of the invisible. In his movement analysis he faced a particular challenge, especially when it was difficult to establish physical contact between the subject and the graphical recording device, as, for example, in the studies of flight of birds or insects. From this perspective it could be said that it was inevitable that he would eventually apply optical and photographic techniques in his work — a circumstance that occurred in his mid-career (around the 1880s) — as soon as they were considered sophisticated enough to be applied to the scientific study of movement.[18] In this respect the instantaneous photographs by the British photographer Eadweard James Muybridge, famous for the depiction of the gait of the horse, attracted his attention in a publication in *La Nature* from 14 December 1878.[19] Marey's commission to Muybridge to develop a photographic rifle based on Janssen's Photographic Revolver failed (Braun 1992: 43ff, 53), as Marey considered the obtained images as not accurate enough for his scientific studies, nor could he use the apparatus developed for Stanford, which triggered the sensors through the horse's movement, for his studies of birds in flight (Marey 1895:108-110). As a consequence,

---

and later microcinematography, which Marey (1895: 291-303) also applied in his 'microscopic chronophotography'.

[18] Fox Talbot claimed in 1844 that he could photograph galloping horses and birds in flight, which shows that even at a time when the exposure time did not allow for any movement capture without blurring the image, the vision of photographing movement had been pursued from the very beginnings (Chanan 1980: 70). Notwithstanding, it is generally acknowledged that it was Muybridge's development of extremely fast shutter speeds — from $1/1,000^{th}$ (Chanan 1980: 72), $1/2,000^{th}$ (Mannoni 2000: 309) to $1/5,000^{th}$ of a second (Larsen 1947: 20) — with an electrically controlled release mechanism developed by John D. Isaac (Ramsaye 1926: 36ff), which made his photographs internationally famous especially in the scientific community following various publications from 1878 onwards. See for example Muybridge (1887); for a chronology of Muybridge's life and work (online) see Herbert (2009).

[19] Muybridge, vice-versa, acknowledged Marey's influence on his work in a letter to Gaston Tissandier, editor of the French journal *La Nature* (Mannoni 2000: 305; Lefebvre 2005). It actually was Marey's publication, *The Animal Machine* from 1874 (*La machine animale: Locomotion terrestre et aérienne,* 1873) that caught Stanford's interest. Stanford consequently commissioned Muybridge to collaborate on capturing the movement of horses through the photographic method (Braun 1992: 47; Lefebvre 2005). Ramsaye (1926: 38-41) credited the French painter Jean Louis Meissonier as co-responsible for Muybridge's development of the projection side of the process, and called the whole investigation the Stanford-Isaacs-Muybridge pictures. He concluded: "A horseman's argument had made Muybridge a photographer of motion. An artist's argument had shown him synthesis of motion".

Marey, together with his chief assistant and collaborator Georges Demenÿ, developed a Photographic Gun based on Janssen's system,
which he altered with a slotted-disk shutter that masked the plate
while it moved, and exposed the plate when it stopped.[20] Marey also
carried this principle of the shutter mechanism forward into his fixed-
plate chronophotographic camera that employed glass plates, which
allowed him to take more than one picture on the plate and produced
the familiar images of superimpositions of single postures in one
frame.[21]

Whereas Muybridge's photographic time-lapse collages and aesthetic narratives were taken from multiple points of view (for which
up to forty-eight cameras were arranged in sequence),[22] Marey, in
contrast, for whom the results of photography were exclusively of interest to his scientific research into movement analysis, used a single
camera for a consistent point-of-view perspective.[23] He superimposed
the images on the carrier to obtain time-images rather than movement
sequences.[24] This approach was consistent with the scientific understanding of a fixed 'objective' position of the observer and reflected
Marey's "disinterested, accurate analytic and systematic" approach to
optical technologies (Braun 1992: 254).

---

[20] Ramsaye's (167) remark that: "… the shutter did not permit the machine to operate
at its full efficiency" is of particular interest for an analogy with the human perceptual
apparatus in that it is understood as filtering out information by eliminating sensory
data in order to suit the capacity of the brain processing.

[21] For an overview on the technological innovations by Marey see Braun (1992); for a
chronological overview on developments of cinema technologies more generally see
Rossell (1995: 121).

[22] See Mannoni (2000: 317), Ramsaye (1926: 37).

[23] Marey at one point also experimented with three-dimensional photography by deploying three different camera angles (front, side, and above) while retaining the single position of each camera. He described this approach briefly in *Movement* including some drawings (1895: 234-237).

[24] Braun (1992: 229-262) has rectified the previous confusion of Marey's and Muybridge's work in the literature and points especially to the misconception of the role
that science played in Muybridge's work. She reminds us that he was a businessman
with artistic ambitions in photographic pictorialism and its commercial exploitation.
He did not pursue a scientific interest in his instantaneous photography, although he
sought acceptance through the scientific community. Braun cites Muybridge from
Anita Mozley's introduction to *Muybridge's Complete Animal and Human Locomotion* (1979: xxxi): "I am neither a physiologist nor an anatomist… [therefore, they] are
assisting in the work to give it additional weight and value" (Braun 1992: 232 — emphasis in the original; with "they" Braun refers to "the scientists").

In Marey's investigations it is obvious that neither the technology nor the images in themselves were of primary interest, but they served his scientific analysis and were continuously modified, refined and altered according to the requirements of the objects of study. Marey recognised the limitations of the provisional character of scientific knowledge and continuously readjusted the shifting boundaries of what was considered as knowable and accessible to the scientific method. In this spirit he developed among many other prototypes a mobile-band Chronophotograph in 1888 using first paper ribbon, coated with a silver bromide emulsion, and later celluloid filmstrips.[25] After the integration of photographic techniques in his work, Marey also applied projection techniques in order to achieve an accurate movement synthesis. Far less important for his own work, but of paramount significance for the development of future cinema technologies, Marey also applied the shutter principle to interrupt the beam of light as one image moved to the next. This patent was used in every subsequent image projector since it effectively decreased the so-called flicker effect. Whereas Demenÿ was much more inclined toward the development of a successful projection technology, for Marey, movement synthesis constituted only a marginal interest in his overall oeuvre.[26] Nevertheless for a short period in the 1890s he paid considerable attention to the technological problems of projection with regard to specific details such as the necessary difference between an extremely short exposure time (for example 1/25,000 of a second for the analysis of an insect's wing) and the extended exposures required during the projection. Marey had proposed some of his early results of projection for a presentation to the *Académie des Sciences* in 1892 (Braun 1992: 173):

---

[25] The publication by Font-Réaulx, et al. (2006), contains a DVD comprising 400 clips of digitised filmstrips from Marey's institute. They originate from continuous celluloid filmstrips (without frames), which were compiled into image sequences through a complicated restoration process. Some single images had to be repeated in order to achieve the current projection speed of 24 frames per second. A further problem consisted in the fact that Marey's camera could capture up to 100 images per second and he would vary the speed as appropriate. For accompanying comments on the restoration of Marey's filmstrips see Font-Réaulx (2006: 191-192).

[26] Marey (1895: 304-318) dedicated the last chapter in *Movement* to projection technologies, entitled 'Synthetic Reconstruction of the Elements of an Analyzed Movement'.

We have therefore constructed a special apparatus, in which an endless length of film containing forty or sixty figures, or even more, is allowed to pass without cessation under the field of the objective. The illumination, which is from behind, and consists either of the electric light or the sun itself, projects these figures upon a screen. This instrument produces very bright images, but it is noisy, and the projected figures do not appear as absolutely motionless as one could wish. (Marey 1895: 318)[27]

Marey's marginal investigation into projection, however, was, and remained, a project for entirely scientific purposes; he did not pursue an interest in the commercial exploitation of the image projection system[28] — in contrast to his assistant George Demenÿ who split from Marey in 1894 to set up his own business (Braun 1992: 183).[29] It seems one of these curious coincidences in history that all subsequent cinema cameras and projectors were based on Marey's basic principles of the single lens, the slotted-disk shutter and the band of sensitized material passing from one spool to another.[30] Marey's own view on projection, particularly once the popularity of image projections on screens had taken off, stood apart from the popular enthusiasm that surrounded the commercial apparatuses, which also featured (sometimes illegal) popular screenings of scientific films. Marey's interest in projection was solely driven by the intent to synthesise his movement analysis for scientific demonstration purposes and he disapproved of an engagement with the general public through an exhibi-

---

[27] Braun (1992: 173) reports that no actual demonstration resulted from the correspondence with the *Académie des Sciences* in that year. It was not until June 29th in 1894 that Marey patented his Chronophotographic Projector (Rossell 1995), and not until 1896 that in his own perception he achieved a satisfactory method of projection (Braun 1992: 173).

[28] Rossell (1998: 48) reminds us that the commercial exploitation was too expensive and Marey tried only very briefly and unsuccessfully to sell his chronophotographic camera for scientific purposes. Also see Braun (1992: 194).

[29] Demenÿ, who was Marey's laboratory chief and assistant from 1881-1893 and greatly supported in his career development by Marey, eventually set up his own company in December 1892, the *Société Générale du Phonoscope*. For a detailed account of the relationship between Marey and Demenÿ, see Braun (1992: 66ff, 173ff).

[30] It is worth recalling that the Lumières Cinématographe provided a most elegant solution in that it was camera, printer and projector in a single device.

tion of his work.[31] He recognised, however, the popular attraction of the emerging cinema in its 'resurrection of movement' in a comment (Marey 1899: 31), in which he differentiated his own interest and his vision of the purposefulness of the apparatus for scientific research:

> The absolutely perfect projections that naturally arouse the enthusiasm of the public are not those, speaking personally, that captivate me the most. *The most appealing chronophotography is not the most useful.* [Marey's emphasis]. Chronophotography provides greater assistance, perhaps, in its simple analytic form than in its synthetic, however satisfying and astonishing that resurrection of movement may be. I make an exception for those cases when, in projecting the representative images of a movement's phases, we modify the conditions of speed in which the movement was produced... It is only there that, facilitating human observation and making it more acute, [chronophotography] is the instrument of scientific knowledge. (Braun 1992: 196 — emphasis in the original)

This reflects a perspective that was shared by other scientists at the time, for example by Albert Londe, expert in chronophotography and director of the photographic service at the Clinic for Nervous Disorders at the *Hospice de la Salpêtière,* with whom Marey exchanged on technological developments in chronophotography and collaborated frequently (Braun 1992: 85). Londe shared Marey's view in a publication in *Le Chasseur Français* in 1896:

> ... from a scientific point of view, it is the photographic analysis of movement which has much greater importance; by this we can discover laws which have been unknown until our

---

[31] It is reported that Marey, at one point, was contacted by the *Musée Grévin* in 1891, famous for hosting Charles-Émile Reynaud's *Théâtre Optique* (with approximately 12,800 performances from 1892-1900 for over 500,000 viewers (Abel 1994: 466; Rossell 1998: 21), but nothing appears to have come from this invitation. The *Musée Grévin* though did eventually show chronophotographs but with Demenÿ's Phonoscope (Braun 1992: 182-183). Other scientists' films were in some cases produced for a general public and commercial display, as in Jean Comandon's collaboration with the *Pathé Frères* film production enterprise that also financed his laboratory, or the collaboration between Francis Martin Duncan (and later Frank Percy Smith) and the entrepreneur Charles Urban (Landecker 2006). Sometimes instead they were illegally exhibited, as it was the case with Eugène-Louis Doyen's documentations of his famous surgeons (Lefebvre 2006, 2004).

times, we enhance our investigative methods; synthesis, on the other hand, if it can serve as a control or verification, if need be, cannot extend the sum of our knowledge. (Mannoni 2000: 352)

In Marey's struggle to reduce the interstices between moments of apparent stability — instances that ordinary human perception was not able to detect — it is important to remember that he deployed the photographic recording devices usually in conjunction with his graphing instruments. Marey's sophisticated set-ups emphasised his understanding of movement as an activity expressed through a variety of parameters and of a particular duration. He usually combined a number of these parameters, for example the relationship between the "frequency and the length of stride, the extent of the vertical head displacements and the various inclinations of the body", or between bodyweight and pressure on the foot, the effect of muscle force on body mass, etc. (Marey 1895: 127). This created complex systems of sensors and wearable instruments for diverse measurements, integrated with the subject's body's activities for capturing data from various kinds of kinetic processes, which in some ways anticipated current wearable technologies.

The performing subjects in Marey's experiments were carefully dressed to produce the optimal contrast in the images and then were often wired up or attached to the apparatus that recorded their movements.[32] With hindsight it can be suggested that his complex set-ups and mise-en-scènes of his experiments in his *Station Physiologique* were reminiscent of the elaborate 'cinema' sets, in which days and weeks of preparation would produce but a few seconds of photographic or filmic capture.[33] Marey's 'positivist belief in objective

---

[32] These included for example arrangements of sensors tracking a runner's passage via telegraph relay poles back to an indoor odograph, an electrical harness or wired sensors loosely attached to certain specific points along the side of the body for geometrical motion studies, a hangar for three-dimensional studies, bodysuits and wired bicycles, and various constructions for experiments with rods or falling objects (Braun 1992: 72-79).

[33] Nicole Brenez (2006: 127) refers to Marey as initiator of a *dispositif* of 'expanded cinema' in his *Station Physiologique*. This resemblance is also exemplified in Albert Londe's set-up — see the photograph published in Braun (1992: 90), on which Marey is captured during a visit of Londe's outdoor photographic laboratory at the *Hospice de la Salpêtrière,* where Londe used his twelve-lens camera for medical photography (85). The set-up with the black screen in the background serving to optimise the con-

quantification as the sole determinant of our knowledge of reality'
was particularly evident in the mise-en-scène for his chronophotographs, which was designed to eliminate perspective and to suggest
the impression of depth and the illusion of a three dimensional space
(Braun 1992: 254). Set against a black background, Marey eschewed
the single frame in favour of the selected time/space continuum in his
superimpositions as geometric expressions. This geometrical basis of
Marey's conception of time is particularly exemplified in his chapter
on the 'Applications of Chronophotography to Mechanics' (1895: 84-
102) and in the motion capture technique called 'Geometrical
Chronophotography', also referred to as *trajectoires squelettiques* or
l'homme squelette (60-61). In this method, the surface of the object
under observation was reduced to a fine thin white line or points. He
used reflective metal or white paper-strips, which in his study of human locomotion he placed along the side of a black body suit.[34] The
images obtained reflected the movement exercised in abstract white
lines against the black background, which according to Marey (1895:
60-61) subordinated space to a more precise graphing of the aspect of
time:

> In the diagram thus obtained, the number of images may be
> considerable, and the notion of time very complete, while that
> of space has been voluntarily limited to what was strictly ne-
> cessary.

Considering that Marey did not study movement in its visual expression alone, but also as through sounds (for example pulses within the
body, insect sounds), frequencies, speeds and flows, the elimination of
space in his set up clearly demonstrates that his main intention was to
increase the perception of movement in relation to time through extension of the smallest measurable intervals. Crary (1990) reminds us
that during the 19th century a severing of vision from other senses
went hand in hand with an increasing distinction of vision of the per-

---

trast with the performing figures, resembled that of a theatre stage including a great
number of props. This performative aspect can also be compared to Muybridge's
work, as well as to Edison's Black Maria or Georges Méliès' studio background on
which the brightly light actors and objects appeared against a non-defined space almost like ghostly apparitions.
[34] For illustrations and context see Marey (1895: 60), Braun (1992: 83-84, 94-5, 98-
103).

ceived object as reliable referent, which he identified as lying at the centre of the changing techniques of the observer.[35] Marey's lack of interest in the emerging public projection practices exemplified the severing of visual perception from the referent in the scientific context, especially since he distinguished his chronophotography from, what he perceived as, the 'realist' representations of movement in the public display of images. Marey expressed in a comment:

> Cinema produces only what the eye can see in any case. It adds nothing to the power of our sight, nor does it remove its illusions, and the real character of a scientific method is to supplant the insufficiency of our senses and correct their errors. To get to this point, chronophotography should renounce the representation of phenomena as they are seen by the eye. (Braun 1992: 255)

As Braun (254) reminds us, Marey opposed the realist, indexical approach to photography, which attempted to align the photographic image with the visual perception of the eye. This was curiously consistent (yet contradictory in Marey's underlying intention) with the prevailing popular taste for the extraordinary in the late 19th century, in that his interest lay in the perception of reality beyond the visibility for the human eye and perceptual capacities of the human senses.[36] At the very beginning of his overview on the technological developments of projection in the chapter 'Synthetic Reconstruction of the Elements of an Analyzed Movement' in *Movement* (1895), Marey briefly referred to the English-Swiss physician and mathematician, Peter Mark Roget's study of Stroboscopy.[37] He emphasised the significance of

---

[35] Crary (1990) alludes to some crucial shifts that took place prior to these developments in the course of the 18th century, whereby vision, as a previously privileged form of knowing, turned into an object of study.

[36] This perspective and Marey's intervention only became possible after the establishment of photography as a viable, reliable 'representation' of reality by the mid 19th century. Before the introduction of the so called 'moving image', the realist paradigm in the discourse of photography (conceived as 'realist medium') had an ambivalent reception since the inception of photographic technologies in the early 19th century, which even their most dedicated defenders were never entirely able to dismiss.

[37] The Stroboscopic effect occurs, when for example spokes of a wheel appeared as either motionless or to be turning backwards. For these studies a variety of rotating discs had been developed to illustrate the stroboscopic effect; these included the Faraday Wheel consisting of two discs that spun in opposite directions from each other,

this phenomenon in its dependence: "… on the physiological property of the retina of retaining for a brief moment the impression of an image after the object which has produced it has disappeared" (1895: 305).[38] Marey pointed to the significance of these studies in their application to the resolution of the discontinuity in single images when projected at a certain speed.[39] In the application for his movement studies, Marey had in the late 1860s (reported from 1867) initially applied the Zootrope (or Zoëtrope), developed by the English mathematician William George Horner,[40] and the further developed device (drawing on the Phenakistoscope and Zoëtrope), the Praxinoscope by the French inventor, artist and showman Charles-Émile Reynaud (Marey 1895: 308ff).[41]

The understanding of what caused the illusion of movement perception was subject to contemporary scientific research into the physiology and psychophysiological processes of visual perception.[42] The alignment of photographic techniques with the mechanistic conception of the eye, to which Marey contributed, provoked extensive controversies around the issues of realism and the subjectivity of the observer, as it was especially manifest in the contemporary discus-

---

and the well-known Phenakistiscope by Plateau, similar to the Stroboscope developed by the Austrian geometrician Simon Ritter von Stampfer, which led to commercial production and exploitation (Crary 1990: 106ff; Chanan 1980: 63-64).

[38] With earlier precedence, the after-image effect was most vigorously studied during the 1820s, most notably by Roget (1779-1869), and followed by the Belgian physicist and mathematician, Joseph Plateau (1801-1883). See also the studies by the Czech psychologist Jan Purkinje (1787-1869), the Scottish natural philosopher Sir David Brewster (1781-1868), the German physician and physicist Hermann L. F. von Helmholtz (1821-1894), the German experimental psychologist Gustav Fechner (1801-1887) and the English physicist Charles Wheatstone (1802-1875).

[39] The projection speed varied at the time, usually between 16-20 images per second, in Europe today the speed in the cinema is 24 images per second, the PAL television standard is 25 frames (field frame of 50Hz) — a difference that has been problematic for audio-visual archives. For an overview on the topic of projection speed in relation to the emerging cinema see Brownlow (1990).

[40] William George Horner of Bristol invented this device that became a very popular toy object in 1834 under the name Daedelum (Rickards 2000: 365) — Marey's spelling in *Movement* (1895) is 'Zootrope'.

[41] Marey's spelling in *Movement* (1895) is 'Raynaud'.

[42] As Chanan (1980: 56) reminds us: "… it would be wrong to imagine that these difficulties were always understood theoretically before their solutions were attempted", since very often, pioneering innovations by engineers (and the experimental sciences) delivered solutions that were theoretically confirmed after the event.

sions of the so-called *persistence of vision*. This myth was based on the conception of the after-image effect, which suggested some form of blending or fusion of visual stimuli on the retina when they were perceived in rapid succession. In the summary of his movement studies, Marey (1895), however, mainly dealt with precise descriptions of the various technological developments and engineering solutions that had taken place in his research laboratory, while the issues of the perception of movement remained rather ambiguous and beyond the scope of his investigations.[43] For the purpose of establishing a stable transportation of the single frames running through the projector's gate step-for-step, the movement had to be intermittently interrupted to avoid the blurring of the images when the filmstrip moved, which Marey solved through applying the shutter technique — one of his most significant technological contributions to the emerging cinema.

In Marey's work, when seen from the perspective of the images that his investigation produced, scientific intention and imaginary dimensions converged in the perception of the beholder. He recognised of course the interpretative potential of his images, which to him was an unavoidable fallacy of perception and — in contrast to Demenÿ — a diversion from the very subject matter that he intended to study beyond the visibility of forms. This diversion needed to be, not only excluded from the scientific agenda for the purpose of the applied method of analysis, but also, overcome through the continuous perfection of technology — a premise that appeared probably most drastically in his geometrical chronophotography and the study of movements in air and water. From this perspective, the materialist tendencies in both the cinema technologies and image productions, and the predominant focus in their theorisation and historicisation (among other things expressed by an overemphasis on the after-image effect in his legacy), can be regarded as a diversion of much more profound processes that lay at the ground of what Marey unearthed with his inventive spirit and interdisciplinary practice. This spectrum of a hidden dimensionality of Marey's work, it can be suggested, constitutes an

---

[43] While Marey focused on the analysis of movement, a more profound investigation into the synthesis of movement would have necessarily led him from physiology into the closely related field of psychology; this is possibly another reason for the marginal position of, and limited interest in projection technologies in his oeuvre. The issue of the after-image effect, however, became most crucial in the reception of his chronophotography, as will be elaborated in the next chapter.

underexplored potential for the scientific study of those phenomena that are intrinsic to the philosophical *dispositif* of the cinema beyond the filter of a putative realism purely sought in the materiality of form. This threshold can be liberated and further illuminated by examining Marey's work in hindsight, through a filter of Bergson's philosophy, in particular through his understanding of the *image* in relation to consciousness. In this context his philosophy can, in a certain sense, be regarded as an extension of Marey's intrusion into those domains where philosophy complements the scientific enterprise — in Bergson's (1998: 344) words, where philosophy completes science.

At a first sight it can be said that Marey and Bergson shared an insistence on scientific rigour through their background in science, which led them both in their own way to very concise and clear analytical thinking. Set in different disciplines, it could be said that their approaches diverged at the locus where philosophy parted from science — where Bergson identified the differing conceptions of time that were frequently confused: time as measurable quantity and time as qualitative intensity. From the perspective of his graphical and chronophotographical method, Marey understood time purely scientifically as a mathematical, measurable and homogeneous quantity. When he wrote about his method as: "... the process which thus serves to register the duration and sequence of events" (1895: 3), he referred to duration in terms of a spatial coordination, a geometrical, chronological conception. This is clearly expressed in the opening of the first chapter in *Movement*:

> Time, like other magnitudes, can be represented in a graphic form by straight lines of various lengths. In this way the respective duration of several events can be gauged by the various lengths of parallel straight lines placed side by side. [...] With regard to the exact order and duration of the events, they can be indicated by means of a scale, subdivided into divisions which represent years, days, fractions of seconds. (Marey 1895: 1-2)

Bergson extended the mathematical notion of time with his definition of *durée* as qualitative experience of time, established in his first major work *Essai Sur les Données Immédiates de la Conscience* from 1889 (*Time and Free Will,* 2001). With his philosophy, Bergson gave credit to science, while at the same time announcing its limits, particularly in the way that he saw that the confined conception of time as measurable quantity limited a full understanding of the extensive dimensions of consciousness in the experience of duration (*durée*). He compellingly showed how 'real time', as we perceive it in action as duration, is elusive to mathematical, scientific and intellectual treatment. Bergson reiterated the reductionism of science in his later publication *La Pensée et le Mouvant* from 1934 (*The Creative Mind: An Introduction to Metaphysics,* 1992) by drawing on his experience from his scientific training:

> Ever since my university days I had been aware that duration is measured by the trajectory of a body in motion and that mathematical time is a line; but I had not yet observed that this operation contrasts radically with all other processes of measurement, for it is not carried out on an aspect or an effect representative of what one wishes to measure, but on something which excludes it. The line one measures is immobile, time is mobility. The line is made, it is complete; time is what is happening, and more than that, it is what causes everything to happen. (1992: 12)

Bergson shifted his original interest in time during his studies in mathematics from the significance of the term *t* in equations of mechanics to an awareness of the impact of perceptual processes on the relativism of time as psychological quality.[44] Already in his earlier works, he frequently referred to the scientific method of movement analysis through instantaneous photography. Thereby he critiqued the commonly confused concept of time, which he distinguished into an externalised quantity (science) versus an internalised quality (metaphysics). According to Bergson, the only dimension that could be measured was the space traversed — in other words simultaneities. He explained:

> We involuntarily fix at a point in space each of the moments which we count, and it is only on this condition that the ab-

---

[44] He particularly referred to Spencer's *First Principles* as the starting point of his philosophical investigation that led him to consider the idea of time (1992a: 12), and pointed to, what he saw as, a major mistake both in philosophy and in science: the overemphasis on and the misunderstanding of movement and the subordination of time.

stract units come to form a sum. No doubt it is possible, as we shall see later, to conceive the successive moments of time independently of space; but when we add to the present moment those which have preceded it, as is the case when we are adding up units, we are not dealing with these moments themselves, since they have vanished for ever, but with the lasting traces which they seem to have left in space on their passage through it. (2001: 79)

Marey's composite chronophotography, when considered as disconnected from his wider research investigation from a purely textual analysis, exemplified the simultaneous appearances of singular instances of movement superimposed in one frame, like several instances of the fingers on the clock next to each other; an analogy that Bergson applied in relation to spatial simultaneities, especially in reference to the paradoxes by Zeno of Elea.[45] These instances, in his view, signify: "... the space traversed, the only thing, in fact, which is really measurable. Hence there is no question here of duration, but only of space and simultaneities" (2001: 116). In this respect Bergson recognised that time as duration fell through the meshes of the scientific method and reiterated in his introduction to *The Creative Mind* (1992) the distinction of the time as conceived by the mathematician or astronomer (or science more generally) from the time as experienced by consciousness. Bergson (1992: 12-13) proposed:

> The measuring of time never deals with duration as duration; what is counted is only a certain number of extremities of intervals, or moments, in short, virtual halts in time. To state that an incident will occur at the end of a certain time *t*, is simply to say that one will have counted, from now until then, a number *t* of simultaneities of a certain kind. In between these simultaneities anything you like may happen. Time could be enormously and even infinitely accelerated; nothing would be changed for the mathematician, for the physicist or for the astronomer. And

---

[45] Bergson referred in particular to Zeno's paradox of Achilles and the tortoise and critiqued the confusion of the indivisible series of acts in Achilles' and the tortoise's steps with the infinitely divisible quantification of the homogenous space that underlay them. He posited: "This is what Zeno leaves out of account when he reconstructs the movement of the tortoise, forgetting that space alone can be divided and put together again in any way we like, and thus confusing space with motion" (2001: 113-114; see also 1991: 191-193 and 258).

yet the difference with regard to consciousness would be profound (I am speaking naturally of a consciousness which would
not be integrated with intra-cerebral movement)... [46]

From this perspective of time, chronophotography in itself, detached
from the wider scope of Marey's oeuvre, merely took the external
passage of a body moving through space into account, as it can be observed from an externalised point-of-view. According to Bergson, it is
instead in our experience that we internally conceive continuous
movement and time as duration (*durée*), as a quality rather than a
measurable quantity. He asserted that:

> When I follow with my eyes on the dial of a clock the move-
> ment of the hand which corresponds to the oscillations of the
> pendulum, I do not measure duration, as seems to be thought; I
> merely count simultaneities, which is very different. Outside of
> me, in space, there is never more than a single position of the
> hand and the pendulum, for nothing is left of the past positions.
> Within myself a process of organization of interpenetration of
> conscious states is going on, which constitutes true duration. It
> is because I *endure* in this way that I picture to myself what I
> call the past oscillations of the pendulum at the same time as I
> perceive the present oscillation. (2001: 107-108)

In Bergson's (2001: 116) view, duration (*durée*) can only be perceived
internally, in the heterogeneity of states of consciousness: "... for the
interval of duration exists only for us and on accounts of the interpenetration of our conscious states". These internal states of consciousness, even though experienced in succession, permeate each other,
which constitutes a sense of *durée*. Only when they are 'measured'
and interpreted (for example through language), time is projected into
space and the whole splits up into single units. Bergson (2001: 112)
summarised it like this:

---

[46] Bergson illustrated this thought experiment also through the projection mechanism
of the cinematograph, based on his elaborations in *Creative Evolution* (1998) which,
in his view, at different speeds adds nothing to the images, since succession marks a
deficit, comparable to the necessities of language and the symbolism of science
(1992a: 18).

> In a word, there are two elements to be distinguished in mo-
> tion, the space traversed and the act by which we traverse it,
> the successive positions and the synthesis of these positions.
> The first of these elements is a homogeneous quantity: the sec-
> ond has no reality except in a consciousness: it is a quality or
> an intensity, whichever you prefer.

From this perspective, the analysis of movement through chronophotography did not allow for movement to appear as duration (*durée*)
in the images themselves, since the separate instances from spatial
configurations would only turn into a whole within the intersecting
conscious states in the internal processes of the beholder. Bergson
(2001: 227) maintained that:

> ... in consciousness we find states which succeed, without be-
> ing distinguished from one another; and in space simultaneities
> which, without succeeding, are distinguished from one another,
> in the sense that one has ceased to exist when the other ap-
> pears. Outside us, mutual externality without succession;
> within us, succession without mutual externality.

As a consequence, Bergson distinguished in *L'Évolution Créatrice*
from 1907 (*Creative Evolution,* 1998) between two types of order,
vital and geometrical order, which he based on his space-time separation and the correlating two opposed tendencies of the human mind:
intellect and intuition. The first is directed externally and constitutes
our social lives, finds expression through language and a grasp of reality according to the scientific method in a spatialised dimension following the movement of matter. The second is directed inwardly, as
an effort to grasp the life-force in its very quality of duration (*durée*)
and intensity, which he called (philosophical) intuition. Bergson insisted that these two tendencies of the mind were intimately entangled
in the basic activities of human cognition, which he conceived as in-
separable from action. He proposed:

> Thus the human intellect, inasmuch as it is fashioned for the
> needs of human action, is an intellect which proceeds at the
> same time by intention and by calculation, by adapting means
> to ends and by thinking out mechanisms of more and more
> geometrical form. Whether nature be conceived as an immense
> machine regulated by mathematical laws, or as the realization

of a plan,[47] these two ways of regarding it are only the consummation of two tendencies of mind which are complementary to each other, and which have their origin in the same vital necessities. (1998: 44-45)

In Bergson's view the intellect is directed towards the outside and examines the external world by splitting the perceived whole into segments and instantaneities in order to impact on material manifestations and their organisation. In this way it processes the most adequate action in the present situation with a tendency towards external material manifestation. From this follows that all knowledge, which the intellect is able to grasp, is purpose- and action-driven, and remains on the surface of things, creating ever more sophisticated perspectives and views. Thus the intellect alone is never able to gain the 'real experience', as it only constructs instantaneities, which are concepts but not the actual parts of the whole. He proposed that the externally oriented lives of our social selves require this necessary tendency of splitting the whole of matter into single sets of movements in space, since: "... life does not proceed by the association and addition of elements, but by dissociation and division..." (1998: 89).

Similar to the conception that every spectator sees a film in slightly different ways, an idea taken up more fully later, Bergson clarified how the heterogeneity of perspectives that split the whole into parts (as in a textual analysis of chronophotography) stood apart from the integrity of the object perceived in duration. In his view: "... it is movement which is anterior to immobility, and the relation between positions and a displacement is not that of parts to a whole, but that of the diversity of possible points of view to the real indivisibility of the object" (1999b: 44). According to Bergson, the division and recomposition of matter, as indicated in the Euclidean understanding of time, will never reveal the principle of its evolution. He suggested instead:

> Making a clean sweep of everything that is only an imaginative symbol, he will see the material world melt back into a simple flux, a continuity of flowing, a becoming. And he will thus be

---

[47] The term "plan" in Bergson did not refer to a predetermined destiny but a decision of free will, which sets the action going in order to realise an idea previously thought out and decided upon.

prepared to discover real duration there where it is still more useful to find it, in the realm of life and of consciousness. (1998: 369)

Bergson exemplified these two tendencies of the mind most explicitly in connection to the cinema as scientific, technological apparatus in the section 'Form and Becoming', in which he wrote about the "cinematographical tendency of our perception and thought" (326), "the cinematographical mechanism of our thought" (313) or "cinematographical habits of our intellect" (312). In his comparison with the single instantaneous frames of the filmstrip, he claimed that: "... the mechanism of our ordinary knowledge is of a cinematographical kind" (306). He regarded the cinematograph as a simulation of the mechanisms that split the whole (of movement) into single instantaneities, which are then synthesised in the projector and create an illusion of movement. This, according to Bergson, is the way science, ancient as well as modern, operates. The intellect, from this perspective, is never able to grasp the profound essence of a thing or an event, as it only works with concepts and language but does not merge with the thing in order to gain an inside view. Bergson (206) exemplified the mutual interconnection between the intellect and matter as follows:

> This alternative consists, first of all, in regarding the intellect as a special function of the mind, essentially turned toward inert matter; then in saying that neither does matter determine the form of the intellect, nor does the intellect impose its form on matter, nor have matter and intellect been regulated in regard to one another by we know not what pre-established harmony, but that intellect and matter have progressively adapted themselves one to the other in order to attain at last a common form. *This adaptation has, moreover, been brought about quite naturally, because it is the same inversion of the same movement, which creates at once the intellectuality of mind and the materiality of things.* (Emphasis in the original)

Not unlike Marey and his exclusive interest in projection for scientific purposes, Bergson referred to the cinematographical method purely in its technological mechanism as scientific apparatus. They both would have also agreed in their lack of interest in the simulation of real movement, imitated by the succession of single frames moving through the projector. With a different intention, however, yet similar to Bergson's (313) notion of an "imitation" of real movement, Marey (1895: 254) made very clear in his comments on movement synthesis that: "... it is useless to attempt to gain a knowledge of the successive phases of movement, by examining the successive photographs of a consecutive series...". The application of projection techniques to achieve an accurate movement synthesis, proved especially problematic in the case of extremely short exposure times. In Marey's examples of insects' flight movements, this discrepancy became most obvious: while the time duration of a complete wing movement occupied for example 1/190 a second, the successive images were separated by a relatively long interval of 1/20 of a second despite the fact that his camera operated at high-speed and was able to capture up to 100 frames per second. The significance of these studies for Marey lay entirely in the movement analysis of the mechanisms of flight, whereas synthesis, it could be said in the most extreme way, formed a superfluous reconfirmation for the habitual assurance of the human reliability on vision — that ordinary spectrum that Marey intended to expand through technological mediation.

Bergson was concerned with a similar problematic in philosophy that he analogously addressed as the reconstitution of the missing movement in the single freeze frames — which Marey only provisionally attempted to reconstitute by the mechanism of the projector. In his comparison of the cinematographical method with the way the intellect obtains knowledge, Bergson (1998: 306) affirmed:

> Instead of attaching ourselves to the inner becoming of things, we place ourselves outside them in order to recompose their becoming artificially. We take snapshots, as it were, of the passing reality, and, as these are characteristic of the reality, we have only to string them on a becoming, abstract, uniform and invisible, situated at the back of the apparatus of knowledge, in order to imitate what there is that is characteristic in this becoming itself. Perception, intellection, language so proceed in general. Whether we would think becoming, or express it, or even perceive it, we hardly do anything else than set going a kind of cinematograph inside us. We may therefore sum up what we have been saying in the conclusion that the *mechanism of our ordinary knowledge is of a cinematographical kind.* (Emphasis in the original)

He exemplified the way in which we take these snapshots of objects around us with another optical metaphor: the shaking of a kaleido- scope, which produces ever new compositions, analogous with the continuous re-arrangement of images between our body and other bodies. In Bergson's view the intellect is not interested in the shakes themselves, but merely in the outcome of the new pictures — which in an analogous transference would shed light on Marey's methods be- yond optical technologies as being led by an intrinsic interest in mo- tion in its indivisibility (the shakes of the kaleidoscope) rather than the images or technology as material outcome. Bergson (306-307) sug- gested:

> In this sense we may say, if we are not abusing this kind of il- lustration, *that the cinematographical character of our know- ledge of things is due to the kaleidoscopic character of our ad- aptation to them.* The cinematographical method is therefore the only practical method, since it consists in making the gen- eral character of knowledge form itself on that of action, while expecting that the detail of each act should depend in its turn on that of knowledge. In order that action may always be en- lightened, intelligence must always be present in it; but intelli- gence, in order thus to accompany the progress of activity and ensure its direction, must begin by adopting its rhythm. (Em- phasis in the original)

From this it becomes apparent that Bergson's view on the function of the intellect, when regarded in an isolated way, was very much in ac- cordance with the scientific principle of observation. It is in this sense also close to Marey's project of chronophotography in its attempts to extend the visible spectrum of the eye's perception via technology. However, a textual analysis of Marey's experiments with composite chronophotography alone, disregards the significance of the broader context of his work, which has frequently led to an overvaluation of the images produced, in the context of teleological histories and theo- ries of the so-called 'moving image technologies'.

Because of Marey's recognition of the representational constraints of instantaneous photography, he very consciously created techniques that would allow him to expose several images onto the same plate (or filmstrip) in order to demonstrate, in the superimposition of single instantaneous attitudes, the simulation of duration — an artificial reconstruction, a synthesis in a symbolic way. The movement that had to be imagined made them appear as if merging into one whole — in other words, they appeared as if representing simultaneity. Marey, rather exceptionally, even referred on one occasion in *Movement* (1895) explicitly to the faculty of perception in terms of affordance, and, in that, he admitted the agency of imagination. In this way he can be said to have sanctioned some aspects of Bergson's philosophy by expanding the scope of his own investigation. This is for example evident in his description of how, in his view, chronophotography superseded ordinary perception. Marey (304) proposed:

> Although chronophotography represents the successive attitudes of a moving object, it affords a very different picture from that which is actually seen by the eye when looking at the object itself. In each attitude the object appears to be motionless, and movements, which are successively executed, are associated in a series of images, as if they were all being executed at the same moment.[48] The images, therefore, appeal rather to the imagination *[l'esprit]* than to the senses. (Insert by the author, see footnote)[49]

This exemplifies among other things, why Marey continued to combine the analysis of photographic images with his other graphing instruments in order to measure the time interval as a whole uninterrupted momentum, "in a single and legible representation" of the various forces at work (Braun 1992: xviii). His graphing methods, in this sense, provided a more perfect way to inscribe time as (measured) duration, since they did not leave any gaps in their inscription as the single attitudes of instantaneous photography did.[50] In this sense, Marey's approach not only continuously attempted to push the limits of

---

[48] It is interesting that Marey seemed to be suggesting here that there occurs a complete collapsing of time in the sense of chronology, pertinent with the period's interests in simultaneity. See for example Kern (1983: 86-88, 314-315).

[49] Braun (1996: 45) cites Marey's remark in the French original: *"Ces images s'adressent donc plus à l'esprit qu'aux sens"*. Significantly Marey used the same term, *l'esprit*, as Bergson did in *Matter and Memory* (1991) with regard to the mind; the dimensions beyond matter.

[50] See also Mary Ann Doane's discussion on the representability versus the legibility of time in Marey's oeuvre. Doane (2002: 61) emphasises that the continuity and discontinuity of the inscription of time in his work reveals his attempt to represent *"all* time" without loss (Emphasis in the original).

the measurability of time, but when taking the wider scope of his oeuvre into account, it can also be said that he was essentially concerned with a measurement of the body state as a whole — not the body in space but the body as a condition. It is an aspect that is unavoidably overlooked when interpreting his chronophotographical images solely through a textual analysis in their apparent single heterogeneous states.

However, any technology merely prolonged the mechanistic process of the visual apparatus, but did not explicitly account for the internally driven mental processes. In this sense, the methods that Marey applied, in themselves, all dealt with time as quantitative expression, and not — although intrinsic to the *dispositif* — with the actual experience of time as duration. Qualitative duration *(durée)* instead, as Bergson defined it, had to be understood in relation to a qualitative experience of conscious states and not as pertaining to an externalised spatial measurement or 'representation' of movement, notwithstanding how continuous this measurement may have been. In his view, the intellect alone was unable to grasp this very activity and creative force, the internal dynamisms of motion such as conscious processes of recollections — memory-*images* drawn from the realms of pure duration. In this sense, the chronophotographical method merely touched the surface of symptoms and actions of a life-force that, according to Bergson, lay much deeper within the internal processes of the psychic life. This, in his view, constitutes the threshold where time is perceived as real duration, as *durée*, and where philosophy proceeds from science.

Marey's acknowledgement of the limitations of his method, are revealed in his main focus on movement analysis and in his lack of interest in projection technologies for public exhibition. In this sense, he deliberately ignored the imaginative dimension of perception that lay at the foundation of ordinary perception and which constituted one of the main attractions of the cinema, as it is proposed here. However, when taking a broader perspective on Marey's whole oeuvre, it becomes paramount that, although he focused on the spatial measurable coordinates in his method, restricted by the constraints of the positivist paradigm, his efforts clearly were driven towards an understanding of duration and underlying forces in relation to the executed movement. He continuously attempted to push the boundaries, and in some way it could be said that technology both liberated and also restricted his investigation in his continuous attempts to establish technologically based observation beyond ordinary perception as standardized scientific method for the discipline of physiology.

Marey and Bergson seemed to work on similar phenomena from complementary positions. Bergson posited, however, that philosophy goes further than science in that it reaches beyond the studies of phenomena apprehended by the senses (natural or technologically enhanced). Marey instead regarded technology as an improvement of the psychophysiological perceptual abilities, while for Bergson, technology did not enhance perception in kind beyond the limits of sensory perception or the intellect. In this sense, technology drew the same criticism as the scientific paradigm of physiological determinism, which Bergson saw closely bound up with mechanistic theories of matter that reduced the human condition in its dimensionality. In his view science reduced psychic states to molecular movements in the brain, as such it followed Auguste Comte's essential biologism that proceeded from the "positive theory of cerebral function" (Stocking 1987: 29). Bergson (2001: 148) instead maintained that: "... in movement we may find the reason of another movement, but not the reason of a conscious state.[51] This insufficiency led Bergson (1992: 13) to search for a solution in metaphysics and concretely within psychic life:

> But this duration which science eliminates, and which is so difficult to conceive and express, is what one feels and lives. Suppose we try to find out what it is? — How would it appear to a consciousness which desired only to see it without measuring it, which would then grasp it without stopping it, which in short, would take itself as object, and which, spectator and actor alike, at once spontaneous and reflective, would bring ever closer together — to the point where they would coincide — the attention which is fixed, and time which passes? Such was the question; and through it I delved deep into the domain of the inner life, which until then had held no interest for me.

---

[51] For Bergson certain cerebral substrata were necessary for psychical states, but that is all that the interdependence of the mental and the physical showed in the pure experience: "From the fact that two things are mutually dependent, it does not follow that they are equivalent" (1998: 354).

Bergson's critique of scientific reductionism offers a significant philosophical underpinning for a critical reflection on the wider intellectual
context of the late 19th century, particularly the prevailing deterministic evolutionist doctrines, which can be regarded as a symptom of
the extreme reductionist, positivist scientific reasoning and the inherent problematic of the grappling with the concept of time. This, at the
time, was particularly evident in the application of, the relatively new
discipline, physiology to physical anthropology through the method of
anthropometry. Against this backdrop Bergson's approach stood in
contrast to the defenders of positivism who in France were strongly
influenced by Comte's *Positive Philosophy* from 1842, which: "…
offered the most systematic and influential model for an ostensibly
scientific study of human progress in civilization" (Stocking 1987:
29). Comte defined the three main stages of human development
through evolution as a shift from the *theological*, to the *metaphysical*
and finally the *positive* phase (Braun 1992: 13). In a broader context
of his evolutionary theory, Bergson (1998: 135) instead countered any
linear biological determinism:

> *The cardinal error which, from Aristotle onwards, has vitiated*
> *most of the philosophies of nature, is to see in vegetative, in-*
> *stinctive and rational life, three successive degrees of the de-*
> *velopment of one and the same tendency, whereas they are*
> *three divergent directions of an activity that has split up as it*
> *grew.* The difference between them is not a difference of in-
> tensity, nor, more generally, of degree, but of kind. (Emphasis
> in the original)

The linear teleological evolutionary perspective of biological determinism supported its ideological framework with data from scientific
research in physical anthropology. The technique of anthropometry
pertaining to the study of ethnicity was also practiced in Marey's *Station Physiologique* particularly by the physician Félix-Louis Regnault,
who started to work in Marey's institute in 1893 and is mostly known
for his chronophotographic movement studies of ethnic groups (Braun
2006).[52]

---

[52] Marey himself related to his work in a foreword he wrote for Regnault's publication
(1897) on the study of modes of walking movements, which he studied across a variety of ethnic groups to mark racial differences. For a critical discussion of Regnault's
ethnographic motion photography see Rony (1996); on anthropometry see Spencer

Like Marey, Regnault regarded observation on film as superior to the best descriptions and regarded moving image technologies as extensions of visual capture devices for uses in medicine, anthropology, prehistory, sociology, history, zoology and psychology. What may read like an indirect reflection on Marey's and Demenÿ's discrepancies, Regnault developed a particular vision of two different kinds of cinema: one he called the Cinématoscope as a cinema of entertainment, and the other the Cinématographe as a cinema of science. He suggested:

> Cinema expands our vision in time as the microscope has expanded it in space. It permits us to see facts which escape our senses because they pass too quickly. It will become the instrument of the physiologist as the microscope has become that of the anatomist. Its importance is as great. (Rony 1996: 46)

Whereas the young discipline of physiology, of which Marey was a supporter, based its observation on the vital functions in individual members of a species (human and animals), the related discipline of social physics was instead concerned with comparative research for wider generalised claims concerning character or race.[53] In this framework, measurements of the body became aligned with culture and race, and psychic processes were understood according to the same laws as the material world whereby the biologically deterministic evolutionist framework was used to underpin the supremacy of the white 'Western' race. Paradoxically, at the same time the particular intimate relationship with the studied peoples' natural environment also served as exemplary model for a healthy and heroic ideal that was contrasted with the weakened, civilised white citizen, prone to illness in, what was conceived as, an unhealthy industrialised, highly artificial environment. This became of particular significance in France during the aftermath of the defeat from the Prussian war and the reestablishment of the nation's self-confidence and self-image. Not sur-

---

(1992). See also Bloom's (2008: 1-33) references to Marey's work in his elaborations on the conception of natural man in the context of the colonial ideology in France in the late 19th century.

[53] For an account on the applications and transference of concepts from physiology to the social sciences see Paul Rabinow (1989).

prisingly, the strand of physical anthropology in the late 19th century was strongly identified with the medical sciences.[54]

Marey's study of physical health, exercise among solders and athletes as well as ordinary men served France's goal to build a strong workforce in all sectors of the State. His physiological research informed the national policy of military training through his longstanding work with the Ministry of War, which adopted his and especially Demenÿ's ideas about physical education in their training programmes. Alongside efficient training of soldiers through physical exercise and gymnastic education, as Rabinbach (1990) points out, civilians who suffered the enfeeblement of sedentary work, were provided the means to recover their strengths through a national health policy of exercise. In this context Marey was a pioneer and proponent of the widespread belief in technical solutions for the acknowledged deficiencies and limitations of the human perceptual apparatus.

Bergson took a different position against the backdrop of this discourse and was at the forefront to postulate a qualitative treatment of subjectivity in relation to free will. In doing so he took a counter position through his critique of biological determinism and radical finalism. In his view, it treated life mechanistically and made it: "... shrink to the form of a certain human activity which is only a partial and local manifestation of life, a result or by-product of the vital process" (1998: xii). He further elaborated:

> Physics and chemistry study only inert matter; biology, when it treats the living being physically and chemically, considers only the inert side of the living: hence the mechanistic explanations, in spite of their development, include only a small part of the real. (1998: 354)

This full dimensionality of Bergson's vision on life is of particular significance for a more complete recognition of Marey's pursuit to study the very complexity of vital forces that drove movement. Marey referred to his interest in these underlying forces in a publication in *Science* in 1883 as: "... the momentum of the opposing forces which represent the power and the resistance in the animal machinery" (Braun 1992: 66). A more holistic approach in Marey's research, still

---

[54] Barbara Larson (2005: 53) addresses this connection and points to the fact that at the time the *École d'Anthropologie* in Paris was part of the Faculty of Medicine.

underexplored in the reception of his work, becomes even more explicit toward the later part of his life, in his pursuit of the study of forces that in themselves remained invisible. His focus turned from the moving subjects to the media or the elements in which they moved, especially in his experiments that made the ephemeral movements of water and air visible.[55]

In his attempts to render the invisible visible, Marey shifted away from physiology and moved more into the terrain of physics as he created wind tunnels for visualising airflow, and where he had previously studied the movement of water animals, he modified the tanks to trace the movement of water itself. Some of the most extraordinary graphic examples of these investigations into the invisible are Marey's studies of smoke trails, produced by obstacles attached to his *Machine à Fumée* — a construction that by 1901 allowed 48 different trails of smoke to be processed. In relation to this, Marey mentioned a research report in a letter to Demenÿ in 1886: "The author has made the air visible by means of smoke fillets of phosphorous vapors, a method for seeing the invisible which quite seduces me" (Braun 1992: 217). Marey was especially interested in the observation of small air currents around plain figures of different shapes, which relayed back to his earlier research into aquatic locomotion and his studies of aerodynamics.[56]

In Marey's later (and most ephemeral) work it becomes evident that there was only a small distinction to be made between his scientific research into energy and the increasing scientific research into psychical phenomena during the late 19th century dealing with invisible forces. When considering them in their own right and original intentions, both these strands of investigations attempted to record the physical expressions of their mediums/ subjects, while of course they entirely diverged in the understanding of what caused these movements and events to happen. It is therefore not surprising that Marey's interests in the scientific measurement of invisible forces is also re-

---

[55] Braun (1992: 214-215) reports that it was following a funding grant from the Smithsonian Institute (for which Marey was persuaded to apply by the third secretary Samuel Pierpont Langley), which made him return to his earlier studies with smoke fillets and wind tunnels.

[56] For an overview on Marey's aerodynamic studies see Braun (1992), Marey (1901). For details on Marey's aquatic locomotion studies, see Braun (1992: 214-221), Marey (1895: 211-225).

flected in his involvement in the rigorous, scientific study of psychic phenomena. It could be corroborated that precisely because of this apparent paradox between his interest in invisible forces and his rigorous scientific methods it had previously been possible for Marey to pioneer in the proof for the contagion through contaminated water, when the cholera epidemic broke out in France in 1884. By mapping the underground flow of different water sources through his hometown and tracing the incidences of mortality, he was able to make the interrelationship between infected water and cholera visible through scientific charts and confirmed the hypothesis of the symptomatic contagion of a hithero mysterious disease. His contribution to an understanding of the contagion of cholera is exemplary for an investigation that combined his rigorous and meticulous scientific approach with the recognition of underlying, temporarly or sometimes even entirely invisible dimensions.

When Bergson was appointed to a Chair of Philosophy at the *Collège de France* in 1900, he joined Marey, who, until his death in 1904, occupied the 'Chair of Natural History of Organized Bodies' in the same institution. From December 1901 onwards they collaborated in a research group at the *Institut Général Psychologique* (General Institute of Psychology) that investigated extraordinary and psychic phenomena.[57] This group consisted of eminent scientists such as Pierre and Marie Curie,[58] Jacques-Arsène d'Arsonval,[59] Charles Robert Richet,[60] Gilbert Ballet,[61] Jean-Baptiste Perrin,[62] Jules Cour-

---

[57] See Braun (1992: 279; 1996: 49-50), Robinet (1972: 509-510), Inglis (1985: 121-122; 1992: 423f).

[58] Pierre and Marie Curie (Maria Sklodowska-Curie) attempted to measure among other things the radioactivity and electrical discharge produced by hysterics; Marey's various graphing instruments were instrumental for their investigations (Braun 1992: 279).

[59] D'Arsonval was director of the Laboratory of Biological Physics, Professor at the *Collège de France,* member of the *Académie des Sciences* and the *Académie de Médecine.*

[60] Richet was professor of physiology at the Faculty of Medicine in Paris and a psychical researcher. He won the Nobel Prize in physiology and medicine in 1913, and was honorary president of *La Societé Universelle d'Études Psychiques,* president of the *Institut Métapsychique Internationale,* and president of the Society for Psychical Research, London in 1905. See Richet (1923, 1930).

[61] Ballet, trained in medicine, became *Chef de Clinique* under Jean Martin Charcot at the *Salpêtrière* in 1883 where he concerned himself extensively with neurology and mental pathology. In 1907 he was appointed professor of medical history, in 1900

tier,[63] Mr. Youriévitch,[64] etc. A letter from the 3rd December 1901, announced the foundation of this research group, called *Groupe d'Études de Phénomènes Psychiques,* with the intention of a rigorous scientific enterprise to study those phenomena that commonly fell outside of the established frameworks and established scientific laws. The main research question reflected a modest and manageable approach in that it aimed to distinguish the objective from the subjective dimensions of these phenomena:

> *Quelle est la part de réalité objective et quelle est la part d'interprétation subjective dans les faits décrits sous les noms de suggestion mentale, télépathie, médiumnité, levitation, etc.?* (Robinet 1972: 510)[65]

This investigation was not an exception, since in the course of the 19th century a variety of institutions were founded to pursue scientific research into 'paranormal' or 'psychic' phenomena; for example the Society for Psychical Research (SPR), founded in 1882 by Edmund Gurney, Frederic William Henry Myers, Henry Sidgwick and Edmund Rogers in London,[66] the American Society for Psychical Research, founded by the eminent psychologist and philosopher William James[67] in 1884 in Boston, the London Dialectical Society in 1869 that promoted psychic phenomena as spiritual manifestations (Inglis 1992:

---

professor of psychiatry. And in 1912 elected member of the *Académie de Médecine.*
[62] Perrin was professor of physical chemistry at the Sorbonne, University of Paris; he won the Nobel Prize for physics in 1926.
[63] Courtier was Professor of Psychology at the Sorbonne.
[64] Youriévitch was General Secretary of the *Institut Général Psychologique.*
[65] "How can the perceptions of objective reality and those of subjective interpretation be differentiated in the occurrences described as mental suggestion, telepathy, mediumship, levitation, etc.?" (Translation by the author). The original group that signed this letter comprised d'Arsonval, Bergson, Branly (Professor of Physics at the *Institut Catholique),* Brissaud (Professor of the Faculty of Medicine), Duclaux (member of the *Académie des Sciences* and the *Académie de Médecine,* Director of the *Institut Pasteur),* Marey and Weiss (affiliated with the Faculty of Medicine).
[66] For an account on the foundation of the Society of Psychical Research see Alan Gauld (1968). See also Luckhurst (2002: 51).
[67] William James (1842-1910) studied among other things the phenomena related to spiritist mediums, particularly the medium Eleonore Piper from 1885 until his death in 1910 (1994: 189). John Durham Peters (1999: 188) reminds us that James' "... psychical research is not peripheral but in many ways is at the center of his thought".

246-249) and The Parisian Society of Psychologic Studies founded by Allan Kardec alias Léon-Dénizarth-Hippolyte Rivail.[68]

At the same time, similar phenomena from the context of studies of so-called 'primitive religions' around the world were reported and became subjected to scientific inquiry, situated within the framework of Eurocentric evolutionary theories in the emerging discipline of cultural anthropology.[69] While the occupation with traditional forms of religious beliefs and rituals both in so-called Western and non-Western societies lay the foundation of the 'science of religions' or 'comparative studies of religions' as an autonomous discipline,[70] it is notable that investigations into the phenomenon of occult practices and spiritist séances were mostly conducted by the disciplines of the 'natural sciences' such as physics, as well as the emerging disciplines of psychology, clinical psychology (and what today would fall under neuroscience), physiology and philosophy (Inglis 1992: 399).[71]

The scientific engagement in studies of so-called psychic phenomena may appear as a paradox or professional schizophrenia in that scientists often occupied a highly eminent position in the scientific community, while at the same time they investigated phenomena that held sway in the popular domain.[72] The meticulous descriptions of séances conducted under the scrutiny of scientific observation in many

---

[68] Allan Kardec's works on spiritism became very famous and popular, most notably *The Spirit's Book* (1989), first published in 1857 as *Le Livre des Esprits,* comprising a series of 1,019 questions exploring matters concerning the nature of spirits and the relations between the spirit world and the material world.

[69] See the references to Tylor (1871) or Frazer ([1890] 1981) in the introduction to Bergson's philosophy in chapter 1.

[70] Mircea Eliade reported that various university chairs in Europe were founded at the time, starting in 1873 in Geneva, followed by four chairs in Holland in 1876, and in 1879 at the *Collège de France* in Paris (1957: 217-218). For a discussion on the relevance of psychical research for religious studies see Jonathan Harrison (1976). Inglis (1992: 399-413) treats the interconnections between the studies of 'primitive religion' and Western spiritist phenomena, among other spirit photography.

[71] Janet Oppenheim (1985: 326-390) elaborates on the relation between physics and psychic phenomena.

[72] This meshing of scientific methods with interests in ephemeral phenomena preoccupied not only scientists from various fields, but was also shared and often preceded by technologists and engineers in their experimental applications of scientific findings. Some of the most technophile scientists were also inclined to investigate psychic phenomena, such as in the case of Thomas Watson, A.G. Bell's assistant who explored the possibility of the telephone to aid in spiritual discoveries (Gunning 1995: 46), however, frequently their investigations were focused on exposing cases of fraud.

scientific reports confirmed that manifestations of spirits, ectoplasm or telekinesis have been achieved by mediums without any aid of hidden mechanisms.[73]

Marey's various instruments were used to measure for example radioactivity and electrical discharge during séances in the studies of the behaviour of hysterics, of "mental suggestion, telepathy, levitation..." (Braun 1992: 279). Gustave Geley (1927: 360-372) included in his publication *Clairvoyance and Materialisation: A Record of Experiments* some original reports of these experiments at the General Institute of Psychology with the medium Eusapia Palladino that took place from 1905-1907, in which Bergson was acting as one of the controllers of the medium's movements.[74] Marey's apparatuses and graphs are described as being used to measure the movement of the teleported objects, such as his *tambour*, in order to measure the phenomena produced by the medium (Chéroux, et al. 2005: 253). In one experiment, Palladino is reported to have stood on one of Marey's weighing-machines, in another experiment again with telekinesis: "... an arrangement was made with a stylus touching blackened paper on a Marey recorder, so that all horizontal movements [of the moving object] could be automatically recorded" (Geley 1927: 364-365 — insert by the author).

Not only in this context, but also in some previously mentioned more generally shared aspects and interconnections of their intellectual interests, it can be said that both Marey and Bergson, although from differing perspectives, most essentially attempted to study those motions and dynamism that constituted life. Bergson defined the underlying drive for this motion, the vital impetus of life, as the *élan*

---

[73] For reports on scientific research into spiritist séances see for example Crookes (1871, 1874), Doyle (1926), Faraday (1853), Feilding (1963), Flammarion (1900, 1907), Geley (1927), Münsterberg (1910).

[74] Inglis (1992: 419-432) dedicates a chapter to Eusapia Palladino that gives an account on the controversy around her séances, but especially the acknowledgement of the widespread support that her prominence gained through serious investigations amongst the scientific community. Palladino was one of the most famous mediums at the time and frequently studied by a variety of scientists and research institutes pursuing research into psychical phenomena. From Geley's (1927) precise reports the set-up of the séances becomes apparent, every single step of the events is recorded, the controllers of Palladino's hands and feet are mentioned each time, the position of her hands are exactly described for example during the levitation of tables or other moving objects. For photographic documentations of events during séances see also Chéroux, et al. (2005).

vital (life-force). He conceived of this force as the storage and release of energy that facilitates the creation of ever new forms, since for Bergson (1998: 262): "… a living being is a center of action". In his view, rational science could not grasp the profound principles of life, only philosophy could provide these methods, while at the same time he attempted to introduce scientific rigour into philosophy: "… philosophers can not to-day content themselves with vague generalities, but must follow the scientists in experimental detail and discuss the results with them" (78). Bergson also referred to this conviction in a thought experiment toward the end of his Presidential Address to the Society for Psychical Research in London on May 28, 1913. He speculated that, if science had taken things at the other end and the human mind had dedicated itself to psychical science at first, then matter, and not mind, would have been considered the realm of mystery. However, what this science would have lacked, Bergson (1920: 82) conceived as:

> … something of inestimable price and without which all the rest would lose much of its value, — the precision, the exactness, the anxiety for proof, the habit of distinguishing between what is simply possible or probable and what is certain.

Bergson, however, set his philosophy against the tendency of contemporary science, which increasingly eliminated and eschewed those dimensions beyond the rationally conceivable and scientifically measurable from their curriculum with full awareness of certain inexplicable phenomena. He directed his critique particularly against the prevailing radical finalism in science and evolutionary theory when he said that:

> It is to believe that life, in its movement and in its entirety, goes to work like our intellect, which is only a motionless and fragmentary view of life, and which naturally takes its stand outside of time. Life, on the contrary, progresses and *endures* in time. (1998: 51 — emphasis in the original)

Marey shared an interest in similar phenomena with Bergson, since, although he situated his work within the scientific framework of positivism, he did not solely proceed from the conceptualisation of the body as a mechanistic apparatus. He rather proceeded from a profound awareness of the underlying dynamic processes of intelligible forces, which shows the influence of Helmholtz' work. The scientific method did, however, not provide him with the framework to venture greatly beyond the surface of material appearances. Notwithstanding, it clearly was the result of his insistence on approaching an understanding of invisible forces through a rigorous scientific method that led to pioneering results and technological innovation in a great variety of disciplines.

Similar to Bergson (42), who opposed extreme vitalism as well as pure mechanism and finalism, the doctrine of teleology, Marey also opposed the neo-vitalism of his time, although he intrinsically pursued a profound research interest in invisible, vital phenomena. Marey, however, drew a different conclusion than Bergson in a comment from 1868:

> I do not recognize vital phenomena, I find that there are only two kinds of manifestations of life: those that are intelligible to us — these are physical and chemical — and those that are not intelligible. As to the latter, it is better to confess our ignorance than to disguise it with a pretense of explanation. (Braun 1992: 12)

In this statement Marey reflected the position of the contemporary canon of the scientific community that subordinated their investigations to the prevailing positivism, although he continuously pushed the boundaries of what was understood as intelligible. Bergson instead much more radically embraced the full spectrum of these dimensions and, very carefully, formulated a much more positive and explorative approach. He admitted:

> Let us confess our ignorance, but let us not resign ourselves to the belief that we can never know. If there be a beyond for conscious beings, I cannot see why we should not be able to discover the means to explore it. (1920: 28)

The famous French physician and psychic investigator, Joseph Maxwell, took a similar stand to Bergson when he pointed out that: "' [i]llusion' could not be used to discredit psychical research in general [...] without undermining the whole foundations of science" (Inglis 1992: 420). Similar to many other scientists, Maxwell did not believe in the supernatural, but assumed that psychic phenomena were based on some kind of natural force, possibly produced within the perceivers' minds.

When looking at Marey's research from a Bergsonian perspective, it sheds light on his intrinsic interests in energy, force and time as duration, while at the same time it reveals the pitfalls of rationalist science in the way it could not accommodate the very profound creative processes of the psychic life particularly in relation to motion in time as experience. By the same token it also illuminates the pitfalls of psychical research or practices that conversely did not proceed from a foundation in science. Moreover, it can be suggested that Marey's scientific perspective in his work, despite — Bergson might have said precisely because of — the positivist paradigm and deliberate reductionism, was prone to meta-discourses of 'another reality' beyond ordinary human perception. This can not only be related to his visions of technology as extended human perception, but also to the various interpretations and reiterations of aspects of his legacy in the early 20th century, particularly in the Arts. It could be suggested that the persistent appeal to reinterpret Marey's work from a mechanistic point of view resulted from the scientific reductionism that did not provide a framework for recognising the cognitive faculties involved in the perception of the beholder but provoked their recognition and inclusion.

More generally, the same exclusion may also have caused a crucial constituent in the discrepancy between the scientific intentions of the projection techniques and their differing reinterpretations through the audiences, conjurers and entrepreneurs.[75] When the cinematograph turned into the cinema, the immediate popularity of the cinema séance reveals crucial philosophical issues at stake in the experience of the audiences, which ties in with an interconnection between Bergson's emphasis on time beyond movement and Marey's understanding of motion beyond the actual appearance of form. Whereas Marey's scientific method touched upon the vital forces foremost in their visible or mediated effect (both in the graphic and chronophotographic method), his rigour, inventive spirit and courageous work at the fringes of the scientific canon at the same time was exemplary for the crucial predisposition of those scientists who investigated invisible, sometimes ephemeral phenomena. Bergson recognised the next neces-

---

[75] See for example Barnouw (1981), Punt (2003b), Solomon (2006).

sary step through his endeavours in a spectrum from science to phi-losophy and provided a conceptual toolset to tackle these forces in their activity. As a starting point he conceptualised the very dynamics of the creative force as it endures in the perceiver's consciousness.

In the context of a broader intellectual perspective on his oeuvre, Marey's interest in invisible forces beyond the appearance of move-ment seems to intersect with the psychical dimensions of the behold-ers in both the experience of movement as duration during execution and the perception of movement during the synthesis of his movement analysis. In some respects Marey did address movement explicitly beyond the mere shift of a body in spatial coordinates in relation to time, but only implicitly as an experienced activity in duration within the perceiver (of both the actual movement and the technologically enhanced mediation). The fact that Marey — who is commonly re-garded as a pure rationalist and orthodox scientist — participated in the study of psychic phenomena from a scientific perspective, should, however, not be confused with phenomenological connotations of an extreme vitalism or the common populist interpretations of spiritist investigations at the time. Not only did Marey proceed exclusively from the scientific positivist framework and methods, but as Bergson has demonstrated, psychic phenomena could be regarded as part of the ordinary spectrum of human cognitive/psychic capacities and mental phenomena. By taking Marey's wider oeuvre into account, it could even be suggested that his research into the cholera epidemic, the in-visible forces in air, water and during spiritist séances, are as — if not more — significant for an understanding of the cinema as philosophi-cal *dispositif* as is his chronophotography for the technological devel-opments of the emerging cinema. It is in this very dimension of a dy-namism rooting in matters of the mind rather than the actual tangible external manifestation — as it is evident in Marey's oeuvre — that the following chapters seek liberation from an overinvestment in materi-alism in the conception of the cinema: through a recognition of the dimension of the spirit *(esprit)*, resituated within the perception of the beholder.

Chapter 3

The Subordination of Time to Movement:
From the Eye-Brain Model
to the Mind-Consciousness Correlate

Ètienne-Jules Marey's interest in the energy and dynamics of move-ment and the effort of the activity involved, reveal an undercurrent in his thinking that brought together two apparently contradictory strands of, one could say, material and immaterial subject areas. This distinc-tion may be as problematic as a strict separation among various aca-demic disciplines, which rather can be regarded as heterogeneity of sometimes converging knowledge practices with distinct methods and epistemologies. Although Marey positioned himself within the acad-emy of the sciences and the discipline of physiology, in some respects his practice operated beyond the established disciplinary boundaries, especially when it comes to his aesthetic concern with chronophoto-graphy and his vision on their significance for the Arts.

Marey's interconnection with this domain not only featured in the frequently cited influence of his legacy on early 20th century art,[1] but also in his own pursuit of a considerable interest in the aesthetic repre-sentation and expression of movement in art as well as in his own work. It is in this cross-disciplinary context that Marey proposed an application of his chronophotographic studies for training artists' visual perception, while at the same time he pursued an explicit con-cern with aesthetics in his chronophotography. To suggest that Marey might have taken inspiration from art for his physiological studies may be far-fetched but not entirely implausible, considering his en-gagement with the academic tradition of the Arts and the fact that the aesthetic quality of his chronophotographs reveals the convergence between the artistic and scientific application of photographic tech-

---

[1] See Braun (1992: 264-318).

nologies. This was certainly not an accident, since he frequently commented on his own work with a serious concern for the artistic quality of photographic images, on the art of lighting, depth and contrast, as for example in the chapter 'Locomotion in Man from an Artists Point of View' in *Movement* (1895: 169-185). His considerations also appear from his correspondence with his Chief Laboratory Assistant Georges Demenÿ, as a very sophisticated and elaborate process of an intentional aesthetic characteristic in his investigations. In a letter during his yearly winter retreat in Naples in 1892, Marey wrote to Demenÿ, commenting on some films that he received from him for examination. They captured sequential facial close-ups of speaking persons, which Demenÿ produced in response to a commission for Marey's laboratory by the National Deaf-Mute Institute. Marey noted:

> *C'est laid... Les ombres portées sont grotesques ou obscènes...*
> *Au point de vue artistique, il y a bien du déchet. La question de*
> *l'éclairage me semble dominer tout et je voudrais bien en par-*
> *ler avec vous.* (Mannoni 2006: 26)[2]

Similarly, Marey described his impression of Demenÿ's capture of speech by the concierge of the *Station Physiologique: "Le parleur Paul est bien affreux ... Quelle horrible grimace! Est-ce un éternuement?"*[3] Nevertheless he also commented positively on this series from a technical point of view, particularly with regard to the amount of detail in the movements (Mannoni 2006: 27). Later on Marey referred to Demenÿ's chronophotographic studies of facial expressions in his publication *Movement* (1895) in a more neutrally assimilated tone, but again called Paul's expressions an ugly grimace, in his view

---

[2] "This is ugly... The shadows are either grotesque or obscene... From an artistic point of view, they are a waste. The use of flashlight seems to dominate everything in my view and I would like to talk to you about this" (translation by the author).

[3] "The speaker Paul is dreadful... What a horrible grimace! Is this supposed to be a sneeze?" (translation by the author). The "sneeze" was not an uncommon filmed subject at the time. Thomas Alva Edison depicted a sneeze in January 1894, recorded by his chief collaborator W.K.L. Dickson. The clip is online at http://catalog.loc.gov/ (consulted 20.03.2009). *Fred Ott's Sneeze* instead was commissioned by the journalist Barnet Phillips to illustrate an article devoted to the kinetoscope in *Harper's Weekly* on March 24, 1894. In Philippe-Alain Michaud's (2004: 56) comment referring to an intercultural comparison of the sneeze, the subject appears as expressing the vital energy of the emerging cinema as an ecstatic convulsion, a state stripped of self-mastery.

caused by the "gradual transitions" of "exceeding fleeting expressions" (1895: 182-183). He was very particular about the "natural look" of the models and movements and suggested that Demenÿ should only use good-looking models to adequately demonstrate the facial expressions from a smile to anger (Mannoni 2006: 27; Braun 1992: 176). One would be forgiven to read the following advise by Marey (1895: 180) as a (film) casting instruction:

> The great difficulty is to find a subject capable of giving these various expressions in a perfectly natural manner. Most people would only produce a grin or a grimace. Clever actors would no doubt succeed better in assuming the various emotional expressions; and the method might even be useful to them in their own studies. But that which is rendered to perfection by chronophotography is the movement which accompanies the act of articulation. M. Demeny has paid special attention to this extension of our method, and he has met with immense success.[4]

The strangeness that the perception of the instantaneous photographs provoked had not gone unnoticed; in 1882 a critical reviewer in a British magazine had commented on a presentation of instantaneous photographs by Eadweard James Muybridge at the Royal Institution in London:[5]

> The first [the paintings] are all movement, activity and elegance; the second [Muybridge's images] are of an unbelievable rigidity and ugliness. ... Perhaps you ask from where this certainty comes? Why, from common sense: the drawings present us with *movement*, the photographs represent still animals,

---

[4] Marey (1895: 181-182) further welcomed the well-directed light in the photographs and the value they had from a phonetic point of view to the service of the teaching of deaf mutes and reports on the positive results obtained from a successful reading of a conversation via chronophotographies by deaf mutes.

[5] This was after Muybridge's successful and widely celebrated visit to Paris where he had been welcomed by scientists and artists alike during a private demonstration at Marey's home with an international audience, a group of "foreign and French savants" in 1882 (Rabinbach 1990: 101). Braun (1992: 52-53) quotes a review of the event in the *Paris Globe* which names some of the eminent scientists and artists present at this presentation, such as Helmholtz, Lippmann, Nadar, Tissandier, Brown-Sequard, Duhousset, etc., and several scientists attending the International Electrical Congress in Paris. See also Rabinbach (1990: 101-102).

fixed in more or less ghastly positions! (Mannoni 2000: 316 —
emphasis and insert in the original)

Marey explained this apparent alienation in relation to his own work
as a matter of the unknown, the unfamiliarity of single positions of the
movement suspended in space, which was reconciled when viewed in
sequence through a Zootrope (1895: 182-183). His sensibility for aesthetics can also be attributed to the way that he claimed that chronophotography had changed the familiarity of visual perception. Marey's
(1895: 183) conception almost anticipated the future influence of his
works on art, particularly in the following comment:

> What does this fact imply? Is it not that the ugly is only the un-
> known, and that truth seen for the first time offends the eye?
> We are often faced by this question while examining instanta-
> neous chronophotographs of horses moving at a great pace.
> These positions, as revealed by Muybridge, at first appeared
> unnatural, and the painters who first dared to imitate them
> astonished rather than charmed the public. But by degrees, as
> they became more familiar, the world became reconciled to
> them, and they have taught us to discover attitudes in Nature
> which we are unable to see for ourselves, and we begin almost
> to resent a slight mistake in the delineation of a horse in mo-
> tion. How will this education of the eye end, and what will be
> the effect on Art? The future alone can show.

While Marey caught the transformative potential in the role of the observer, in that his vision did quiet accurately reflect on the future shifts
in the representational forms in the visual arts, his own interest in art
stood in stark contrast with the interpretations of his legacy. As Véronique Rollet (2006: 106-107) points out, Marey's artistic interest was
influenced by ancient paintings of Italian origins, as well as those by
some contemporary artists, especially by Gaetano Esposito and Mari-
ano Fortuny, with whom he was acquainted. In the chapter 'Locomotion in Man From an Artistic Point of View' in *Movement* (1895: 169-
185) Marey compared movements of horses and human locomotion in
artworks from Antiquity (in several monochrome reproductions) with
the movement analysis in his chronophotographs. Modestly admitting
that he felt unqualified to speak of aesthetics (167), he emphasised the
exactness as well as the distortions of certain representations of
movements in the arts from a point of view that seemed to bring to-

gether paradigms of science with a considered interest in the artistic expressions of movement. Marey (170-171) compared, for example, the exact postures of an instantaneous photograph of a runner with the drawn postures of Ocydromes (swift-runners) on a Greek vase in which he pointed to the accuracy of one runner's position and reminded artists not to forget: "... that one of the characteristics of running, and even of walking, is to maintain a continuous position of unstable equilibrium".

Marey (205) considered the issue of aesthetics in close alignment with the scientific quest for truth and claimed that: "Art and Science join hands in searching after truth". He saw his contribution to the arts foremost in the application of the exact scientific studies of movement in chronophotography for artists' training in the perception and representation of movement, which would serve in particular to identify the most "expressive attitude" (179). He suggested that some of the attitudes shown in chronophotographs might be acceptable to artists "without transgressing the laws of aesthetics" (172). In this context he conceived of the advancements in physiological studies not only as a direct link to, but also as a modern version of, the anatomic studies of life-model drawing. This approach led to a very successful publication by Marey and Demenÿ: the portfolio *Études de Physiologie Artistique Faites au Moyen de la Chronophotographie* in 1893 (Braun 1992: 268).[6] In 1888 Marey had written to the *Académie des Sciences* to explain his view on the use of chronophotography for artists to study and analyse a more precise presentation of movement and 'animated beings':

> Certain artistic representations of walkers or runners are sometimes bothersome to the physiologist familiar with the succession of movement in human locomotion. The impression is somewhat analogous to what we feel in front of those landscapes painted when the laws of perspective were observed less than they are today. The difficulty artists find in representing men or animals in action is explained when we realize that the most skilled observers declare themselves incapable of seizing

---

[6] Marey did not follow up this first volume after Demenÿ's departure from the *Station Physiologique,* however Albert Londe and Paul Richer published their *Atlas d'Anatomie Artistique* and *Physiologie Artistique de l'Homme en Mouvement* in 1895, capitalising on the popularity of Marey's and Demenÿ's previous port-folio (Braun 1992: 269).

the successive phases of locomotive movements. To this end, photochronography seems called to render services to art as it does to science, since it analyzes the most rapid and most complicated movements. (Braun 1992: 267-268)[7]

At one point in the late 1890s, Marey (1895: 236-238) deployed three cameras from different angles in order to use these perspectives for a comparative analysis, which he illustrated in *Movement* in a case study of birds in flight, such as gulls and pigeons. He then sculpted plaster models of a particular single phase of a wing and finally mounted the sculptures into a large Zootrope in order to create what he called a "synthesis in relief" (Braun 1992: 136,141-142, 267). Rollet (2006: 106) highlights Marey's considerable artistic skill, which is particularly evident in a plaster bust of his son in law and a painter, Noël Bouton. Marey himself, however, mistrusted his talent, as Braun (1992: 137) reports, and chose to collaborate with the academic sculptor Georges Engrand to produce bas-reliefs.[8] It is of particular significance that Marey also had these models cast in bronze during his winter stays in Naples. Although they were not intended as artworks in themselves, they raise a consideration of the artistic dimension in his work, since professional sculptors regarded bronze as the most difficult material to manifest movement as a consequence of the apparent immobility its presence suggested (Pisano 2006: 95). It can only be assumed here that Marey may have chosen bronze in order to make an intervention in support of the academic tradition of the *Beaux Arts* by showing how bronze could capture the precise movements of birds and transform its material appearance.

Notwithstanding his realist approach to the artistic representation of movement, Marey was not interested in a, what he called, 'realistic' representation of objects and things in the sense of ordinary sensory perception. Rather, he understood chronophotography as superseding ordinary perception in that in his view it allowed for greater details

---

[7] Marey called his instantaneous photography at first "photochronography", emphasising the aspect of time (*chronos*), which was sometimes also applied as the term "time photography". The term chronophotography eventually became the standard term, which was decided in 1889 on behest of Marey by the International Congress of Photography headed by Janssen (Braun 1992: 396, footnote 46).

[8] Engrand made for example bas-reliefs of a runner in a specific posture according to Marey's chronophotographic analysis. See Marey (1895: 176), Braun (1992: 137, 267, 144 Fig. 81).

and precision, which normally gets lost in the speed of movement. In the case of the singular photographic postures transferred into plaster casts, such as Engrand's sculpture of the runner, one might say that Marey fell into the trap of realist orthodoxy since the sculpture arrested movement and did not, as his composite photographs suggested, express the succession of movements. A discussion of the representation of movement in the arts and science raises questions, first and foremost of what was considered as 'real' — movement in the experience of the beholder or in the dissection of material forms as science executed in its methods; exactly the threshold where Bergson situated his philosophical intervention. In this sense, Marey's intervention into the arts really was limited to instructions for movement analysis as a tool for artistic training. His bronze models merely represented copies of the frozen figures of instantaneous photography and in this way dissected the movement into sequential figures in frozen postures. This stood in sharp contrast to the transitory conception of time in sculpture achieved through movement in flow over a time duration, as it was for example expressed and championed by Marey's contemporary, the famous sculptor Auguste Rodin (1840-1917). The simultaneity of transitory states within a figure was precisely why Rodin's artistic intervention has been claimed to be so radical; especially in his *Balzac, The Gates of Hell* or *L'Homme qui Marche,* movement supervened posture, and time crystallised in form. Rodin explained in a conversation with Paul Gsell in 1910:

> And even in those of my works where action is less stressed, I
> have always sought to include some indication of gesture; it is
> very rare that I have represented complete repose. I have al-
> ways tried to express interior feelings through the mobility of
> the muscles. (Gsell 1986: 27)

Not surprisingly, Rodin almost obsessively criticised chronophotography for suggesting a veridical relation with nature in a pure copy of reality, while reality for him, like Bergson, was life itself, movement and duration. Pisano (2006) reminds us that for Rodin sculpture petrified time through the specific instant that stretched in duration and underwent a metamorphosis in its transfer into matter, in contrast to the *'instant quelconque'* ('instant whatsoever') in instantaneous photography. Rodin gave art a particular status in its preservation of psychic states through the inscription of time in its material form, which also reflected in his support of photography as an emerging form of art that he applied and exploited in his own creative processes in his atelier (Elsen 1980). In this sense, Rodin took a similar position to Bergson with regard to his understanding of psychological time as dynamic, as flux and continuous change. The contrasting of the quality of time in sculpture as duration with the instantaneity of quantitative time in the freeze frames of instantaneous photography, is reiterated in a comment by Rodin in conversation with Gsell (1986: 32):

> "No", responded Rodin. "It is the artist who tells the truth and photography that lies. For in reality, time does not stand still. And if the artist succeeds in producing the impression of a gesture that is executed in several instants, his work is certainly much less conventional than the scientific image where time is abruptly suspended."

Rodin, moreover, emphasised the immobility of the figure in chrono-photographs and counter-argued against instantaneous photography by illustrating how in his *Saint Jean-Baptiste,* 1877, both feet were on the ground and suggested the simultaneity of a succession of movement resulting in a perceptual process by which the figure shifted its weight in a sequence of intentional duration (Gsell 1986: 30-31; see also Pisano 2006: 99). Gsell (1986: 31) quotes Rodin saying:

> And this confirms what I have just stated about movement in art. In high-speed photographs, although figures are caught in full action, they seem suddenly frozen in mid-air. This is because every part of their body is reproduced exactly at the same twentieth or fortieth of a second, and there is not, as in art, the gradual unfolding of a movement.

While Rodin commented here on instantaneous photographs, as Muybridge most famously exhibited them,[9] Marey's superimpositions of

---

[9] Muybridge's horizontal and vertical instantaneous photographic narratives illustrate the previously mentioned analysis of Bergson in their concern with external movement in space, constituted by never more than single positions of the moving body in space, like the hand of the clock at a particular point. In Muybridge's work, scrutinised through a Bergsonian filter, the movement of animals and humans is reduced to single, distinct units in space, which, in contrast to Marey, were taken from a multiplicity of perspectives through the deployment of dozens of cameras. In this sense

single instances in one frame seemed to support — although merely in an analytical way — Rodin's intention to incorporate various instances of a movement in his sculpture. This attempt of an inscription of time into movement of the figure, as a passing from the past into the future captured as a transitional state, however, only becomes transparent when the perceptual processes of the beholder are incorporated in the consideration of how movement actually was produced. For Marey the single instant of a frozen posture had to proceed from a particular instantaneous posture in the past in order to create a simulation of movement, and this achievement of a sense of duration implicitly referred to the involvement of cognition in the perceptual process. This not only defined his continuous deployment of his graphing methods, but also informed his conception of the succession of movement when modelling instantaneous positions in sculpture. Although the result seemed to contradict his intentions, Marey (1895: 173) suggested: "… it might be said that the modelling of a limb not only expressed the action of the time being, but also suggested, to a certain extent, its immediate successor".

While it is not always clear in Gsell's account if Rodin criticised Muybridge's instantaneous photography or Marey's composite chronophotography, Rodin, in any case, rejected the view that photography, driven by scientific realism, would achieve this progressive unfolding of a gesture in the images themselves. He explained to Gsell in reference to the sculptor's (or painter's) role:

> He makes visible the passage of one pose into the other; he indicates how imperceptibly the first glides into the second. In his work, one still detects a part of what was while one discovers in part what will be. (Gsell 1986: 29)

With reference to Marey's chronophotography, George Didi-Huberman's notion of the "perpetual indiscernibilities between the near future and the persistence of the present" in the transitional moments in between events (Pisano 2006: 97),[10] reflects Bergson's re-

---

they did not constitute movement at all, but instantaneity and a rupture in the flow of time, as best exemplified through the celluloid filmstrips with single still frames.

[10] *"En réalité, puisque nous ne connaissons pas le nombre d'intervalles possibles d'une position à une autre – l'œuil nous restitue un mouvement dans sa continuité –, l'artiste ne peut penser le mouvement qu'en termes de métamorphose et de 'perpétuelles indiscernabilités entre le bientôt et l'encore'"* (Pisano 2006: 97). — "In reality,

cognition of the artist's ability to catch the moment of transition; the state of flow as a creative act with indeterminate outcome. Bergson addressed the shortcomings of the scientific method in his postulate of the indeterminacy of the future, which confirms Marey's previously cited comment on the predictability of future movement through scientific analysis:

> This is, in fact, quite natural; the role of science is to foresee. It extracts and retains from the material world that which can be repeated and calculated, and consequently that which is not in a state of flow. (Bergson 1992: 13)

Bergson's notion of flow referred to his concept of *durée,* which he elaborated in connection with an engagement in the intrinsic pleasure of an aesthetic experience. In this regard he gave an example of the experience of the quality of grace in *Time and Free Will* (2001: 11-13), which counters Marey's view that each position in chronophotography allowed the perception of the following one, and redirects our attention to the significance of Marey's graphing methods instead. Bergson (2001: 11-12) visualised:

> At first it is only the perception of a certain ease, a certain facility in the outward movements. And as those movements are easy which prepare the way for others, we are led to find a superior ease in the movements which can be foreseen, in the present attitudes in which future attitudes are pointed out and, as it were, prefigured. If jerky movements are wanting in grace, the reason is that each of them is self-sufficient and does not announce those which are to follow. If curves are more graceful than broken lines, the reason is that, while a curved line changes its direction at every moment, every new direction is indicated in the preceding one. Thus the perception of ease in motion passes over into the pleasure of mastering the flow of time and of holding the future in the present.

---

since we do not know the number of possible intervals from one position to the next – the eye restores to us a movement in its continuity – the artist can conceive movement only in terms of metamorphosis and 'perpetual indiscernibilities between the near future and the persistence of the present'" (translation by the author). Pisano cites from Didi-Huberman and Mannoni (2004: 226).

Bergson situated this sensation — what could be extended to the conceptions of 'precognition' or 'presentiment' — within the conscious states and internal flux of time of the beholder, signified by the management or mastering of the flow, or as he expressed in others words, *"le plaisir d'arrêter en quelque sorte la marche du temps"* (2005: 9).[11] He continued his exemplification of the sensation of grace by drawing in yet another element, which bears a particular relevance to the emerging attempts to synthesise the capture and projected representation of image sequences with synchronous sound from the 1890s onwards.[12] Bergson (2001: 12-13) proposed:

> A third element comes in when the graceful movements submit to a rhythm and are accompanied by music. For the rhythm and measure, by allowing us to foresee to a still greater extent the movements of the dancer, make us believe that we now control them. As we guess almost the exact attitude which the dancer is going to take, he seems to obey us when he really takes it: the regularity of the rhythm establishes a kind of communication between him and us, and the periodic returns of the measure are like so many invisible threads by means of which we set in motion this imaginary puppet. Indeed, if it stops for an instant, our hand in its impatience cannot refrain from making a movement, as though to push it, as though to replace it in the midst of this movement, the rhythm of which has taken complete possession of our thought and will. Thus a kind of physical sympathy enters into the feeling of grace.[13]

It becomes evident that the aesthetic quality, which some of the critiques of instantaneous photographs at the time have identified as lacking, concerned the very perceptual processes when motion turns

---

[11] The original French expression could literally be translated into "the pleasure of arresting the passage of time" (translation by the author).

[12] For research into sound technologies see Richard Abel and Rick Altman (2001, 1999).

[13] While continuity editing attempts to draw the spectator ceaselessly into the flux of the film, in which music and sound play a most crucial role, experimental filmmakers in particular have revealed and playfully as well as critically engaged with the spectator's agency in the perceptual processes by separating image and sound from their continuity. John Smith's *The Girl Chewing Gum* (1976) for example evoked a simulation of control reminiscent of Bergson's suggestion of the agency of the spectator in the anticipation of the future — an effect that the cinema has adopted and developed into very sophisticated techniques.

into a qualitative experience of time within the interpenetrating states of consciousness — which involves the active engagement of the perceiver in order to synthesise the mechanistic dissection of movement in the pictures. While this may seem too obvious to mention, it can be identified as the crucial pivot where the diverging views in the discussion on the representability of time parted company. From this perspective, it follows that the perception of seeming jerky movements might lie in the discrepancy between the integrity of the object (and its familiarity) and the dissection into parts, seen from unfamiliar perspectives. Moreover, Bergson's insights suggest that the reason may lie in the inability to master the flow of time in terms of internalised, qualitative conscious states that impinge on the perceptual processes. This perspective illuminates Marey's position in that he distinguished the photographic perception from the much more limited visual perceptual abilities of the human apparatus and claimed to have made accessible a dimension beyond the visible; a super-ordinary reality. Whereas Marey sought a solution for the deficiency of the human perceptual process in technology, Bergson situated his philosophical intervention by taking up the issue of consciousness.

Bergson (2001: 15-16) addressed the issue of movement in the materiality of art at the very beginning of *Time and Free Will* (2001) and shared his observations in a shift of attention from the artwork to the spectator:

> While the works of ancient sculpture express faint emotions which play upon them like a passing breath, the pale immobility of the stone causes the feeling expressed or the movement just begun to appear as if they were fixed for ever, absorbing our thought and our will in their own eternity. We find in architecture, in the very midst of this startling immobility, certain effects analogous to those of rhythm. [...] Thus art aims at impressing feelings on us rather than expressing them; it suggests them to us, and willingly dispenses with the imitation of nature when it finds some more efficacious means.

It can be further implied that the unfamiliarity and ugliness conceived in the unusual postures of instantaneous photography temporarily inhibited the development of an affinity, or even sympathy, with the perceived.[14] This impact, caused by the forced, unexpected arrest of time, afforded a counter movement of the mind in its natural tendency or bend in the experiential motion of movement (which later the projector would take over to compensate for this required effort). Bergson, however, suggested that the conscious extension into the object, accompanied by sympathy (which he also referred to as aesthetic intuition), went much farther than the re-education of the senses that Marey proposed in relation to the experience of 'ugliness', of a 'truth' seen for the first time that offends the eye (Braun 1992: 271). Bergson (1998: 176-177) instead conceived of the aesthetic faculty in the perceptual processes in a close relationship with the creative intention of the artist:

> That an effort of this kind is not impossible, is proved by the existence in man of an aesthetic faculty along with normal perception. Our eye perceives the features of the living being, merely as assembled, not as mutually organized. The intention of life, the simple movement that runs through the lines, that binds them together and gives them significance, escapes it. This intention is just what the artist tries to regain, in placing himself back within the object by a kind of sympathy, in breaking down, by an effort of intuition, the barrier that space puts up between him and his model.

Evocative of Rodin's proprioceptive approach in its chiming with Bergson's conception of sympathy and affinity between subject and object, Gsell described, how Rodin spoke with admiration and great sympathy in his reflection on the *Vénus de Médicis* and the statue's curvatures, when observed under the dim light of a lamp at night:

> "Isn't it marvellous?" he said. "Admit that you did not expect to discover so many details. Look! Look at the infinite undulations of the valley between the belly and the thigh. Relish all the voluptuous curvatures of the hip. And now, there, in the back, all those adorable dimples." He spoke softly with a devout ardour. He bent toward this marble as if he were in love

---

[14] This raises the question if Marey's concern with good-looking models could be related to Bergson's notion of sympathy as a point of intersection in a discussion of aesthetics, which would require a much closer examination of the specific discourses regarding aesthetics in the context of the late 19th century.

with it. "This is real flesh!" he said. Beaming, he added: "It must have been moulded by kisses and caresses!" (Gsell 1986: 23)

Curiously parallel with Rodin's remark, although shifting the attention entirely away from the object to the perceptual processes of the beholder, Bergson (1998: 248) asserted:

> It is natural to our intellect, whose function is essentially practical, made to present to us things and states rather than changes and acts. But things and states are only views, taken by our mind, of becoming. There are no things, there are only actions.

In between things and states lies Bergson's conception of the *image*, which neither stands for the thing or the object in itself, nor its representation, but rather for an existence halfway in-between. Once incorporated through the processes of perception, a purely qualitative differentiation by being *in* time results in a multiplicity of conscious states in constant change: *durée* as it constitutes 'becoming'. Bergson asserted, similar to Rodin's position, that the flow of time could not be achieved through a fixed posture of the past, as exemplified in instantaneous photography. He acclaimed the indivisibility of the qualitative experience of time, *durée,* pertaining to the indeterminacy of the future, which contrasts with the intellect's processes of dissection:

> ... our intelligence images its origin and evolution as an arrangement and rearrangement of parts which supposedly merely shift from one place to another; in theory therefore, it should be able to foresee any one state of the whole: by positing a definite number of stable elements one has, predetermined, all their possible combinations. (1992: 96)

In Bergson's view the very forces of life could not be grasped by the intellect alone, which operated according to the scientific method and split the whole into single instances. He asserted that:

> We hold, on the contrary, that in the domain of life the elements have no real and separate existence. They are manifold mental views of an indivisible process. And for that reason there is radical contingency in progress, incommensurability

between what goes before and what follows — in short, duration. (1998: 29 footnote 1)

Bergson's understanding of duration as non-quantifiable entity, which
he defined as a quality of internal conscious states, had a significant
bearing on his conception of the discrepancy between the material
form and the experience of an actually 'lived duration' (*durée*):

> But in reality the body is changing form at every moment; or
> rather, there is no form, since form is immobile and the reality
> is movement. What is real is the continual *change of* form:
> *form is only a snapshot view of a transition.* (1998: 302 — em-
> phasis in the original)

Bergson's evocation of a camera's "snapshot view" seems to bear a
critique of the increasing subscription to photographic realism that
was closely aligned with the scientific attempts to establish proofs for
a causal relationship between the perception and its referent. This veridical connection was shattered and challenged through the changing
role of the observer in the 19th century, as mentioned earlier, and not
least by the emerging cinema itself. Similarly, Rodin shifted the attention from the object to the proactive perceptual processes of the beholder, guided to follow the development of an act through a character
in the sculpture. He suggested: "The sculptor obliges, so to speak, the
spectator to follow the development of an act through one figure"
(Gsell 1986: 29-30). This indivisibility of movement that Rodin meant
to achieve in an art object in combination with a proactive receiver,
according to Bergson, defines not the object in itself, but constitutes
the enduring subject in a constant flux of becoming.

  In this sense, everything is truly in motion in terms of time not
space (reminiscent of Marey's elimination of space in favour of time).
This internal flow — that is the realm of the spirit — had to be understood immanent within matter and not detached on a transcendental
plane. This ever-changing reality in constant flux and vibration was
'knowable' and accessible in the two familiar ways of the mind: on
the surface and its material form through the intellect, and in its duration and profound vital force and being, through intuition. In this dynamic process that expresses the very motion of creativity, matter and
spirit (*l'esprit*) connect, touch, and enable synergies of shared consciousness. In this sense, according to Bergson, human beings are

born both artisans and geometricians in a metaphorical sense. As geometricians we reject the unforeseeable; as artisans (or artists) we accept indeterminacy drawing on creation and spontaneity.[15] Consequently Bergson (1992: 93-94) understood human beings as continuous creators and inventors:

> Call it what you will; it is the feeling we have of being creators of our intentions, of our decisions, of our acts, and by that, of our habits, our characters, ourselves. Artisans of our life, even artists when we so desire, we work continually, with the material furnished us by the past and present, by heredity and opportunity, to mold a figure unique, new, original, as unforeseeable, as the form given by the sculptor to the clay.

Each material form derives from a previous form in a continuous flow of changing states by adding each time something new; this is how Bergson proposed to understand *durée*, the quality of time, as lived 'reality'. This reality could only be grasped in its fullness through an internal motion (what he later called intuition), a counter movement to the externally oriented intellect. He proposed:

> Reality is global and undivided growth, progressive invention, duration: it resembles a gradually expanding rubber balloon assuming at each moment unexpected forms. But our intelligence imagines its origin and evolution as an arrangement and rearrangement of parts which supposedly merely shift from one place to another; in theory therefore, it should be able to foresee any one state of the whole: by positing a definite number of stable elements one has, predetermined, all their possible combinations. That is not all. Reality, as immediately perceived, is fullness constantly swelling out, to which emptiness is unknown. It has extension just as it has duration; but this concrete extent is not the infinite and infinitely divisible space the intellect takes as a place in which to build. Concrete space has been extracted from things. They are not in it; it is space which is in them. Only, as soon as our thought reasons about reality, it makes space a receptacle. (1992: 95-96)

---

[15] Bergson (1998: 341) referred in *Creative Evolution* to that: "… unforeseeable nothing which is everything in a work of art".

Bergson's view of space as being contained by consciousness put the agency of the observer in a whole new perspective with significance up to today. It had a particular bearing on the way he uniquely managed to embrace the contemporary scientific knowledge on the psychophysiological processes of the human mind (increasingly sought in the brain), together with a philosophy that proposed insights into the body-mind interconnection — the so-called 'hard problem' in consciousness studies today.

Marey's work can be regarded as pivotal in the indication and crystallisation of the shifts that took place during the 19th century in the conceptualisation of the observer alongside with the rupture between perception and the object, which also reflect on some of the driving forces of the emerging cinema. His intention to deconstruct movement in order to uncover the dynamic principle of motion can be more profoundly understood in terms of the two distinct principles of time by Bergson: time as an externalised measurable quantity in space, and time as an internal qualitative experience of duration *(durée)*. This philosophical position suggests that Marey's work, especially his composite chronophotographs, can not only be read as symbolic representations of movement instants in space, but also as indicators for two kinds of multiplicities that have continuously been mixed up in the discourse. First, that the perception of movement is conceived internally as duration of an undivided whole and simultaneity within the beholder, and secondly, as an external multiplicity of single images, as distinct parts of the whole of a movement. These dimensions of the processes involved during perception, as exemplified by Bergson, were not accounted for and remained obscured in the scientific studies of movement analysis in physiology, which likewise also led to significant oversights in some of the theoretical conceptualisations on how the cinema emerged. The focus in the discourse lay (and often still does) on the textual analysis of the images themselves. Marey's composite chronophotographs, however, much more profoundly hint at, and trigger, the recognition of the perceptual processes involved.

It is not coincidental that both Bergson and Marey referred to art in some of the most crucial moments of their thinking — the very discipline that over centuries had cultivated a serious consideration of the internal states and psyche of the human mind. In his arguments against determinism with regard to both the issues of form and movement, Bergson proposed that it is especially the philosopher and the artist[16] (and the artist philosopher) who remind us that the temporality of duration cannot be found in space. As the previous discussion exemplifies, the misunderstanding of time as measurable quantity, as Bergson proposed, seemed to lie at the core of many controversies between distinct knowledge practices during the late 19th century.[17] In a Bergsonian manner the disciplinary distinctions could rather be regarded as navigational coordinates that indicate a tendency toward an externalised multiplicity of perspectives segmented by the intellect (spatial/quantitative) or toward internalised characteristics of creative processes conceived as a flow within the conscious states of the acting individual (qualitative, as *durée*). Bergson saw both these tendencies as mutually inclusive; hence they neither formed a dichotomy nor an unsolvable paradox, when looked at from the perspective of the very experience of the mind in its oscillating processes of execution. Bergson separated these two tendencies merely schematically, in their essential manifestations and outstanding intensities relating to matter and spirit (in particular those of time and memory) in order to ultimately reconnect them through the activity of consciousness that embraces both motions. He achieved this without the invocation of an external absolute or transcendental entity, but through an inclusive metaphysics operating through immanence.

The confusion between the conceptions of time, matter and spirit that Bergson so elegantly untangled, is apparent in most accounts of the discussions on time and movement in relation to art and the cinema — historical and contemporary. The contradictory potential of this confusion surfaced most explicitly — not coincidentally — when the global standardisation of time liberated alternative speculations, which culminated among other things in extensive discussions on relativity or the fourth dimension. This potential did not only reflect in the reinforcement of the separation between the arts and the sciences, but also in the controversies around the interventions of some of the most prominent thinkers and practitioners, of whom Marey's work in this context appears as paradigmatic. By separating the two modalities of

---

[16] For a more general discussion on Bergson's conception of art see Ruth Lorand (1999).

[17] This may be most obvious in the oversimplified separation between the arts and the sciences, which overlooks that their distinctions constituted parts of a "single interlocking field of knowledge and practice", as Crary (1990: 9), Punt (2000, 2004b) and also Doane (2002) among other theorists alert us to.

time, as Bergson envisioned, the apparent contradictions in Marey's work dissolve in the perspective of the wider framework of interdisciplinary connections, not least since his interest in the forces of life constituted the very movements he analysed.

Similarly, there is also an apparent paradox in Rodin's conception of photography. On one hand he vehemently criticised instantaneous photography and a scientific realist approach to photography's technique to freeze movement into a virtual halt in time, which disavowed time as duration in the instant. On the other he applied photography in his own work processes and supported the emerging artistic approaches to photography as art form. This appears most explicitly in his concurrence with Edward Steichen's photographs of his *Balzac* for example, which in his view represented exactly the way he wanted his *Balzac* to be seen.[18] The grainy, low contrast photographs made his *Balzac* appear as if moving — as though alive — and evoked the way in which Rodin wanted his sculpture to be perceived (note: not simply 'seen') by the human observer. It posed the question of the distinction between an instant photograph taken of an executed movement and that of a 'still' yet seeming animate image of a sculpture?

An indicative answer to this question seems to lie in the particular aesthetic qualities that evoke a differentiation between the textual analysis of the photographs themselves and an inclusive, transparent account of the experience of the beholder during the perceptual process within the expressiveness of the image. Photographs may be captured in a smallest instant of a second; the perceptual processes still involve a certain trajectory of duration within the internal processes of consciousness, however short they may seem. These two separate conceptions of time, as Bergson has identified them — time as spatial measurement and as duration *(dureé)* — are commonly mixed in the discourses on various media technologies.

As soon as the active participation and specific affordance of the beholder is taken into account in reference to instantaneous photogra-

---

[18] For an example see *Balzac Toward the Light, Midnight,* 1908 by Edward Steichen, Alfred Stieglitz Collection, 1933, The Metropolitan Museum of Art, New York; online at: http://www.metmuseum.org/toah/hd/rodn/ho_33.43.38.htm (consulted 14.03.2009). Rodin had expressed to Steichen: "Your photographs will make people understand my Balzac". Cited from an exhibition at the Musée Rodin on the role of photography in Rodin's work (Nov. 2007 – Feb. 2008) online at: http://museums-in-paris.com/sub.php?action=musee&code=291 (consulted 14.03.2009). Also see Pinet (2007).

phy, some of the controversies in the contemporary discussions on the perception of movement and time in art and science (in relation to photography) appear to dissolve. In this respect it can be said that Rodin's rejection of Marey's and Muybridge's instantaneous photography, as much as Bergson's critique of the subordination of time to space (and externalised movement), profoundly countered the increasing materialism and certain formalism in both the arts and the sciences. Moreover, once the beholder is included in the discussion, it becomes transparent how both Rodin and Marey in similar ways alluded to the cognitive processes of perception in their synthesis of movement (as distinct from Marey's analysis) and eschewed a realist approach to optical technologies. From this exclusive perspective only, their work seems to differ in the degree in which they were able to incorporate a certain suggestion of duration; Marey by rendering the invisible visible, and Rodin by externalising internal states and the passage of time in his sculptures. In both cases movement and other forces became alive in the perception of the beholder, constituting the dimension of a qualitative experience of time that Bergson called *dureé*. From such a perspective, it becomes transparent how both, the conceptual periphery of Marey's work, and Rodin's implication of duration in sculpture, pointed to the realms in between the figure and, beyond the text. This interpretation seems especially apt when recognising that the perceived *image* always outruns perception (both human and technologically enhanced), in the sense that perception is always fuller than conscious recognition, and that an effort is required by the perceiver to connect the single instances and perspectives to one another. From the perspective of Marey's own references to art and his interest in the aesthetic quality of his images, it could be suggested that cinema not merely took on Marey's technological base into cinematography, as it is most obvious on a material level, but also some of the inherent aesthetic aspects of Marey's scientific images and a profound recognition of the spaces for interpretation and imagination that found a great resonance especially in the popular reception of the emerging projection technologies.[19]

---

[19] Georges Méliès' oeuvre in particular could be interpreted as a synthesis of Marey's and Muybridge's work that combined some of Marey's sophisticated techniques of superimpositions and transformations of single states taken from a single camera point of view, while it also was reminiscent of Muybridge's interest in narration and

The underlying dimensions and the controversy around the representability of time in relation to Marey's work in particular were more explicitly addressed during the various interpretations of his work during the early 20th century. They revealed the philosophical appeal of his work, which found manifold adaptations and reinterpretations in a variety of domains, scientific as well as artistic: from ergonomics, medical instrumentation, aeronautics, photography, sculpture, avant-garde movements to rapid- and slow-motion cinema. Braun elaborates on some of the most obvious appropriations of Marey's work in the Futurist and Cubist interventions that used his movement analysis techniques. These art works intellectually and formally challenged the idea of representation by accommodating ideas such as simultaneity, speed, mobility, acceleration or the fourth dimension (Braun 1992: 264-318).[20] The sublimation of reality as perceived by the 'eye' stimulated metaphysical interpretations of Marey's work and the epitomising of the subjective and dynamic sensation of felt time in art.

The reception and various interpretations of chronophotography, similar to the reception and theorisation of the emerging cinema, has been influenced and supported by the widespread assumption that the perception of movement was caused by the after-image effect. The materialist scientific understanding of vision as retinal mechanistic process in the late 19th century reinforced the overvaluation of movement over time. It was supported by a misconception of how movement is perceived and has persisted throughout the literature on visual culture.[21] This myth had been debunked already through Marx Wert-

---

the reconstruction of events within a personalised framework of characters and plotlines.

[20] As Brenez (1992) reminds us, this widespread appropriation included the film avant-garde, for example Eisenstein's montage technique, deploying repetitions and successive short sequences in order to achieve a sublimation and transformation of a mere 'representation' of reality. Another example is the application of Marey's chronophotographic method by Frank Bunker Gilbreth who was concerned with the capturing of time and economic movements in the processes of mechanisation. This resulted among other things in the development of his three-dimensional chronophotography called the "chronocyclegraph method", which produced images that are reminiscent of certain types of spirit photography and can also been in relation to Anton Giulio Bragaglia's work. See Braun (1992: 340-8).

[21] This is especially the case in the literature of cinema and film studies, which (even today) uncritically draws on Frederick Talbot's early cinema history of 1912. The endurance of the myth of the so-called *persistence of vision* in cinema studies has been critiqued and rectified by several authors, among others by Bill Nichols and

heimer's experimental studies into a complexity of effects intrinsic to the perception of motion, by which he recognised that the theory of *persistence of vision* was insufficient to account for movement in visual perception. At the time, Wertheimer (1912) developed a distinct range of effects, among which the B and *phi* movement, today summarised as the so-called "apparent motion".[22] His findings still underpin the current understanding of the perception of movement, and are particularly significant for the illusion of movement in standard film projection, when in fact nothing is actually moving except the film-strip through the projector gate.

The phenomenon of the positive after-image effect, it is now commonly acknowledged, merely relates to the retention of the colour and brightness relations of the original stimulus; it occurs regardless of whether motion is perceived or not and hence is distinct from the perception of movement (Nichols and Ledermann 1980: 97). The perception of movement has been recognised as at least two distinct elements; the perception or processing of form and the perception of motion (of still and moving objects). Apparent movement in the cinema occurs mainly between the displacements of an object in space through single-frame images when no intermediate points are presented to the retina, as it would be the case in real movement. The illusion of the apparent movement makes us see the object moving from one place to another even though the intermediate positions are lacking. This phenomenon, which Wertheimer recognised as beta movement, is often compounded with another effect of apparent movement called *phi*. This refers to an illusion of 'pure' motion when two or more objects are stationary but blinking (or as in the cinema, interrupted through a shutter), at a frequency that creates an illusion of movement around the objects and inbetween them.[23] As a conse-

---

Susan J. Ledermann (1980), Joseph and Barbara Anderson (Anderson and Fisher 1978), and Michael Chanan (1980: 54-68).

[22] Both, the *beta* movement and *phi* phenomenon are classifications of apparent movement and often summarised with the term "phi phenomena". See also Steinman, et al. (2000). David Parkinson summarises the current understanding of the illusion of "apparent motion" in the cinema perception as follows: "Flicker fusion prevents us from seeing the lines between each frame, while the phi phenomenon... provides a mental bridge between the frames to permit us to see a series of static images as a single continuous movement" (Greenaway 2004: 3).

[23] See Nichols and Ledermann (1980: 100-101), Greenaway (2004: 3), and also Chanan (1980), Anderson (1980), Aumont (1991), Mannoni (2000: 201).

quence, the impression or illusion of the perception of movement in the cinema occurs foremost through the involvement of two distinct perceptual phenomena; the effect of the "visual flicker", which disappears after a certain projection speed through so-called "flicker-fusion"[24] or "fusion masking" (a threshold that is called the Critical Fusion Frequency, CFF),[25] and the phenomenon of "apparent motion".

While the endurance of the myth of the so-called *persistence of vision* in film and cinema studies could be seen as disciplinary blindness, it is all the more puzzling since one of the very early and well known theoretical works on the cinema, *The Photoplay* (1916) by the German psychologist Hugo Münsterberg, already included a critique of the insufficiency of this conception, which, in addition to his own experiments, also drew on Wertheimer's research.[26] A pioneer in the fields of industrial, experimental, and clinical psychology,[27] Münsterberg (2001: 29) accordingly considered the *persistence of vision* as too simplified a conception to do justice to the actual experience of the perception of motion:

> ... the apparent movement is in no way the mere result of an afterimage and the impression of motion is surely more than the mere perception of successive phases of movement. The movement is in these cases not really seen from without, but is superadded, by the action of the mind, to motionless pictures.

---

[24] "Flicker-fusion" bridges the distinction between single still frames, it does not yield the impression of movement.

[25] CFF signifies the point when the flicker of single frames becomes indistinguishable; a threshold that is dependent on the degree of illuminance (Nichols and Ledermann 1980: 98).

[26] Münsterberg (2001: 26) moreover referred to scientific research from the previous thirty years, such as by Stricker, Exner, Hall, James, Fischer, Stern, Marbe, Lincke, Wertheimer, and Korte, who according to him: "... have thrown new light on the problem by carefully divised experiments". Both Marey and Bergson were aware of the contemporary psychophysiological research and also cited some of these authors in their own work.

[27] Münsterberg was trained in medicine and psychology and was invited by William James in 1892 to run the psychological laboratory at Harvard. While this position made Münsterberg a forerunner of behaviourism, in the way that he saw mental phenomena they necessarily correlated with psychological processes. In this regard he did acknowledge the human agency of freedom in relation to values and was like Bergson and Marey involved in research of parapsychological phenomena; he also studied one of the most famous mediums of the time, Eusapia Palladino (Münsterberg 1910).

This reference is reminiscent of Bergson's (2001: 111) earlier elaborations on the perception of movement, in that he understood motion as
a mental synthesis, in so far as it concerned a passage from one point
to another.[28] In a similar sense, Münsterberg (2001: 26) asserted that:

> ... the perception of movement is an independent experience
> which cannot be reduced to a simple seeing of a series of dif-
> ferent positions. A characteristic content of consciousness must
> be added to such a series of visual impressions.

Münsterberg (30) referred to the conception of apparent movement in
his claim that: *"... the motion which he [the spectator] sees appears
to be a true motion, and yet is created by his own mind"* (Emphasis in
the original, insert by the author). Following this notion, the film his-
torian Terry Ramsaye (1926: 170) accordingly replaced the concept of
persistence of vision in his cinema history with the notion of a "persistence of optical imagination". Both Münsterberg's and Bergson's elaborations on the issue of perception in relation to instantaneous photography and film, critiqued some of the enduring discussions and
perspectives that had brought forth great controversies among the intellectual elite at the turn of the century.

The theory of *persistence of vision* was especially foregrounded in
the vigorous debates around visual perception in the discourse on art
and photography at the late 19th and early 20th century. Novel optical
technologies, such as those developed by Marey, played a crucial role
in this controversy, fuelled by the increasing acknowledgement of the
relativism of subjectivity and a persistence of the mechanistic conception of the retinal functions. As Braun (1992: 272ff) extensively demonstrates, the reception of instantaneous photography in particular
continued to support the ambivalent, but increasingly strategic, split
between the sciences and the arts, which consequently anticipated the
ambiguous position that the emerging cinema took in between these
fields. The endurance of the myth of the *persistence of vision* had a

---

[28] Bergson's early writings preceded Wertheimer's publication *The Photoplay* (1916)
and in his scientific rigour of incorporating the most current studies into psychophysiology he cited some earlier works by Münsterberg, for example his *Beiträge zur experimentellen Psychologie* from 1889–1892 ('Contributions to Experimental Psychology') in *Matter and Memory* (1991: 103). When he published *Matter and Memory* in
1889, he was well aware of the cognitive processes involved in the perception of vision and the occurrences with memory functions, as they were known at the time.

particular impact on the artistic interpretations of instantaneous photography, especially those that translated Marey's chronophotographical superimpositions into a conception of multiplicities perceived in simultaneity. It found increasing resonances in new formalistic depictions of movement and time in artistic expressions, a tendency that Braun (1992: 276-277) has identified in the shifting understanding of aesthetic truth from empiricism to subjectivity. In the continuous controversy around the representability of time, the retinal after-image effect provided a mechanistic interpretation of the perception of instantaneous photography, which was both used and vigorously criticised by some artists with regard to the scientific conceptions of realism. The aesthetician Paul Souriau, for example, promoted the merging of scientific truth with subjective choice based on the theory of the persistence of retinal images, in that he proposed the artistic use of chronophotography in representations of movement. He concurred with Marey to regard the camera as: "... an ideal eye that sees everything at one glance and permanently retains what it has seen" (276).

As mentioned earlier, Marey (1895: 179-180) saw great benefit for the arts in the opportunity to select from the broad spectrum of attitudes of the moving body in composite chronophotography in order to interpret them through the artist's individual choice. In this anticipation of the artistic implications and applications of chronophotography, he suggested that the individuality of an artist's expression could be found in the aspect of time as it is expressed through the speed of a particular movement and the specific time interval. Against the background of a widespread refusal in the arts to accept the camera as a truthful instrument to represent the reality that the human 'eye' sees, Souriau picked up Marey's suggestion and reiterated the judicious use of chronophotography in terms of a choice of attitudes rather than a direct translation into a blurring of objects. He proposed in *L'Esthétique du Mouvement* (1889) that the artist should make a choice among the 'truths' of chronophotographic representations of movement — but not as Marey envisioned, as singular states. Braun cites Souriau who suggested that:

> ... the literal representation of appearances would be no less implausible than that of the truth. For the watching eye, the flying bird does not have two wings, it has at least four; the trotting horse does not have four legs, it has at least eight, since, in any rapid alternative movement, the eyes conserve at the same

time the image of both extreme phases of the oscillation. (Braun 1992: 276)

Souriau's vision was taken up by the Futurist movement in their reiteration of the conception of the after-image effect in their 'Technical Manifesto' from 1910:

On account of the persisting of an image upon the retina, moving objects constantly multiply themselves; their form changes like rapid vibrations in their mad career. Thus a running horse has not four legs, but twenty, and their movements are triangular. (Doane 2002: 85-86)

The theory of *persistence of vision* supported the transposition of Marey's chronophotography into an obsession with the instant and the simultaneous in early 20th century art. However, at the same time, the very principle (in its misunderstanding of the perception of movement) was used to critique instantaneous photography, since from this perspective, a realist approach to the human eye would mean that it could only perceive blurred, superimposed images and not single positions. It becomes apparent how Marey's composite chronophotography could evoke such speculations, since he relentlessly attempted to improve the superimposition of the single images into tighter sequential simulations, leading to his geometrical method that was also frequently depicted and reinterpreted in early 20th century art.

The contradictions in the various interpretations of the after-image effect in the foundation of contemporary discourses seem to pivot on the problematic of different understandings of time. In order to perceive a horse with eight legs, the single chronophotographs had to be understood as simultaneities (supported by the theory of the *persistence of vision*) — that was precisely, according to Bergson, what the measurement of movement through the intellect and the scientific method simulated. The discrepancy between the conception of multiplicity and a monorealist argument manifested precisely in the changing conception of the observer — in the shift from the object to the subject. In his critique of the chronophotographic analysis of movement, Bergson (1998: 332) implicitly addressed the scientific method, as in the example of the horse's gallop:

Of the gallop of a horse our eye perceives chiefly a characteristic, essential or rather schematic attitude, a form that appears
to radiate over a whole period and so fill up a time of gallop. It
is this attitude that sculpture has fixed on the frieze of the Parthenon. But instantaneous photography isolates any moment; it
puts them all in the same rank, and thus the gallop of a horse
spreads out, into as many successive attitudes as it wishes, instead of massing into a single attitude, which is supposed to
flash out in a privileged moment and illuminate a whole period.[29]

These insights led Bergson (362) to his postulate of multiplicity by
which he conceived a plurality of durations, understood as qualitative
multiplicity.[30] He differentiated multiplicity in:

... that of material objects, to which the conception of number
is immediately applicable; and the multiplicity of states of consciousness, which cannot be regarded as numerical without the
help of some symbolical representation, in which a necessary
element is space. (2001: 87)

With regard to Marey's oeuvre, Bergson's differentiation of two kinds
of multiplicity reveals the particular significance of the imaginary
qualities in respect of chronophotography. Similarly, Rodin emphasised the observer in the discourse of art reception and the process of
intuition in the creative process of the artwork in his comment on the
depiction of the gaits of the horse through instantaneous photography:

And this is what condemns certain modern painters, who re-
produce poses provided by high-speed photographs when they
want to represent galloping horses. They criticize Géricault because in his *Race at Epsom* in the Louvre he paints horses gal-

---

[29] Marey also referred to the depiction of the horse's gaits on the Parthenon in *Movement* (1895) in the chapter on the 'Locomotion of Quadrupeds'. While Bergson saw a
certain duration of time inscribed in these sculptures, Marey (1895: 204) mentioned
how even in gallop they do not seem to be moving: "... if they appear to move at all,
at nothing more than a processional pace".

[30] In this regard Bergson made a distinction from Spinoza's view on form as being
deduced to a manifestation of one complete Being — what Spinoza called the One —
and his view that there was no previous given, neither a Platonean 'idea' or concept,
nor a general substance.

loping at full speed with their fore-and hindlegs thrown out simultaneously. They say that the photograph shows that when the front legs of the horse are stretched forward, the back legs, having sprung to propel the entire body, are already beneath the belly again ready to begin a new stride. Consequently, the four legs seem almost to meet in mid-air, giving the animal the appearance of having jumped up on the spot and having been immobilized in this position. Yet, I believe Géricault rather than the photograph is correct because *his* horses have the appearance of running. This comes about because the spectator looks from back to front. He first sees the back legs make the effort to spring. Then, he sees the body stretch, and the forelegs reach for the ground in front. Géricault's representation is false in showing these movements as simultaneous; it is true if the parts are observed in sequence. Only this truth matters since it is what we see and what impresses us. Note, furthermore, that when painters and sculptors bring together different phases of an action in the same figure, these do not proceed by reason or by artifice. They express quite naively what they feel. Their souls and their hands seem to be drawn to this gesture, and it is by instinct that they translate its development. Here, as everywhere in the domain of art, sincerity is the only rule. (Gsell 1986: 32-33 — emphasis in the original)

Rodin implicitly touched here on the perception of movement in the cinema where the afford of sequential observation had partially been taken over by the technological mechanism of the projector, while the jumps between scenes as well as superimpositions within the images, etc. introduced new forms of associative and imaginative requirements of cognitive activity.

The appropriation of Marey's work, however, stretched far beyond his conception of visual perception and drew particularly on his interest in dynamism and duration as continuity. This is particularly evident in the Futurists' works by Giacomo Balla and Anton Giulio Bragaglia, which differed from the more commonly adapted sequential separations of instant attitudes in simultaneity, as exemplified in Cubism. Comparable with Gilbreth's approach and aesthetics, there is even a certain resemblance with spirit manifestations (so-called doubles) of mediums in trance in spirit photography.[31] This is particularly

---

[31] Initially a member of the Italian Futurist movement, they soon strictly distinguished their arts movement from Bragaglia's photodynamism in a manifesto from 1913

evident in the work of Bragaglia, who pursued an interest in para-psychological phenomena (Braun 1992: 296). He criticised photography as realist medium and was outspoken about the insufficiency of "instant chronophotography", which in his view: "... ridiculously kills live gestures: in its desire to grasp the whole gesture it blocks and immobilizes only one of its hundred thousand fleeting *states*" (299 — emphasis in the original). Braun also points out that Bragaglia saw chronophotography as an intermediary state between instantaneous photography and his photodynamic expression of duration in the blurring of the moving postures, of which Demenÿ's sword sequence is possibly the closest precedent example.[32] Bragaglia put Marey's chronophotography in contrast to his own method of photodynamism:

> With photodynamism we have freed photography from the indecency of its brutal realism, and from the craziness of instantaneity, which, considered to be a scientific fact only because it was a mechanical product, was accepted as absolutely correct. (Braun 1992: 299)[33]

Bragaglia was concerned with the dynamics of motion, speed, energy, and their urban manifestations, in which he was influenced by Bergson, Spencer, and James, and also by the popular idea of the fourth dimension (291ff).[34] The conception of an underlying invisible

(Braun 1992: 309). Braun elaborates on the interrelation of Marey's work with Bragaglia's in *Fantasmes des vivants et des morts: Anton Giulio Bragaglia et la figuration de l'invisible* (1996), where she cites from Bragaglia's articles *I fantasmi dei vivi e dei morti* ('The phantasms of the living and the dead') and *La fotografia dell'invisibile* ('Photography of the invisible') published in 1913, in which he particularly addressed his interest in the occult in relation to photography (translations by the author). For illustrations of Bragaglia's photographs see Braun (1992: 297-298, 303).

[32] It is not suprising that Marey would have used a similar expression, "exceeding fleeting expressions", to critique Demenÿ's chronophotographic studies of facial expressions as in the case of the concierge Paul, as cited earlier, since he insisted on the precise demarcation between the single postures. The increasing disagreement between Marey and Demenÿ, which in 1893 led to their separation, manifested particularly in Demenÿ's chronophotographic style that showed dissolves between instants in the composite photographs, while Marey aimed to keep the single shifts of the figures precise and sharp.

[33] Braun cites from Bragalia's manifesto *Fotodinamismo Futurista* from 1911. See Bragaglia (1970: 23, 18).

[34] For literature on the fourth dimension, see for example Hinton (1912), Philmus (1969), Ouspensky ([1909] 2005), Henderson (1983).

spiritual principle of nature was a common theme at the end of the 19th century[35] and Bragaglia's work in particular expressed this profound curiosity into the realms beyond the visible, into the interior essence of things, the dynamic sensation of life, or as Bragaglia expressed it, in: "... the pulsing rhythm of the blood, the unceasing breath, the vibrant energy of gestures, for actions" (299) — notions that are reminiscent of Marey's own research interests. Although Bragaglia referred to time in terms of space as the "intermovemental fractions" between seconds, and the "infinitesimal calculation of movement", he also attempted to embrace Bergson's postulate of the subjective qualitative duration of time *(durée)*. This was particularly expressed in a concern with, what Mary Ann Doane (2002: 87) describes as, the: "... inner, sensorial, cerebral and psychic emotions that we feel when an action leaves its superb, unbroken trace".

At first 'sight' (indeed when considering a visual image analysis alone) the reinterpretation of Marey's work during the early 20th century avantgarde in the context of metaphysical concerns such as in Bragaglia's photodynamism, appears as a contrast with his scientific paradigms and intentions. It can be suggested, however, similar to the earlier suggestion in regard to his involvement in psychical research that it only appears as an illogical leap, when neglecting or marginalising the intrinsic dimensions of the immaterial in his work. These dimensions were not only evident in his studies of movement in the air and water, or in his pursuit of aesthetics in his work, but they also anticipated the shift from a mechanistic conceptualisation of vision (the eye-brain correlation) to the subjective perception of the beholder (the issue of mind/consciousness). The latter appeared most explicitly in Marey's (1895: 304) statement that the: "... images, therefore, appeal rather to the imagination than to the senses". The question if chronophotography, as well as Marey's legacy in art, either annihilated or, more positively, stimulated the position of the observer and active perceiver, can be classified as an issue of perspective, which distinguishes those discourses that separate the object from the subject. At this threshold lies Bergson's ingenious intervention: by redefining *images* as something inbetween an object and its representation, he situated the perception as an extension of consciousness into

---

[35] This went along with a revival of Goethe's, Schelling's and Hegel's *Naturphilosophie* in which spirit and physical nature were conceived as deriving from the same source, recalling Spinoza's philosophy of a universal substance (Larson 2005: 183).

the object. It is in this respect in particular that a reconsideration of Bergson's philosophy can be so fruitful for contemporary art and media theory, which sometimes seems to be caught in a similar paradoxical entanglement of seeming contradictory perspectives and forces, as they were evident around the turn of the century regarding the issues of movement and time.

Contrary to his main intentions, when seen from a wider perspective, Marey's focus on a scientific materialist approach ultimately remained vulnerable to phenomenological connotations and rhetoric of a technological enhanced supra-reality. Bergson's philosophy instead took materialism back from its extreme and introduced a metaphysics of immanence, which accommodated a perspective that did not allude to any extra-ordinary, supra-ordinary, altered or potentially fictitious dimensions. In this respect his conceptions are particularly significant and insistently contemporary, since it allows us to approach the dimension of the spirit within the ordinary processes of the human mind, immanent in matter, while at the same time depriving science of its involuntary mysticism. In this sense, it can be said, his work is closely aligned with Marey's rigour and research interests, although they took very different approaches to venture into the unknown and invisible.

The misunderstanding of time, which Bergson so consistently criticised, further reveals the deadlock of materialism and the dominance that the rationalist paradigm gained in the arts since the beginning of the 20th century. Not surprisingly, the positivist framework either produced ignorance toward an experiential dimension of life, or it brought forth obtrusive fabulations of ephemeral phenomena, which can be regarded as attempts to reanimate a mechanistic worldview. Considering the persistent misunderstanding of the perception of movement as mechanistic issue, it is comprehensible why the issue of movement and motion perception — rather than time —has historically been foregrounded in those theories of the cinema that were aligned with technological determinism. The conception of movement on the surface of a textual analysis, as well as the intrinsic mechanisms of the apparatus, however, appear as superficial readings of phenomena that crucially draw on the experience of time, memory and consciousness. This becomes particularly obvious when additionally considering that some of the diverging scientific interests into the study of forces, energies and invisible phenomena were closely followed and fuelled by the general public, especially those concerns that sanctioned alternative understandings of reality, time and related issues. This observation is also in harmony with Bergson's critical argument confronting the subordination of time to movement, and that of the internal, subjective experiences to the dominant paradigm of scientific realism, materialism and rationalism.

It becomes once more apparent in the controversy around photography, the issue of realism and the subjectivity of the perceiver, that the spiritualist manifestations and practices at the late 19th century can be regarded as subversive attempts in order to regain a lost dimension, which the reductionism of the positivist framework of science necessitated and the increasing economic rationalisation imposed on the modern citizens' lifestyles. In this apparent vacuum, the synthesis of the scientifically grounded movement analysis in projection reconstituted and facilitated this lost dimension in the subjective experience of time within the perceptual processes of the beholder, by resisting the exclusive control and rationalisation of positivist imperatives. The rapid diffusion and manifold developments around the emerging cinema, implicitly as well as explicitly, built on this powerful *dispositif* which embraced both the rational and the irrational, the introspective and the extrospective, the scientific and the popular, and, in a Bergsonian reading, both tendencies of the mind, the intellect and intuition.

A Bergsonian take on film and cinema history proposes an understanding of the emerging cinema that supersedes the realist and idealist divide by creating a 'third' form, something oscillating 'in between' these aspects — a view that is consistent with Bergson's conception of the *image* in respect of the *dispositif* of, what could be called, the 'human perceptual apparatus'. The emerging cinema, in this sense, can be regarded as having undergone certain transformations through the recognition of a threshold by which the spectators could engage actively with the dimension of *l'esprit* (spirit). Hence it is not so much the distinction between science and art, neither the 'real' versus the 'illusionary', nor the 'transcendental' versus the 'materialist' that marks out the fullest recognition of the emerging cinema's significance and particularity. Its crucial potential rather can be situated in its ability to merge the extremes of several competing strands of thought in one apparatus — the idealists' metaphysical aspirations as well as the rationalist scientific paradigms — by allowing a broad spectrum of conscious engagement of the mind, as will be discussed more specifically in the following chapters. Through this apparent stabilisation, the cinema was able to provide a conduit for the conduct of this dispute, which was able to serve and suit both constituencies — the believers in technological, economic, scientific progress and those who continued to seek alternative models to understand the world.

Chapter 4

The 'Image in Motion' Beyond the 'Cinematographical Tendency' of the Intellect: Dynamism, Intuition and Consciousness in Warburg, Marey and Bergson

This chapter takes up the resonance of the prologue in a more systematic treatment of the interconnections between Marey, Bergson and Warburg in regard to ideas around time, dynamism and perception. The previous chapters have emphasised that Marey's movement studies constituted fundamentally an inquiry into the issue of time and underlying forces in conjunction with a particular engagement with the arts through his explicit views on aesthetics. These dimensions in his work and his specific treatment of dynamism in relation to time bears an intrinsic relationship to an art discourse, conceptualised by a key contemporary thinker, the art-historian Abraham (Aby) Moritz Warburg (1866-1929).

Warburg's work is considered significant for this discussion not only because he was concerned with the interconnection of single images, which in his *Mnemosyne Atlas* were assembled from sources differing in form, content, medium and period, but also because of his successful attempt to address the immaterial dimensions of art from within the discipline of art-history by opening it up to related subject areas. In a similar way Marey operated within his own discipline by extending it into other areas, but most importantly, his wider research interests concerned the activity of movement as invisible forces beyond the movement of objects or the figure. It is in this sense, it could be suggested, that Marey's work in a certain sense has set out and anticipated some aspects of Warburg's concerns, particularly in his major project during the last years of his life, the *Mnemosyne Atlas*. A reinterpretation of the experience of this significant intervention from the perspective of the perceiver resonates with the discourses in the previous chapters. However, some of these issues can only be touched upon selectively here for the purpose of the development of a meta-discursive approach — almost in form of a conceptual *Mnemosyne* or a zig-zag doctrine, to use Bergson's expression. Rather than setting up a consistent commonality between these thinkers, the related points of reference in their work, as well as inherent contradictions, concerning key ideas around movement and time, will be woven into a network of ideas and forces to which in some pivotal crossings the emerging cinema is connected, without being its key agency or a straight-forward consequence.

To start with some contextualisation, it is worth pointing out that there is a significant, although indirect connection with regard to an interdisciplinary, intercultural approach to the production of images, between Aby Warburg and Albert Kahn (1860-1940) who was a friend and colleague of Henri Bergson.[1] A banker and, what at the time was called, a philanthropist, like Warburg, Kahn dedicated his interests to the foundation of the *Archives de la Planète,* a vast collec-tion of 183,000 meters of filmed-footage and 72,000 autochromes captured between 1909 and 1930 from around the world (Cœuré and Worms 2003: 132; see also Rohdie 2001: 9). While Kahn established himself in the banking business, he commissioned others to contribute to his archives and financed a chair at the *Collège de France* for Social Geography, awarded to Jean Bruhnes to direct the commissions for the *Archives de la Planète.*[2] Kahn was convinced of the transfor-mative power of knowledge and considered his archive to be a signifi-cant resource for philosophy, social studies and in particular geogra-phy. It was a project pioneering some of the key concerns of France's national reform and modernisation, especially in the fields of physical mapping in geography, physiology and movement studies. With a similar family background, Warburg dedicated his entire life to re-search as a full-time occupation, which he financed through his

---

[1] Albert Kahn and Henri Bergson shared a friendship since the time when Bergson became Kahn's private tutor in philosophy when he was a student at the Sorbonne. Sam Rohdie (2001: 7) refers to them as 'liberal internationalists' regarding their shared philanthropic activities in their pursuit of international affairs in politics, fi-nance and economics. For a publication of the correspondence between Kahn and Bergson between 1879 and 1893 see Sophie Cœuré and Frédéric Worms (2003).

[2] Among those commissioned by Kahn were camera operators, production companies such as Gaumont, as well as scientists such as the physician and biologist Jean Co-mandon.

family's banking business run by one of his brothers.[3] In the later part of his life, between 1924 and 1929, he created a *Bilderatlas,* an 'atlas of images' from various cultural contexts with a similar impulse, although of a different method, different intention and different result to Kahn's. Working at the fringes of a variety of disciplines Warburg expanded art-history with aspects drawn from cultural anthropology, sciences of religion, and psycho-historical studies.[4] He reflected on his interdisciplinary approach in his notes 'On Planned American Visit' from 1927:[5]

> When I look back at my life's journey, it seems that my function has been to serve as a seismograph of the soul, to be placed along the dividing lines between different cultural atmospheres and systems. (Michaud 2004: 332)

Guided by a profound interest in images and their relationships with human consciousness, both Kahn's and Warburg's concerns interconnect with the interests and intellectual project of Bergson, not least in that they shared an interest in cultural, psychological, and philosophical concerns of humanity, art, technology, and the transformative power of knowledge.

It is now well accepted that Aby Warburg's syncretic approach and personality revitalised art history by opening it up to insights in particular in connection with cultural anthropology. This followed his reflections on fieldtrips to New Mexico and Arizona undertaken in 1895-1896 and his correspondences with some of the most esteemed anthropologists such as Franz Boas.[6] It was not until the 1920s, how-

---

[3] As the eldest of seven children Warburg renounced to take over the family business in exchange for the financial support of his research project during his entire lifetime, which led to the establishment of the *Kulturwissenschaftliche Bibliothek* in Hamburg.

[4] Warburg (1992: 70) described the strict distinction in disciplines as *'grenzpolizeiliche Befangenheit'* (literally meaning 'border-policed inhibition') and *'einflussreiche Grenzwächtertum in unserer heutigen Kunstgeschichtsschreibung'* ('influential frontier guard in the contemporary historicisation of art') — literal translation by the author.

[5] 'On Planned American Visit' is an unpublished text of five typewritten pages, kept in Warburg's personal archive (catalog number 93.8), printed in Michaud (2004: 331-335). Warburg's writings are preserved in the Warburg Institute, London, in the form of notes that would fill up to seventy books if they were published.

[6] Warburg was introduced to cultural anthropology by Cyprus Adler, Frank Hamilton Cushing, James Mooney, Franz Boas (Agamben 1999: 91). He was in correspondence

ever, that Warburg (2002) situated the meaning of the Hopi serpent ritual and the Pueblo Kachina dance ritual in his work on Renaissance art, in which he recognised as the transformative period from the pre-modern to the modern.[7] Matthew Rampley (1997: 50) reminds us that for Warburg: '"... the Renaissance constitutes a period of conflict between magical-associative (symbolic) and logical-dissociative (allegorical-semiotic) modes of representation" through which he traced the transition from the symbolic to allegorical signs in the history of art. Michaud (2004: 222) notes how in Warburg's work the transitory states of the dancers were metamorphosed into the images of the nymphs and Intermedi figures of Renaissance paintings, in which Warburg saw the "... "universal pathetic form" of the representation of movement in the crucial symbol of the serpent". With a resonance of an anthropological approach, Warburg suggested that art should be understood as an impulse and activity rather than a collection of icons. In this respect he criticised the categorisation, periodisation and focus on style of the contemporary art-historical practice; he wrote:

> ... I had developed a downright disgust with aestheticizing art history. The formal contemplation of images — not conceived as a biologically necessary product situated between the practices of religion and art (which I understood only later) — seemed to me to give rise to such as sterile trafficking in words that after my trip to Berlin in the summer of 1896 I tried to switch over to medicine. (Michaud 2004: 177-178)

Warburg revitalised the art history discourse through a recovery of 'spirit', which he defined as an enduring momentum and trace throughout the various cultural expressions and styles of the particular periods. Resonant with the 19th century practice in cultural anthropology of cross-cultural comparison, he explained in his notes: "We attempt to grasp the spirit of the age in its impact on style by comparing the same subject as it is treated in various periods and various count-

---

with Boas, famous for his pursuit of cultural relativism that established modern cultural anthropology with an interdisciplinary approach reaching from archaeology, geography to what today is called museology. Cited in Michaud (2004: 177-179, 301, 331); for a monograph on Boas see Stocking (1989).

[7] One of Warburg's inspirations is reported to have been the German philologist Hermann Usener who traced a parallel between the Hopi Indians and the peoples of Antiquity (Michaud 2004: 265).

ries..." (Rampley 1997: 55). Like Bergson, Warburg saw in the notion of 'spirit' the driving force beyond cultural manifestation, and both grounded their work in 19th century science such as psychology, psychophysiology and anthropology. Whereas Bergson advanced a novel conception of phenomena related to 'spirit' *(l'esprit)* in philosophy, Warburg founded a unique method in his dynamic library in Hamburg, the *Kulturwissenschaftliche Bibliothek* (KWB),[8] and particularly through the *Mnemosyne Atlas,* his major occupation during the last years of his life between 1924 and 1929.

With the *Mnemosyne Atlas,* Warburg created a gallery of his personal image-memory in a sophisticated composition, which Didi-Huberman refers to as an "aphasic and anachronistic montage" (Michaud 2004: 17-18). On large wooden frames covered with coarse black linen, Warburg arranged photographic reproductions of artworks and images of disparate origins, such as art reproductions (forming the largest image source of the atlas), newspaper clippings, geographical maps, advertisements, astrological charts, play cards, images of coins, stamps or emblems, etc. which, as the books in his library, he continuously rearranged according to new clusters of ideas and insights.[9] Warburg conceived these image panels as an "iconology of intervals" *('Ikonologie des Zwischenraumes'),* as he expressed in

---

[8] Warburg's library, toward the end of his life containing around 60,000 volumes of books and 20,000 photographs, was organised according to ideas instead of categories or subjects, and therefore underwent a continuous process of rearrangement according to new insights and emerging ideas. One of Warburg's main purposes in the library's organization was, as he noted in his fieldnotes, "a primary collection for studying the psychology of human expression" (Michaud 2004: 313). The library, today in the Warburg Institute in London, is still mainly organized around the original four floor levels with the dedicated indicative areas labled as action, orientation, word and image. For more information see The Warburg Institute, located at the University of London, http://warburg.sas.ac.uk/ (consulted 10.03.2008). For an examination of the KWB from the perspective of library science see Schäfer (2003).

[9] Only very few of the original panels have survived; Warburg drew on approximately 2,000 reproductions of which the *Mnemosyne Atlas* (which remained unfinished by his death) comprised around 1,000 pictures on 79 panels. A reconstruction of the *Mnemosyne Atlas* can be studied in the Studienabteilung of the Albertina in Vienna, originally reconstructed for an exhibition of the *Transmedialen Gesellschaft daedalus* in 1993 at the Academy of Fine Arts Vienna (concept and organisation by Werner Rappl and Gerhard Fischer). As basis served a photographic documentation by Warburg from 1929. A published reproduction of the *Mnemosyne Atlas* can be found in Martin Warnke's *Gesammelte Schriften* (2000).

his 1929 journal (244).[10] Their significance lay not in the representations of images themselves; their sophisticated arrangement rather enabled a reflection upon the analogies, tensions, anachronisms, or contrasts among them. This method reiterates Warburg's earlier established approach to art-history in which he similarly favoured displacements and ruptures over the transmission of forms in his uncovering of the underlying Dionysian principle and dynamics in art, which he sought in the apparent motion beyond the visible appearance of art forms and content. According to his insights, an artwork constitutes not a closed totality but a juxtaposition of elements in tension — an intellectual, cultural and philosophical *dispositif.*

In the broader discourse of the visual arts of the later 20th century, the *Mnemosyne Atlas* has frequently been compared with various forms and techniques of audio-visual media and has led to reflections on image archives, conceptually as well as in contemporary artistic practice.[11] Rampley (1997: 55) shifts the focus from formal and content-related interpretations of the *Mnemosyne Altas* to a consideration of the unconscious in relation to the magical-associative symbols of images, in order to avoid the more common approach that he characterises as "an exercise in art historiographical archaeology".[12] Michaud (2004) seems to have taken up this call and puts Warburg's work and commentary in a dialogue with some of the developments of the period of the emerging cinema. For example he compares the collage of collective and personal memories in the *Mnemosyne* method with Marey's geometrical chronophotography, Dickson's early film experiments in Edison's studio Black Maria, the 1920s' artistic photomontage, experimental film montage, and Jean-Luc Godard's *Histoire(s) du Cinema* (1988-98). He proposes:

---

[10] Michaud cites from Gombrich (1970: 253).

[11] See for example *Altas* by Gerhard Richter (Richter 2008; Zweite 1990), or *Light\Image Atlas* by Gustav Deutsch and Hanna Schimek, exhibited at the Lentos Museum, Linz, 2004 and Kunsthalle Wien, 2005.

[12] Warburg's methodology has become well established in art history, following on from his doctorial thesis in which he uncovered a Dionysian component in interpretations of Antiquity in Quattrocento artists' works, especially through his students Fritz Saxl and Erwin Panovsky, or Ernst Hans Josef Gombrich. Georges Didi-Huberman, however, points to the incomplete application of Warburg's concerns in their work and formulated his intention as an attempt to recover a more profound strand that Warburg (2002: 180) called "dynamic symbolism". For an online overview on Warburg's oeuvre online see Bruhn (undated), or for a biography see Gombrich (1970).

> If we relinquish defining the cinematographic apparatus on the basis of material determinations — film as the conjunction of a supple celluloid medium, perforation, and rapid emulsions — and instead consider it, in a more unusual and larger framework, as a conceptual interrelating of transparency, movement, and impression, we will discover, within the field of cinema, the same categories Warburg used in the history of art. In the last decade of the nineteenth century, the filmmaker and the historian apply identical procedures in separate fields that reveal a common orientation. (2004: 39-40)

Michaud has opened a new set of interconnections with Warburg's work, which ask for further elaboration, especially from a new historicist perspective on, and critical revision of, the emerging cinema[13] and those discourses that foreground its characteristic expression of energy and force rather than the performances of moving figures on screens or the visual construction of narratives. This connection with the impulse behind early attempts at image projection not only recalls Thomas Alva Edison's vitalist interest in creating, what we now might call, a simulacrum of the living through the preservation of life in the survival of the 'body', but also Georges Demeny's vision of extending his movement studies of speech for deaf-mute communication aids to the creation of family albums for the purpose of recording and replaying the gestures of ancestors in a more vivid and vital form than previous mediations had achieved. In Michaud's (2004:88-89) comparison between Warburg's and Marey's intentions in their treatment of movement as a force or energy, he focuses on Marey's geometrical chronophotography and the graphical notation of motion capture as a particularly obvious example, since they most explicitly display the apparent absence of the figures through the eclipse of the captured bodies to mere abstracted white lines or singular time-lines in the graphs.

The interconnection between Warburg's and Marey's intentions, however, can be seen as more profound when separating the immaterial implications from the material manifestations and techniques.

---

[13] The commonly recognised view on the emerging cinema as an expression of a vital force rather than a representation, is in the literature frequently characterised as 19th century curiosity. It is often subsumed in the common foregrounding of the issue of movement, based on a mechanistic relationship between that of cause and effect in relation to both the technology and the performance.

Warburg approached the notion of movement beyond the figurative surface in an iconology of the interval by questioning the very idea of stability in material forms, which recalls Marey's concern with the aspect of instability in the figure during movement itself and Bergson's discourse on the contingency of form, as elaborated earlier. When Marey (1895: 171-172) commented on the representations of runners in contemporary art, he insisted that we: "… seem to forget that one of the characteristics of running, and even of walking, is to maintain a continuous position of unstable equilibrium". Beyond his interest in the analysis of singular positions, Marey distinguished the differences of these various time intervals between the resting and the moving positions. This particular concern with time is most explicit in a statement in the chapter 'Locomotion in Man from an Artistic Point of View' (Marey 1895: 169-185) in which he referred to a composite photography of Demenÿ's chronophotographic study of 'A Sword Thrust' (178).[14] Marey (179) described how the most extended positions in terms of duration (measured time interval) are the best visible and the most "expressive attitudes" with regard to the exposure time, whereas the instances in-between are blurred, signifying the velocity of the movement: "… there are some attitudes which last longer than others, and which may be called "positions of visibility". Chronophotography would determine these with the greatest precision". He considered these differentiations as potentials of variable expressive attitudes in the captured instantaneous positions on which the artist could base her/his individual choices. Michaud compares these expressive instants with the expressiveness of frozen moments in the Japanese Kabuki theatre, in which the actors stop in a frozen pose, the *mié*, from the height of one tension to the next. He connected this expressiveness to Warburg's *Mnemosyne Atlas:*

> In *Mnemosyne,* Warburg sought to juxtapose figures caught at the culminating point of their expressivity by using the black spaces between them as visual ruptures, disjunctions in which diminution of slackening energy was annulled. Thus if one were to express *Pathosformeln* in Japanese, one might translate

---

[14] Marey's intermediary states in the figure's displacement were generally characterised by very precise, sharp and distinct postures, while Georges Demenÿ's, in contrast, were blurred and they much more obviously expressed the movement's speed in terms of time intervals.

it as "*miē*", a movement frozen in the instant of its greatest intensity. (2004: 272)

It is easily overlooked that it is not the figures in themselves, but the invisible movements inbetween the states that constitute the very forces that Marey sought to study, which bring about the ecstatic state of the single expressions, the very dynamism driving the visual forms exemplified in what Warburg called *pathos formulas (Pathosformeln)*. It can be corroborated that the recognition that Warburg studied motion beyond the surface of appearances liberates a consideration of movement from the dominant materialist constraints of both the technology and the index.

A foregrounding of the immaterial dimensions in Warburg's oeuvre also steers us away from the common emphasis on Marey's chronophotography to his wider oeuvre and research interests, as suggested earlier, as well as from the common misconception of his significance in regard to traditional interpretations of the emerging cinema in its material outcomes. The frequent, rather mechanistic, comparison of movement beyond the figure with technologies of interruption is often related to the discourse of the *persistence of vision*, as discussed in the previous chapter.[15] A revision of this misconception through a shift from a mechanistic model of vision to the domain of the mind *(esprit)* reveals some crucial resemblances of Warburg's intervention with Bergson's interests in a liberation of the dimension of the spirit, which in the wider context of this book, moreover, points to an understanding of the emergence of the cinema as a philosophical *dispositif.* The dominance of a mechanistic reading of the emerging cinema, from which Michaud partially succeeds in escaping, has inhibited a more profound interconnection between Warburg's momentum and the moving image from a perspective that includes the experience of the beholder. This is especially relevant when considering that, while Marey was concerned with the smallest possible distinct intervals for his movement analysis, his movement synthesis and particularly his graphical methods of time measurement were concerned with dynamism and flow.

---

[15] Proceeding from the common misconceptions around the emerging cinema, Agamben (2004) for example relates the heuristic of the *Mnemosyne Atlas,* particularly Warburg's idea of the "afterlife" *('Nachleben')* of the retinal after-image effect.

The growing interest in Warburg in the context of visual culture, media studies and more generally the studies of culture in various disciplines, calls for an extension of the reconsideration of his oeuvre, which seems not only appropriate but also, first and foremost, consistent with Warburg's own transdisciplinary intentions. Such a consideration could for example extend from the *Mnemosyne's* cinematographic layout in its resemblance to Marey's, Méliès'[16] and Dickson's studio set-up to that of the mise-en-scène of spiritist séances, in which space became isolated in favour of the representation of the performance, and above all in the experiential perception of movement and apparitions. In this context it is not surprising that Warburg called the *Mnemosyne Altas* "a ghost story for truly adult people" *(eine Gespenstergeschichte für ganz Erwachsene)* (Agamben 1999: 95). Brian Dillon (2000) picks up the notion of the "ghost" as phantom of the image in the recovery and reinvention of its underlying 'spirit' through the experience of the *Mnemosyne Altas:*

> The Atlas, wrote Warburg, was 'a ghost story for adults': it invents a kind of phantomic science of the image, a ghost dance in which the most resonant gestures and expressions its creator had discovered in the course of his career return with a spooky insistence, suddenly cast into wholly new relationships.

When relating Warburg's notion of motion beyond the figure to Marey's aspirations to study the very principles of life in order to advance an understanding of the cinema *dispositif,* the differences in their overall scope and purpose of their oeuvres and disciplines can, however, not be neglected. The scientist Marey transposed his interest in the study of the underlying dynamics of movement from the mere figurative to a technological solution by implementing a complex network of apparatuses to measure these various effects.[17] In a certain sense Warburg seems to have extended some crucial aspects of Marey's underlying conceptions and met those objectives in a cultural historical context of art. In this way Warburg made explicit what Ma-

---

[16] For works on George Méliès see for example Bessy (1961), Cherchi Usai (1991), Frazer (1979), Hammond (1974), Jenn (1984), Maltête-Méliès (1973), Méliès (1945).

[17] Be it coincidence or not, it is worth noting that George Didi-Huberman mentions in the foreword to Michaud's publication that the Warburg Institute published the first studies on the history of chronophotography (Michaud 2004: 341 footnote 33).

rey only exceptionally expressed: that a consideration of movement in art as a dynamic force needs to be situated beyond the mere appearance (in the materialised form) but rather in the beholder's mind. The inclusion of Warburg's approach into the context of the emerging cinema therefore illuminates some underexplored dimensions in Marey's research as well as their implications for an understanding of the emerging cinema as philosophical *dispositif.* Rather than an overemphasis on its material aspects (technology and image) it figures the experience of the beholder, the domain of the spirit *(l'esprit).*

Considering the interpretative activity of the perceiver, it is of particular interest with reference to Bergson's thinking that Warburg transferred movement to an inner principle and saw it no longer as an external force. He understood it, in his own words, not as: "... the embodiment of life in motion but the psychology of the interior" (Michaud 2004: 132),[18] which in some respect anticipated Edgar Morin's (2005) anthropological/ psychological approach to cinema studies in the 1950s. In this respect Michaud (2004: 56) tracks the cinema as a form of thought rather than as a spectacle, reminiscent of Bergson in his reference to the cinematographic method of an arrangement in thoughts (of the intellect). This significant undercurrent in Michaud's book needs to be uncovered and further explored in order to move from an emphasis on the image text and its inherent techniques of montage, etc. to the interpretive activity of the spectator. Michaud (2004: 38) refers, for example, to a lecture by Warburg in 1912 where he projected autochromes and made a comment with reference to the "cinematographic spotlight". He suggests that Warburg's use of slides: "... is not enough to explain the term *kinematographisch,* which seems to designate not a material apparatus of projection but a mental apparatus, a dynamic manner in which to apprehend the works". The suggestion to shift the focus from the material to immaterial considerations of the emerging cinema along with Didi-Huberman's (2002) emphasis on Warburg's "dynamic symbolism" of a magical-associative assemblage segues the here suggested turn from a consideration of movement, time and montage in the text, to that of the mind. This is of particular significance with respect to a consideration of the conceptual space between the subject and the object in the

---

[18] Warburg's note derives from "Flemish and Florentine Art in Lorenzo de'Medici's Circle Around 1480" (1901), published in Warburg (1999).

context of a discourse relating to the interpretation of the 'image' beyond the text. In this way a reconsideration of the *Mmenosyne Atlas*
can be situated within the perceptual qualities during the experience
itself as an epistemology of aesthetics.

Pisano (2006: 93) reminds us that Warburg understood the underlying dynamism in art as archaic forms of thought that endure
throughout the cultural history of humankind. Pinotti (2003, 2006)
discusses this as the problematic of the material inscription of memory
versus the immaterial transfer through collective and individual consciousness, whereas Agamben (2004) relates this issue to the conception of Benjamin's dialectical image, a widespread reference from the
perspective of a dialectics of culture.[19] Consistent with Bergson's elaboration on time and space, Warburg's work can be read as a critique
of the mechanistic understanding of movement in its material form, in
particular in the way they both understood movement as the very emergence of motion, dynamics and underlying energy of the creative
processes of art. In this sense, the juxtaposition of single postures and
frames in the image panels of the *Mmenosyne Atlas* provoke a consideration of time as duration in a Bergsonian sense. Let us recall how
Bergson described the experience of duration, or real motion, when
the attention is directed internally:

> Finally, let us free ourselves from the space which underlies
> the movement in order to consider only the movement itself,
> the act of tension or extension; in short, pure mobility. We
> shall have this time a more faithful image of the development
> of our self in duration. (1999b: 27)

Bergson's exemplary introspective method, suggested in this citation,
provides a model for a personal experience of a historical momentum
in the present, as soon as memory processes are replaced with an intuitive extension of consciousness into the object to be perceived. An
application of Bergson's philosophy at this nexus might offer a recon-
ciliation of the established dichotomies in relation to these distinct
processes in Warburg's work, especially when treating the immaterial,
invisible forces from the past not merely as an individual experience
but as an invigoration of a collective cultural history beyond text.

---

[19] For reflections on Benjamin's dialectics in relation to Warburg's oeuvre, see Rampley (2000).

Considering that Warburg's intellectual concern in his *Mnemosyne Atlas* was to articulate a new approach to the cultural significance of the function of the human image memory, this seems to map out a promising field of study to apply Bergson's philosophy to the perceptual processes of the beholder of the *Mnemosyne Atlas*. Such a reading could provide the liberation of a philosophical understanding of the underlying spirit *(l'esprit)* that Warburg sought through his work. Although such a consideration would expand the scope of this book, a few initial thoughts are necessary to more fully underpin the significance of Warburg's intervention for this study.

By taking the perspective of the beholder and the very experience of the *Mnemosyne's* method and heuristic into consideration, the issues of perception and related mental operations such as associations, memories, repetitions, or focalisations, arise as a crucial pivot in Warburg's conception of the *Atlas*. Warburg struggled to reconcile contemporary scientific research into memory phenomena with his innovative approach to the thrust of memory from the past into the present, and consequently he was obliged to reinterpret some of the theories he borrowed from the sciences. He was inspired by the German psychologist Richard Semon's approach to memory, who conceived that every event that affects a living being leaves a trace in memory, which he called an *engram*. By leaving a material effect, according to Semon (1904),[20] this "ecphoric stimulus" constitutes the cue or pattern that helps in retrieving a specific memory (Pinotti 2003). In this Semon was influenced by the understanding of memory as biological inheritance and as a general function of organised matter following the theories of his teacher, the physiologist Ewald Hering (1834-1918). As Michaud (2004: 255) emphasises, Warburg was particularly drawn to Semon's conception of the function of memory as being: "… charged with preserving and transmitting energy temporally, allowing someone to react to something in the past from a distance". What Semon described as a psychical phenomenon, Warburg transferred to an externalised deployment in his study of cultural history, in which he reinterpreted Semon's original approach (Böhme 1997: 29).

---

[20] The original title of Semon's work *The Mneme* is *Die Mneme als Erhaltendes Prinzip im Wechsel des Organischen Geschehens,* meaning in a literary translation: *'The Mneme as sustaining principle in the changes of organic activity'* (translation by the author).

In Warburg's application of Hering's approach to memory in particular, an underlying strand of the issue of consciousness becomes paramount, as well as a more fluid conception of memory that contrasts with Semon's consolidated term of the *engram*. It is evident that Semon's biological understanding of the *engram* or trace would have been too materialist and mechanistic a concept for Warburg's intentions. In this respect Böhme (1997: 29) reminds us that Warburg's use of biological terms, such as mnemic heritage *(mnemisches Erbgut)*, neither relates to a Darwinian nor an ethological understanding of its meaning, but rather to a metaphorical transcription of a historical transference of powerful affects through cultural media. In this sense, Semon's or Hering's conceptions of memory only refer to the representations of images in the *Mnemosyne Atlas* themselves, which constitute *engrams* — which Warburg referred to in his notes also as reproductions, or photograms. As they are capable of re-creating an experience of the past through a spatial configuration in the present moment of perception, according to Warburg, they signified a revival of an original energy in a contemporary context, which reconstitutes a new kind of subject.[21]

Warburg's treatment and reinterpretation of memory processes, at least in how far they are consistent with Semon's biological and in some respect rather mechanistic, materially based conceptions, asks for a more immaterial, cultural or, as it is proposed here, philosophical interpretation of knowledge transfer. Bergson's conception of memory as the virtual potentiality of the mind, independent from matter, offers an alternative to phenomenological or metaphorical approaches. It constitutes an intimately connected approach to Warburg's method, especially since memory, for Bergson, extends into the present and does not conversely appear through a reaction to something past. It is not conceived as a purely imaginative realm since its actualisation is always coexistent with the present moment of action or cognitive activity; nor is it to be situated in a material form or space to which the popular notion of the trace in the literature alludes.[22] It follows that

---

[21] Pinotti (2003) highlights the distinction between the original and originary in the individual and collective heredity of memory, in particular as they are manifest in their cultural translation in Warburg's approach to images.

[22] Bergson (1920: 50-53) also rejected any theories that regarded memory as contained by the brain, such as the consideration of imprints, using analogies such as phonograms, the phonographic disk or sensitive plates; since for Bergson (73) all that

Warburg's notion of a "ghost story for truly adult people" can be related to Bergson's virtual. Firstly, in the sense that it constitutes a revival of past memories in the present, of an energy that not only persists but also continuously pushes evolution forward in multiple pathways and hence leaves traces in cultural forms. Secondly, in the sense that the virtual constitutes a quality of the whole of matter, of all images impinging on one another, the very vibration of a life-force, it could be said, which Warburg conceived in his seismographic activity, and whose sedimentations he identified most evidently in art and religion.[23]

In a similar way Edgar Morin's notion of the psychic flux into which the perception of the film enters seems closely connected to Warburg's psychological approach and resonates with Michaud's (2004: 273) elaboration on Antonin Artaud's term of the 'secret psychic impulse'— a view that most crucially addresses Warburg's revival of art history beyond language and text. As Michaud cites, Warburg referred in his notes to a symbolic form of thought prior to language:

> All humanity is eternally and at all times *schizophrenic*. And yet an attitude toward memory images may be designated ontogenetically as prior and primitive, while it nevertheless remains secondary. In the later stage, the memory image does not release an immediate practical reflex movement — whether combative or religious — rather, memory images are consciously accumulated in images or signs. Between these two stages stands the treatment undergone by the original impression, which can be designated as a symbolic form of thought. (2004: 314 — emphasis in the original)

Warburg's differentiation between the meaning of a memory image in its original context of perception and that of recollection reveals his intention to seek the significance of an image in its difference from the original narration by which it was inspired (Michaud 2004: 77). A Bergsonian perspective would underline this distinction; moreover, it

---

the brain 'contained' were the necessary connections for motor habits. For elaborations on the notion of 'trace' see for example Doane (2002), specifically in relation to Marey's work see Dagognet (1992).

[23] Note that the 'trace' here indicates the material (visual) manifestation and not memory in itself as a trace of the present or lived experience.

would drive the discussion beyond the image as 'material' form in its constitution as a representation or signifier. Notwithstanding, Warburg's thinking is in that sense close to Bergson's philosophy in how far it acknowledges the accessibility of memories beyond a direct indexical relationship with the present moment and this is a significant aspect to be recognised.

According to Bergson, memory-*images* impinge on the present moment and overlap with perception and in this way transform into new forms of thought and consequently stimulate new forms of body-states including affects, eventually leading to actions and 'material' manifestations. This flow of memory-*images* continuously performs a creative activity, ideally steered by free will. Bergson suggested:

> ... there is no state of mind, however simple, which does not change every moment, since there is no consciousness without memory, and no continuation of a state without the addition, to the present feeling, of the memory of past moments. It is this which constitutes duration. (1999b: 40)

Memory-*images,* according to Bergson, are formed coextensively with the present moment through the processes of recollection and the activity of attentive recognition, within the vast range of our conscious states. In his conception of pure memory instead, there are no *images* to be distinguished, pure memory precedes *images,* it is entirely unconscious, as Bergson (1999b: 27) maintained: "The inner life is all this at once: variety of qualities, continuity of progress, and unity of direction. It cannot be represented by images".

Warburg conceived of the mnemonic techniques as a threshold that did not indicate a linear development from the Dionysian to the Appolonian principle, but rather a rhythmic pulsation back and forth in a continuous retrieval of the archaic affective powers (Böhme 1997: 31-32). Similarly, Bergson did not understand progress as a uni-linear forward development. He insisted instead in the context of his theory on creative evolution that:

> Evolution is not only a movement forward; in many cases we observe a marking-time, and still more often a deviation or turning back. [...] No doubt there is progress, if progress mean a continual advance in the general direction determined by a first impulse; but this progress is accomplished only on the

two or three great lines of evolution on which forms ever more and more complex, ever more and more high, appear; between these lines run a crowd of minor paths in which, on the contrary, deviations, arrests, and set-backs, are multiplied. (1998: 104)

Warburg's *Mnemosyne Atlas* refers to the perception of the affective quality of images through a certain detachment indicative of a "history of experience",[24] which has to be understood as a form of active intervention in the processes of understanding and interpreting, which takes place in the spaces in between the symbolic order and their material forms — which Warburg (1992: 267) referred to as *'Andachtsraum'* or *'Denkraum der Besonnenheit'*.[25] In Bergson's view the perceived *images* are always already memory-*images* as soon as we become aware of them, since memory-*images* from the past overlap with the pure perception of the present moment. At the same time, the very formation of memory itself happens contemporaneous with perception, and not as a posterior occurrence, as Bergson (1920: 109-151) proposed in his essay on false recognition. Michaud (2004: 40) interprets Warburg's elaborations in a similar perspective, as being directed less toward the definition of knowledge in the past than towards its reproduction in the present. This reproduction, however, is not to be understood as manifest in the 'image' (as text) itself, but can be grasped as an *image* in a Bergsonian understanding, at the moment of contact between matter and spirit within the perceptual processes of the beholder. In this sense, the notion of 'reproduction' could be interpreted as a recollection, an actualisation of a memory-*image,* triggered, mediated or amplified by the art-work (or the film), evoked by the tension of our consciousness towards the requirements of the present moment of perception (and the desires and imagination of the spectators). This reading would also indicate that what Warburg described as *Zwischenraum,* as the space 'in-between', cannot simply be read as the black spaces in between the images on the panels (as some

---

[24] Rampley (1997: 55) defines the continuous strand of thought running through Warburg's oeuvre as: "... the analysis of the transformation of symbols, in particular, the transformation of their function from magical-associative symbols to logical-dissociative allegorical signs. In turn, this transformation of function is indicative of a history of experience, in which the mimetic identification with phenomena passes over into a sense of distance from them".

[25] This can be translated into an intermediary (mental/virtual) space for reflection.

of Michaud's interpretive analogies with the emerging cinema suggest), but rather as moments of reflection in the sense of an intuitive
effort to achieve a grasping of the whole — as a qualitative rather than
quantitative (intellectual) event in the perceiver's mind. The conception of memory retrieval, in this sense, can be read as an effort beyond
language into the deep realms of 'pure memory' where from a flux of
pure duration memory-*images* emerge that allow new meanings and
connections to be made and infiltrate into the present moment of perception in preparation for action and intellectual reflection. Rather
suitable to Warburg's reference to the seismographic activity of the
mind, Bergson (1991: 104) proposed that: "... reflective perception is
a *circuit,* in which all the elements, including the perceived object itself, hold each other in a state of mutual tension as in an electric circuit..." (emphasis in the original).

Warburg conceived the retrieval of affective dynamograms through
the archaic symbolism in images, which he called *Pathosformeln (pathos formulas)* (Böhme 1997: 30). He interpreted these *pathos formulas* that emerged through the method of the *Mnemosyne* as incorpora-
tion of the tensions between the Apollonian and Dionysian principle
embedded within the image. Warburg sought this search for a 'gestural pathos' in the transitory state of movement in art, most explicitly in
the snake's symbolism, especially expressed in his studies of the *Lao-
coön Group.* The definition of art as a persistence of intermediary
states in the displacements of the figures, recalls Rodin's conception
of movement in art, as flowing mobility and fluidity[26] and especially
his invocation of a scene in Dante's Inferno in a response to Gsell's
question on movement in bronze sculpture:

> "Since you take me for a sorcerer, Rodin responded, "I will try
> to honor my reputation by performing a task that is much more
> difficult for me than animating bronze: explaining how I do it.
> First, note that *movement is the transition from one attitude to
> another.* This simple statement, which sounds like a truism, is
> indeed the key to the mystery. [...] You remember how in
> Dante's Inferno a serpent is glued to the body of a damned man
> and is converted into a man, while the man is changed into a

---

[26] It also recalls the distinction between the 'movement in paintings' in contrast to the
stillness of instantaneous photography, as it is posited in the review on Muybridge's
presentation at the Royal Institution, cited in chapter 3, p. 107.

reptile. The great poet describes this scene so ingeniously that in each of the two beings, one follows the struggle of two natures, which progressively invade and supplant one another. It is basically a metamorphosis of this kind that the painter or sculptor executes in making this personages move. He makes visible the passage of one pose into the other; he indicates how imperceptibly the first glides into the second. In his work, one still detects a part of what was while one discovers in part what will be." (Gsell 1984: 28-29)

This is similar to Marey's intention in his geometrical chronophotography and most evident in his graphical method. Rodin's suggestion of a metamorphosis describes an intervention against the subordination of time to movement that becomes alive in the perceiver's active engagement. This dimension needs to be emphasised in relation to Michaud's (2004: 278) consistent reference to the medium of photographic reproduction in Warburg's image panels as: "... not merely illustrative but a general plastic medium to which all the figures are reduced before being arranged in the space of the panel". The movement beyond the figures in each image as well as the motion created among the juxtaposition of the images needs to be separated as two levels of an interactive momentum, continuously recreated in the perceiver's mind.

The survival of the past in the present in Warburg's conception, according to Pinotti (2006: 10-11), has to be understood in Nietzsche's sense of a 'becoming',[27] since these formulas can only be conceived within the very processes of transformations in the perception of the viewer. By taking the perspective of forces embedded in experience, in resonance with Bergson's own conception of 'becoming', the discourse shifts a contemplation of the *Mnemosyne* from a textual analysis to a focus on the cognitive processes of the beholder. It is this dimension that is implicit and persistently provocative in the work of Marey and Warburg, and which constitutes the crucial lever to liberate the dimension of the spirit beyond the material form. Michaud (2004:84) refers to the perceptual processes of the *Mnemosyne Atlas* as a form of interaction:

---

[27] Pinotti (2006) emphasises the influence of Nietzsche's philosophy in Warburg's thinking.

> Warburg defines the recording of motion as a persistence of
> intermediary states in the displacement of the figure: for the
> onlooker, its perception requires an identificatory attention —
> of an almost hypnotic type — through which an exchange
> takes place between the subject and the object.

Instead of a form of hypnosis, however, when proceeding from
Bergson's treatment of the cognitive processes of recollection and remembering, the cinematic arrangement of the *Mnemosyne* in its 'mental montage' stimulates associative trajectories of meaning and suggests rather a consciously intuitive approach to the appreciation of
Warburg's intervention. Bergson's philosophy on time and the bifur-
cation of memory in the present provides a lever for closing the common problematic particularly evident in visual studies relating to the
dualism of the subject and the object relation, or in other words the
distinction between the material and the immaterial. Michaud's and
Didi-Huberman's reading of Warburg's work in particular suggest to
some extent a consistency with Bergson's concept of intuition, since
for Warburg the production and perception of art is constituted by a
creative (e)motion, guided by empathy in its grasping of the qualitative intensity of life or spirit. An explicit connection with the concept
of intuition is evident in Warburg's description of the Kachina dance
ritual in his field notes from the region of the Pueblo Indians, on
which Michaud (2004: 203) comments:

> In dressing like the doll representing him, the dancer produced
> an intermediate being between the body and the image and
> transformed himself into a representation. This intuition, di-
> rectly inspired by Burckhardt, who discovered in Renaissance
> festivities a path leading from life to art, was reversed by War-
> burg, who saw in the Oraibi ceremony the opening of a path
> leading from art to life.

The transformative qualities of the image (here a performance), recalls
the earlier discussion on the interrelation between the artist and the
model, the performer and the perceiver, in the reflections on movement in art by Rodin and Bergson. It is also reminiscent of Marey's
(1895: 304) statement that chronophotography appeals rather to imagination than to sensory perception. Warburg has elaborated this

interrelationship in his notes entitled, 'Spectator and Movement' (revised into 'Movement and Spectator') from 1890:

> To attribute motion to a figure that is not moving, it is necessary to reawaken in oneself a series of experienced images following one from the other – not a single image: a loss of calm contemplation. (Michaud 2004: 83)

This quotation from Warburg almost contains the discussion of this chapter (in reference to the emerging cinema) in a nutshell, so to speak, in his treatment of the composition of movement taking place in the beholder, the reawakening of experienced images reminiscent of Bergson's notion of the actualisation of memory-*images*. Michaud (2004: 260) suggests that Warburg's 'despecification' of discourse and disciplinary boundaries:

> … makes it possible to recharacterize the metadiscursive discourse of the historian or the philosopher as a form of authentic poetic expression; and an implicit critique of the philosophy of the subject: the author is less the master of his words than he is a receptive surface, a photosensitive plate on which texts or images surging up from the past reveal themselves.

Michaud's citation recalls spiritist practices whereby the mediums acted as "seismographs of the soul", to use Warburg's words, to function as receptacles for certain forces from other realms, the past, such as spirits, departed souls, etc.[28] Warburg's notion of the "loss of a calm contemplation", however, speaks of a proactive engagement rather than passivity and also provides an alternative model to rethink the spectators' involvement in spiritist practices, and the performances of mediumship and mediating technologies.[29] Like Warburg, Bergson suggested that the very processes of the creative activity — which according to him constitute the ordinary workings and proceedings of our consciousness — were expressed most tangibly through the aes-

---

[28] The term 'seismograph' was widely used in a transitive sense at the turn of the century in literature (Hofmannsthal), philosophy (Bergson) as well as science (Marey).

[29] The term 'active' and 'passive' are used as contingent concepts, in the case of intuition a certain passivity of the acting self does not exclude a heightened activity of mental processes — this kind of awareness and conscious effort is addressed here when referring to memory processes as proactive engagement.

thetic faculty as a constituent part of intuition in the production (and it could be added, in the perception) of the artwork. A treatment of the aesthetic perception of art cannot be further addressed in this context. It should be noted, however, that art as an aesthetic experience, in particular the cinema, as it is suggested here in the context of an inclusion of the perceptual processes, constitutes a paradigm for the contact between subject and object, matter and spirit. It is worth recalling in this place that, for Bergson (1991: 102), every attentive perception involves a reflection, which he conceived in the etymological sense of the word: "… that is to say the projection, outside ourselves, of an actively created image, identical with, or similar to, the object on which it comes to mold itself". This recalls the earlier discussion on Bergson's (2001: 13) reflections on the experience of aesthetic pleasure in the example of grace, in which he suggested that the conscious subjective processes bear a tendency toward an affinity with sympathy:

> But the truth is that in anything which we call very graceful we imagine ourselves able to detect, besides the lightness which is a sign of mobility, some suggestions of a possible movement towards ourselves, of a virtual and even nascent sympathy.

It is questionable if Bergson's (2005: 10) use of the French term *sympathie* implicated a connection with the notion of 'empathy', which was a concept used in psychology at the time, most notably in Robert Vischer's influential work *On the Optical Sense of Form* from 1873. It can be suggested, however, that Bergson's conception of sympathy, in connection with an aesthetic experience, appears certainly reminiscent of Vischer's notion of empathetic symbolism and imagination, which constituted a significant influence on Warburg's work. Rampley (1997: 45) notes how for Vischer: "… through the artistic imagination the mimetic assimilation of the subject to the object occurs in its most intense form".[30] With some overlap with Bergson's conceptions, Warburg exemplified, as it can be proposed with Rampley (50), the subject-object relationship in view of a development from a magical-

---

[30] Rampley remarks in this respect that Warburg has extended Vischer's concept of empathy in two ways, one in giving it a greater role of symbolism in the rooting of identification in the unconscious, the other in historicising the phenomenon of empathy.

associative to a logical-dissociative rhythmic progression in arts practice. Warburg addressed this oscillation explicitly in a sketchy note from his field-trip to the Hopi and Pueblo Indians in New Mexico and Arizona in 1895-1896:

> Incorporation is a logical act of primitive culture...
> Incorporation is a process that occurs between a human being and a foreign being, animate and inanimate...
> ... Communion rites...
> 2. Appropriation through incorporation. Parts of the object remain as associated foreign bodies, thus inorganically extending the ego-feeling. Manipulating and carrying.
> 3. The subject is lost in the object in an intermediary state between manipulating and carrying, loss and affirmation. The human being is there kinetically but is completely subsumed by an inorganic extension of his ego. The most perfect form of the loss of the subject in the object is manifest in sacrifice, which incorporates some parts into the object. Mimetic and imitative transformation: example; the mask dance cult.
> The scientific worldview presupposes that an actual transformation of a human into a plant, animal, or mineral is, by the laws of nature, impossible. The magical worldview, however, is based on the belief in the fluid borders between human, animal, plant, and mineral, such that man can influence becoming by means of a voluntary connection with the organically foreign being. (Michaud 2004: 325)

Warburg's comment to some extent seems to go along with Bergson's (1998: 178) understanding of perception, which takes place in the object to be perceived by way of an extended consciousness — or, as Bergson called it, by "reciprocal interpenetration". This bears relevance to Warburg's notion of the *dynamogram,* which rather than a means of signification for him expressed a morphology or an aesthetic of forces. What Warburg understood as a dynamic symbolism, as Didi-Huberman (2002: 176ff) emphasises, became particularly evident in Warburg's later metapsychological approach as an intervention in the historical study of the human psyche, which led him to inscribe an understanding of the image with an oscillating polarity between an interiorised and exteriorised vibration. Didi-Huberman's interpretation of this later bias of Warburg's work interconnects with the convergence between Marey's and Warburg's interests in underlying life forces and dynamisms beyond the appearance of movement in the displacement of the figure. On a more philosophical level it exemplifies Bergson's distinction of the interdependent yet contradictory tendencies of the mind in a continuous fluctuation. Moreover, what in the citation above may seem reminiscent of James Frazer's ([1890] 1981: 9-13) notion of "sympathetic magic" (also referred to as "contact-magic") can be translated into a grounded understanding of cognitive processes in constant negotiation between perception and recollection. Bergson suggested that reality could only be grasped through an oscillation between the virtual (all qualities, *images,* of matter, including the past, memory) and the actual (present, action). He conceived of the constant bifurcating oscillation between the commonly assumed dichotomy between internal and external, spirit and matter, subject and object, past and present, as constituting tendencies of a creative evolutionary process. This constitutes a vibrating 'object' of inquiry, on an experiential level of virtual contact, which in the perceptual processes of the *Mnemosyne Atlas* can be interpreted as the conscious entanglement with the survival of the past in the present. Warburg's intervention in this way can be seen as an attempt to organise the, sometimes, overwhelming flow of the virtual in order to manage the affections created by the vibratory activity of life in the human body. It is worth repeating in this place how Bergson conceived of the whole of matter as an aggregate of *images* and that he proposed that:

> The qualitative heterogeneity of our successive perceptions of the universe results from the fact that each, in itself, extends over a certain depth of duration and that memory condenses in each an enormous multiplicity of vibrations which appear to us all at one. (1991: 70)

Even more dramatically, Warburg's fluid conception of the interconnection between the subject and the object seems to open an abyss between the unsettling, even potentially dangerous, power of the affective pulse from the past and the symbolic detachment of its cultural expression as intermediary spaces for reflection. He regarded the inference of the retrieval of the archaic affective powers in their ecstatic ruptures in the present as pathological — a schizophrenia of an intrinsic human condition, as he called it, expressed in the *pathos formulas* (Michaud 2004: 314). Bergson instead distinguished two tendencies of the mind, intellect and intuition (formerly instinct), which in their schematic opposition, if balanced, appear less dramatically, since in his view they constructively constitute and complement each other throughout the evolutionary process (on a macro-level) and within the creative processes of the mind (on a micro-level). He proposed a solution for the commonly assumed dichotomy between mind and matter through his conception of intuition, which supplements and ultimately contains the intellect in that it enables us to grasp what intelligence fails to give us but which it stimulates us to seek in the first place (1998: 177ff, 200). This dual movement of the mind is exemplified in the way that, for Bergson, intelligence is directed towards inert matter, whereas instinct and intuition are directed towards life. He asserted that:

> If, as I have tried to show in a previous work *(Creative Evolution),* matter is the inverse of consciousness, if consciousness is action unceasingly creating and enriching itself, whilst matter is action continually unmaking itself or using itself up, then neither matter nor consciousness can be explained apart from one another. (1920: 18)

It is clear that Bergson did not posit intuition as more important than intelligence, and consequently neither the related knowledge practice of metaphysics over science, rather, as he saw them, they are essentially complementary. The distinction of these two tendencies in his philosophy merely served as a schematic analysis in order to separate them as complementary tendencies of the human mind. Bergson elaborated on this topic in *Creative Evolution* (1998 [1907]) which led him to introduce the concept of the *élan vital* as the driving creative impulse of consciousness, guided by free will and accessible via intuition, set within the framework of the body's necessities and directed by the intellect toward activity and the manipulation of matter. He proposed that:

> In reality, life is a movement,... [...] The impetus of life, of which we are speaking, consists in a need of creation. It cannot create absolutely, because it is confronted with matter, that is to say with the movement that is the inverse of its own. But it seizes upon this matter, which is necessity itself, and strives to introduce into it the largest possible amount of indetermination and liberty. (1998: 249, 251)

Within this spectrum, he asserted, the conscious activity based on the liberty of will pushes the life of the spirit (the virtual, the past) constantly into the present moment of action and by way of a conscious intervention (reflection) can enable the human spirit to liberate itself from the constraints of the material form in terms of pure necessities. In the way that both tendencies constitute quotidian occupations, they complement each other as two necessary movements of the mind. By aligning the scientific knowledge practice with the tendency of the intellect, Bergson (1998: 198-199) suggested that:

> ... it must be understood that the further it [science] penetrates the depths of *life,* the more symbolic, the more relative to the contingencies of action, the knowledge it supplies to us becomes. On this new ground philosophy ought then to follow science, in order to superpose on scientific truth a knowledge of another kind, which may be called metaphysical. (Emphasis in the original)

Although Bergson (1998: 178) maintained that intuition transcends intelligence by the way it introduces us into "life's own domain" — by which he understood the continuous flux of creation, experienced as *durée* — he found that:

> ... it is from intelligence that has come the push that has made it rise to the point it has reached. Without intelligence, it would have remained in the form of instinct, riveted to the special object of its practical interest, and turned outward by it into movements of locomotion.

Bergson's approach to perception in the way it straddles a discourse on (formal) images (or technology and quantitative methods) and the perceptual faculty of the human mind concerns a dimension of which both Marey's and Warburg's work was indicative and evocative. Some of the crucial concerns in Marey, Bergson and Warburg converge in their acknowledgement that a certain pulse or dynamism constitutes activity (mental, affective, physical, etc.) at the very threshold of the intersection between psychical and physical life. This triangle provides a sophisticated interrelated network that accommodates both their speculative and their applied knowledge practices in a range from peripheral to centrifugal forces. It could be said that Bergson's philosophy constitutes a bridge between Marey and Warburg, particularly through his investigation into the temporality of movement as an internal quality of *durée* by connecting the intellectual grasping of movement external in space and the internal qualitative experience of consciousness. With regard to the investigations of motion beyond the appearance of movement, it seems that in a certain sense Warburg takes off where Marey's investigation stopped, particularly in relation to their shared interest in force and energy as a life principle that manifested in their pursuit of motion beyond the surface of forms within the specific paradigms of their assigned knowledge practices. Whereas Marey touched upon this issue in places where his investigations exceeded the intellectual framework of science and extended into a discourse of metaphysics, art and aesthetics — reminiscent of Warburg's syncretic approach — Bergson at the same time was working at the root of a similar problematic to investigate the very principles of life. He saw the reasons for the unresolved problem in dualism and the consequent assumption of a mysterious relationship between matter and spirit, the body and the mind, in a misunderstanding of time as solely externalised in space. Besides the significance of the issue of time, the recurring themes of life-force, energy and dynamism are evident in the works of all three thinkers as an underlying principle beyond the image as text, which figured merely as a symptom of an acknowledgement of a deeper relational dimension.

Bergson and Warburg, more explicitly than Marey, recognised these very driving forces that precede the actual material form and its manifestation, a perspective that is, however, also traceable in Marey's studies of water, air movement and of cholera, especially once his oeuvre is extended into the broader intellectual context of his concerns. Pisano (2006: 98) confirms this view when he relates Rodin, Muybridge, Marey, and Bergson (and Warburg tangentially) to one another in the convergence of their shared interest in the simultaneous progressions of the future in the present and the notion of time crystalising in form or matter by escaping its continuity. By recognising the entanglement of these innovative thinkers in some of their core conceptions in relation to the perception of images, Pisano's assumed vantage point, however, necessitates a distinction from the intentions that lay in the production, methods and context of their works. This goes along with a specification of the inherent contradictions and differing objectives that distinguish the work of Marey from Bergson's philosophy as well as from Warburg's specific understanding of motion beyond visible appearance in the context of an art-historical enquiry. In the scientific knowledge practice, the investigation ends at the material surface of its exploration, as it was the case in Marey's major works considered from the limitations of the positivist framework and the technical application of his ideas, although he continuously pushed the limits and saw technology as a solution for the deficiencies of the human apparatus and as a challenge to instrumental realism. In the reflection of scientific positivism in the mechanisation of modern technology, Warburg, on the contrary, saw a danger in technology along with an obliteration of the tension between affect-energy and the provoked cultural sublimation in artistic or spiritual symbolism. The domestication of wired electricity in his view destroyed the "tele-sensory" capacities of the *Andachtsraum.*[31] Bergson also saw an imbalance between the intellect and intuition, however, for him the issue did not result in an antagonism toward technology but rather in questioning the equilibrium of conscious states, between matter and spirit, intellect and intuition in contemporary knowledge practices.

From Bergson's point of view, which claimed the essence of life as a force *(élan vital),* a continuous flux that endures, a constant becoming, Marey's studies of movement in their material, technological manifestations appear as merely the graphical traces of an effect whose origin remains implicit, although it nevertheless lay at the core of his interests. Only in this sense did his investigation remain on the surface of the exteriorisation of motion, which for Bergson in its origins derived from a decisive action based on free will. In Bergson's (1998: 337) view: "… real time, regarded as a flux, or, in other words, as the very mobility of being, escapes the hold of scientific knowledge". From this perspective, it can be suggested that Marey achieved the study of the very activity of movement in its physical expression and effect, whereas Bergson regarded the physical movement as a mere sensori-motor effect of a decisive action formed by the intrinsic processes of consciousness. While Marey acknowledged the underlying dynamism, core to his research, for Bergson the underlying forces could not be described nor expressed, never be measured, but only

---

[31] Warburg (1988: 58) spoke about the telephone, telegraphy and the aircraft as the *Ferngefühl-Zerstörer* ('destroyers of tele-sensation' — literal translation by the author).

lived and relived through experience. This was the ingenious intervention of Warburg's *Mnemosyne Atlas* as a gestural cataloguing of an exemplary cultural history; to create a platform for accessing these invisible, intangible forces beyond or rather between the images through the affective power that lies in the perceptual tensions of consciousness within the beholder. In addition, when considering the fragile balance in Warburg's mental condition and sensitivity, it also may have served as a way to manage and organise these affective forces that afforded a particular perceptive address, a tension with a potential for resistance, in the encounter with artistic and religious image culture. Finally, it might be held that in a reflection on Agamben's (1999) call for a reconsideration of Warburg's approach as a 'nameless science' lies the paradox of life itself; the continuous effort of spirit shaping matter, always striving for a fuller *image* of reality, which Bergson conceived as essential for his vision of a new science that embraced metaphysics through philosophy.

Chapter 5

Time, Memory, Consciousness:
Resituating the 'Spiritual' Dimension
in the Perceptual Processes of the Spectators

The previous chapters have contextualised Bergson as among those scientists who considered the cinematographical technology from a scientific point of view alone. A re-reading of Bergson's philosophy beyond his references to the technology of the cinematograph in the context of the cinema as a philosophical *dispositif,* however, reveals how through an application of his philosophy, the cinema can be regarded as a paradigm relative to understanding it as a model of consciousness. This becomes evident in the creative processes that interconnect matter and spirit within the spectators' cognitive activities. The necessary move within the discourse on the emerging cinema, as it is suggested here, requires a temporary shift from the focus on the 'spiritual' as 'belief', as an essential quality of 'apparitions' or other 'paranormal' phenomena, as well as a shift from the focus on the film as content and a phenomenology of the image, to a refiguring of the 'spiritual' within matter, as 'spirit in action'.

Although Bergson did not make this move with regard to the cinema, this approach does, however, closely follow his intention in the deployment of a metaphysics, which for him naturally emerged from a scientific engagement with matter.[1] Taking up this view, it can be proposed that the cinema as a philosophical *dispositif* could be regarded as a metaphysics in practice. The following citation could be

---

[1] For Bergson (1999b: 52-53), quantities, like mathematics as a science of magnitudes, were qualities in a nascent state; hence it was only natural: "…that metaphysics should adopt the generative idea of our mathematics in order to extend it to all qualities; that is, to reality in general. […] It will have seen with greater clearness what the mathematical processes borrow from concrete reality, and it will continue in the direction of concrete reality, and not in that of mathematical processes".

read as an analogy for the divergence between Marey and Demenÿ, when Bergson (1999b: 52) claimed that:

> ... metaphysics, which aims at no application, can and usually must abstain from converting intuition into symbols. Liberated from the obligation of working for practically useful results, it will indefinitely enlarge the domain of its investigations. What it may lose in comparison with science in utility and exactitude, it will regain in range and extension.

As starting point for this move served the observation that, although certain aspects of the immaterial, so-called spiritual, dimensions of the emerging cinema *dispositif* have been recognised in film and cinema studies, the treatment of its audiences in the context of this discourse has overly remained one that undermined agency in the spectator's share even to the extent of assigning the fascination with these dimensions to naivety or a question of belief. By drawing on the understanding of the cognitively impenetrable experience of the cinema *dispositif* as one of the core assets to its popularity, the prevailing interests in the immaterial have in the previous chapters been situated in some selected case studies within the wider context of the scientific community. A reconsideration in particular of Marey's interest in the underlying dynamisms and forces beyond the visibility of movement through the filter of a re-reading of Bergson's philosophy, led to an integration of Warburg's *Mnemosyne* method as key to establish a discourse of spirit beyond belief and beyond a phenomenology of the film text. Set against this context the following reflections will outline an approach to a Bergsonian cinema ontology by resituating some core aspects of the discourse of the immaterial/spiritual within the perceptual processes of the spectator's engagement during the screen event.

Even when departing from a purely technical perspective on the cinema experience, the necessity for an inclusion of the concept of time as experienced quality, *durée,* and the agency of choice within the perceptual processes becomes paramount, which will be illustrated with the following two thought experiments. The recording process of the analogue camera cuts an event into a small amount of instances: of the real-life movement only approximately three percent are actually recorded in assimilated duration. In the synthesis through analogue projection, a film today, according to the European cinema standard projection speed, is composed of 24 single still frames per second. Each image, momentarily arrested in the gate of the projector, is, moreover, interrupted twice by the shutter, from which it follows in a schematic calculation that we only perceive 1/500 *samples* of a second of real-time movement — when taking an average of light intensity as Terry Ramsaye (1926: 170-172) suggested. Therefore in a film of 90 minutes we only perceive in all 172.8 seconds of *samples* of actual time-duration (in the common 'spatial', measurable sense), which makes in total only 2.88 minutes screen time of fragmented actual 'movement' out of a 90 minutes film.[2] It follows that what the cinema provides is an amplified process of ordinary perception, since the spaces in between the perceived images require an enactment of lived experience, *durée,* empowered by memories through recollection, association and recreation, accompanied by affections and various body states — with an intensity depending on the spectators' choice to engage. This further finds an equivalent in the way the perceptual processes line up dispersed, unconnected single instances of ordinary perception through intellectual analysis and reflections, which only in the conscious states of duration consist as continuity and flow. Beyond a mechanistic reading of the technology in a more dynamic view, as Marey's critical negotiations with instrumental realism has exemplified and Warburg has so adequately shown with his *Mnemosyne Atlas,* it is the perceiver who makes the states beyond the figures move.

What is common knowledge today, Bergson (1991: 205-206) suggested in 1896 through a thought experiment that illustrated how, what we perceive consciously, is only a very small part of our entire perception. He gave the example of the perception of one second of red light, understood as the frequency with the longest wavelength and the least frequent vibrations of 400 billion successive vibrations a second. If we were able to conceive this frequency in our conscious per-

---

[2] This is reminiscent of the reversed effect in Comandon's and Carrel's time-laps microcinematography where cell life was observed over a long period of time and compressed into a couple of minutes screen time. Dr. Green, professor of Chemistry at Leeds University commented in 1925 on his experience of Carrel's films: "It was one of the most amazing things I ever saw... The film of the growth of the tissue was taken during twenty-four hours and must have involved a vast amount of reel. What takes place in the twenty-four hours is reduced in it to a comparatively few minutes... Dr. Carrel introduces immortality in a physicall (sic.) sense" (Landecker 2005: 927-928; see also 2006).

ception, according to Exner's calculation of the smallest interval of perceived time of 0.002 seconds, it would take more than 25,000 years in order to perceive the full frequential range of one second of red light — if they were laid out in a succession of instantaneously perceived vibrations. According to Bergson it is only a tiny part of perception that is consciously distinguished, a much greater part of what we perceive are qualitative states in duration *(durée)* — qualities that are sometimes felt rather than consciously grasped but remain accessible if later on required for a nascent action. The conscious processes themselves in ordinary perception, so Bergson (1991: 179), are limited in order to achieve the most economic way to act upon the present moment of perception; he proposed that: "... the body, always turned toward action, has for its essential function to limit, with a view to action, the life of the spirit".

In the cinema this situation is reversed and amplified and since no immediate action is required, it consequently encourages the most abundant and fullest engagement with spirit — if the spectator chooses to. Certainly, almost inevitably, the cinematic experience stimulates and necessitates at least some of these internalised processes, even if only in an automatic response — if of course the spectator is willing to engage in an attempt to understand the construction of a film. This engagement consequently opens up a spectrum of ever deeper and more complex layers, through which individually differing experiences can be created exponentially relative to the creative effort of the mind.

Set in the external circumstances of a shared context (not least through the cinema as communal space, which despite its sensory deprivation, accommodates publicly expressed utterances), a Bergsonian reading of the cinema experience accommodates the individual perception of a film, as well as the particularity of each perception of the same film on different occasions. Bergson (1991: 179) reminded us that:

> ... our past experience is an individual and no longer a common experience, because we have always many different recollections equally capable of squaring with the same actual situation...

The difficulty with this issue of course lies in the fact that the heterogeneous states of consciousness within the perceptual processes of the cinema experience cannot be homogenised in a generalising category. At least, the level on which Bergson situated these processes is onto-logical and operates beyond or before the point where experience be-comes transferred and expressed through the intellect. The dimension of internalised experiences instead, in this view, belongs to the spirit, a domain that in the discourse has by and large been ignored, not least due to the difficulties of addressing and communicating subjective and intimate states and encounters. Notwithstanding this needs to be fac-tored in when addressing spectatorship and the 'spiritual' dimensions of the cinema experience, which surfaces in the amplified arena of the conditions of the ordinary processes of perception and, as it is pro-posed here, can lead to a fuller engagement with this domain.

Given the comfortable arrangement of seats in most cinemas today (we should not forget that this has not always been the standard even in Metropolitan picturehouses), the cinema accommodates the disinte-rested body and the curious mind. It facilitates the internalised en-gagement and enjoyment of the various stages of the perceptual pro-cesses that Bergson exemplified in *Matter and Memory* (1991): the vast spectrum from the modality of an automaton to the dwellings of the dream-state. Bergson chose the issue of memory as one of the most accessible objects of study in the context of internalised pro-cesses of consciousness; not surprisingly this choice is mirrored in discourses on the perception of audio-visual media, although mostly with a focus on the film content. The cinema experience from a spec-tator's point of view provides a model for the workings of memory as primary constituent in the recollection and mnemonic recreation of the perceptual processes, both during and after the cinema event. Bergson (1991: 150) asserted:

> Your perception, however instantaneous, consists then in an incalculable multitude of remembered elements; in truth, every perception is already memory. *Practically, we perceive only the past,* the pure present being the invisible progress of the past gnawing into the future. (Emphasis in the original)

Bergson further posited that every *image,* in the moment in which it is consciously perceived, has already turned into memory; the formation of memory is, in this sense, coexistent with perception and does not come to life as a posterior occurrence, as he explained in an article on false recognition (1920: 109-151). Memory-*images* are constantly seemingly conjured up in the present moment of perception, in reality triggered through similarity or association, repeated or recreated and further amplified by processes of identification with the characters and events in the screen.

As we have seen earlier, the most crucial move in this respect that Bergson made is that he distinguished between the body (matter) and the mind in terms of time, not in terms of space. He claimed that a common mistake lies in the perception of movement as instances across space, which leads to a dualistic view in regarding matter in space, and unextended sensations in consciousness. To solve this problem Bergson introduced the term *durée* as a qualitative experience of time, a heterogeneity characterised by a melting of interiorised states of mind into one another. These states in continuous flow, in his view, only become distinguished through analysis by the intellect and reintroduced into space through actualisation in the present moment in preparation for action. Since the medium of film consists of arrangements between parts edited together, both on a micro-level of single frames, and on a macro-level of edited scenes and sequences, it can only be within the perceptual processes of the spectator's mind that a temporal qualitative experience of the film's reception can be sought. This adds another dimension of time to the established time coordinates of film and cinema studies, such as the material length of the film (meters), the duration of the screen-time, plot-time or story-time (minutes): the qualitative time dimension within the individual duration of the perceiver. Such an approach treats the cinema perception beyond the image as text, as complementary dimension, in addition to the analysis of the technological apparatus or other externalising attributes to spectatorship. The latter more common approaches to spectatorship, to the social, cultural, gendered, etc. 'self' — which Comolli (1980: 138) called the "ideological and social subject" — provide an interface for reception studies in combination with tangible empirical data.

A pioneering psychological approach was published by Hugo Münsterberg in 1916 (2001), entitled *The Photoplay,* in which he applied experimental psychology to the 'moving pictures' — a scientific study of the cognitive faculties of perception during the cinema experience with reference to the particular viewing position of the spectator. He suggested:

> Depth and movement alike come to us in the moving picture
> world, not as hard facts but as a mixture of fact and symbol.
> They are present and yet they are not in the things. We invest
> the impressions with them. (2001: 30)

An underexplored anthropological-psychological approach, for example, in the study of cinema spectatorship has later been offered by Edgar Morin in *Le Cinéma ou l'Homme Imaginaire: Essai d'Anthropologie* from 1956 (*The Cinema or the Imaginary Man,* 2005). Morin focuses on the cinema *dispositif* rather than the film content, which in his view constitutes a historical mirror and, at the same time, a harbinger of mechanisation. He refers to the cinema as a "personality factory" that externalises the psychic processes of the human mind (2005: 213). Rather interestingly from a Warburgian perspective, he consequently addresses the issue of aesthetics in the cinema not as an original human given, but as "the evolutionary product of the decline of magic and religion" (211). Reminiscent of Warburg's conception of the purpose of the *Mnemosyne Atlas,* according to Morin (2005: 181-182), cinematic (affective): "... participation equally constructs magic and reason, ... that finally, magic, sentiment, and reason can be syncretically associated with one another". For Bergson, however, since there was no distinction in kind between an actually lived experience and perceptions integrated from the cinematic experience, consequently there was no framework for 'magic' neither in terms of an epiphenomenon of consciousness nor in terms of external forces. Notwithstanding, Morin describes a similar process to Bergson (whose philosophy actually informs some of his elaborations) of an expansion of consciousness where the internal and the external merge — or in other words: spirit and matter touch.

However, these culturally informed readings of the cinema experience need to be seen as the consequence of these internalised processes through the contact of the spectator's perception *in* the screen. They can be regarded as an externalised result of the internalised processes of qualitative, conscious experiences, which surface during and after the cinema event. Among those are the various forms of identification, which concern a process of reflected projection of self-images, desires and wishes into the screen, as an act of externalisation on a 'meta-psychological' level, in which the cinema functions as an "individual wish-machine", as Siegfried Zielinski (1994a: 8) suggests.

In order to avoid a normative homogenisation, "domestication" or "pacification of memories", through which Johannes Fabian (2007: 103) warns against a convergence of memory and culture, Bergson's philosophy offers a strategy to identify instead those processes that are characterised by multiplicity, bifurcating, repetition, contradiction and recirculation in the activity of memory as it actualises in the present moment in the subject *before* it becomes manifest in cultural expressions such as language. Likewise it would be a reductive reading of Bergson's philosophy if the cinema would be perceived as a mere subjective experience, as a capitulation into a kind of dream-state, into a dwelling of memories without any relation to sensori-motor links, without agency to prefer one memory-*image* over the other. The cinema spectators are in a fully alert state, fully aware of how the cinematic apparatus works and of the implicit contract between the audiences' share and the cinema performance. The sensori-motor links are intact and linked to the present moment in conscious awareness in order to make choices in relation to the interpretation of the perceived present, which do manifest in concrete bodily states. However, in the cinema situation the spectators are liberated from the necessity to take action, which enables those virtual *images* to actualise and to be re-created, which suit the present circumstances of the spectators' desires, imaginations and (conscious and unconscious) choices. The spiritual (virtual), in this sense, is as vast a domain as the so-called positivist 'reality' in its material manifestations. The common associations regarding the cinema experience with the realms of illusion, dreams and imagination, in a Bergsonian reading, form scales within the spectrum of the conscious interaction with memories from the past, which constantly push into an actualisation in the present moment.

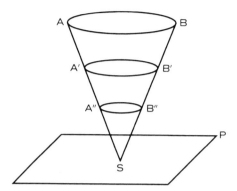

If we visualise Bergson's (1991: 162) inverted cone again, it schematises on the one extreme end automatism or habitual memory, the orientation beyond the cone at the focal point (S — the schematic present moment of action), on the other end the plane (A-B), the depth of pure memory within the multiple layers of memory-*images*. The cinema perception mostly does not have any direct impact on the immediate future of the spectators' external lives since they are not expected to act according to the perceptions received. But it has an inevitable, immediate impact on their internal, virtual lives, on processes of becoming in duration; each *image* perceived in the cinema becomes part of their individual memory, of the whole that constitutes their past, their personality.

As soon and as long as these past, lived experiences endure within the states of consciousness, these memory-*images* remain an internalised quality of becoming. This so-called 'spiritual' life resides in the deeper layers of pure memory, which reaches further than the layer of body-memories, which are mostly triggered automatically and constitute habitual activity. Memory-*images* contain a qualitative fullness that is accessible to recollection; in this sense, they provide a 'surplus-potential' through which additional and complementary recognition and subsequent interpretation and innovation at will occurs. Consequently, in a future engagement in any moment in the experience of the present (S), it is possible that some of those *images* turn into memory-*images* in order to actualise in perception through recollection and recreation, if they either show a great contiguity with the present moment or certain similarities in their inherent processes of remembering. The *images* in themselves are 'neutral' it could be said, however, they become recreated in manifold ways when they actualise and when, by conscious choice, they steer sensations and possible future actions.

Bergson's approach to perception suggests that cinema spectators touch the screen with their (inner and outer) senses and briefly become one with the object — in this case with projected images, as they are perceived *in* the object, the screen. This outreaching of the mind and perceiving through the sensory system instantaneously is impinged upon by memories from the past to actualise in the present moment through processes of recognitions, recollections and recreations. The perceiver's mind is continually stimulated to draw memory-*images* from the depth of pure memory in order to recognise, recollect and recreate in the sense-making of the filmic image sequences. In this way, the cinema perception, as any other kind of ordinary perception, constitutes an activity of extended consciousness reaching out into the object. The screen in itself is an *image* on to which images (by the technology) and *images* (by the mind) are being projected. In this sense, the projection of personal memory-*images* into the screen places the spectators within a *dispositif* of virtual processes of manifold projections and recreations of *images* onto other *images,* in constant negotiation between the screen and the mind.

The actualisation of personal recollections are additionally reinforced by gaps in the flow of the film, when ruptures occur and the stream of film memories is not sufficient to create the necessary resources in order to make sense of what is perceived. In these gaps and spaces between the sensori-motor reactions and the habitual mechanisms, the dimensions of the spirit become more fully activated and relayed into the present moment. Along with memories directly related to the perceived moment, associative and imaginative (virtual) *images* are created and recreated through the choice and the liberty of the will, wherever the meshes of necessity for (virtual) actions provide some space to innovate and intervene. As a consequence, it could be said that the activity of the spectator is doubled with two repositories to draw upon — the past *images* perceived *in* the screen as well as the recollections from the spectator's personal life, as they both intermingle and intersect as a double stream that impinges on the ongoing perception of the film. This is, it could be suggested, where the dimension of the spirit in the cinema experience can be situated.

Bergson introduced experience as a most crucial heuristic, which he understood as related to a conscious act of free will, an action that brings us in contact with duration: "... with *faits internes* (internal states), with the concrete self in action" (Guerlac 2004: 37).[3] It is, in this sense, that Bergson regarded spirit as independent but connected with matter, through the experiential dimension of our body that is expressed through activity. He critiqued the "great error of the doctrines on the spirit", which were: "... isolating the spiritual life from all the rest, by suspending it in space" (1998: 268). Bergson (268) instead proposed to: "... see the life of the body just where it really is, on the road that leads to the life of the spirit". In contrast to the conception of a transcendental subject in cinema theory (Metz 1975, 1986b; Baudry 1986a), Bergson's immanent discourse allows and favours the dimension of experience *within* and through the framework, necessities and utilities of material reality and not *beyond* or through an alteration. An awareness of the embedded transformative processes of the mind rather provide, in their extension in duration through aesthetic or philosophical intuition, the grasp of pure memory and pure perception, which exceed subjectivity and the personal by an experience that is, at least partially, unencumbered by the cognitive constructedness of reality.

In this way Bergson critiqued theories that saw perception as mere projections of internal states. He emphasised instead the partial coincidence of the moment of pure perception in the object to be perceived with the impinging of memories and affections that merge with the perceived *image*. He asserted:

> My consciousness of matter is then no longer either subjective, as it is for English idealism, or relative, as it is for the Kantian idealism. It is not subjective, for it is in things rather than in me. It is not relative, because the relation between the "phenomenon" and the "thing" is not that of appearance to reality, but merely that of the part to the whole. (1991: 230)

---

[3] Suzanne Guerlac (2004) has undergone a revision of the question of 'experience' in Bergson's philosophy emphasising its undervaluation as for example in Deleuze's Bergsonism.

Whereas from a psychoanalytic point of view, as pioneered by Christian Metz (1975, 1986b), the cinema experience remains one of loss, since the 'object of desire' always escapes the subject's grasp, Bergson's philosophy instead departs from a conception of subjectivity as fullness, an immanence that precedes the individual externalisation processes and constitutes the depository for the life of spirit. Pure memory, for Bergson, is always complete and whole, comprises all details of past experiences. It follows that a person's character is the synthesis of all past states, of all memories. As a consequence, the *image* in duration, which is intrinsic to the enduring self, is always fuller than the spectrum that the conscious processes reveal within the necessary framework for action. These processes occur on deeper layers than the consequential emotional, affective responses to the film content. This focus on the spectator's perception could suggest a revealing 'misreading' of a comment by Jean-Louis Comolli (1980: 141), which instead of his reference to the screen event and its representation could rather be reinterpreted in reference to the internalised processes of perception and the fullness of memory-*images:* "It is what resists cinematic representation, limiting it on all sides and from within, which constitutes equally its force; what makes it falter makes it go".

While semiotic film theory has revealed how the sign in the film image can never accommodate the fullness of its referent,[4] Bergson's unique conception of *images* as existing independent of us, has informed Deleuze's conception of the cinema as a composition of images and signs as 'preverbal material', which in his critique of a linguistic and 'representational' approach to film studies he also coined as "pure semiotics" (2007: 274). However, what is proposed in this book, shifts the attention away from the screen content all together into the internalised processes of perception and to the fact that the *image* can never be fully embraced by conscious awareness, since we never: "... perceive more than a very small part, whereas, on the contrary, we use the whole of our lived experience" (Bergson 1991: 146). Bergson (49) maintained that perception always remains partial and

---

[4] See for example Metz' (1975, 1986b) reference to the 'imaginary signifier'; Comolli (1980: 141) remarked similarly: "The cinematic image grasps only a small part of the visible; and it is a grasp which – provisional, contracted, fragmentary – bears in it its impossibility".

limited in contrast to the fullness of the *image* as a whole (and our becoming in light of the life of the spirit):

> The diverse perceptions of the same object, given by my different senses, will not, then, when put together, reconstruct the complete image of the object; they will remain separated from each other by intervals which measure, so to speak, the gaps in my needs.

This is how Bergson has related the cinematographic apparatus (perceived as the technological apparatus) to the mechanism of thought, as elaborated in a previous chapter, in the way it runs single images through the gate of the projector, comparable to the analytical processes of the intellect that singularise the impressions of sensory perceptions through reflection before they once again merge within consciousness. An intellectual assemblage, in his view, cannot provide a complete *image* of the objects we perceive, similar to that of a depiction of a 'real-life' action, captured by the camera and projected on to the screen. In order to construct stable appearances in the perception of *images,* a re-assemblage of the sensory data is necessary, which Bergson also referred to as "education of the senses". He suggested that:

> ... we must bring together all sensible qualities, restore their relationship, and reestablish among them the continuity broken by our needs. Our perception of matter is, then, no longer either relative or subjective, at least in principle, and apart, as we shall see presently, from affection and especially from memory; it is merely dissevered by the multiplicity of our needs. (1991: 49-50)

This could be interpreted as an anticipation of, or reflection on, the function of editing and the specific way in which spectators make sense of the film sequences through their cognitive engagement by encouraging the perception of an apparent continuity of separate entities. The intervals between the *images,* in a certain analogous sense, measure the gaps in the spectators' needs or interests (desires). However, as we saw earlier, according to Bergson (1920: 77), we perceive virtually many more qualities and dimensions than we actually become aware of through consciousness, whose function it is to shut everything out that does not contribute to the momentary interests for action. In the citation above Bergson (1991: 50) established an understanding of "consciousness as virtual action", since he defined perception as a preparation for action. In this activity, he situated the threshold of 'spirit' as creative activity, or it could be said that, when the gaps between the *images,* which refer to the sensory data perceived, are too big to enable assemblage, these spaces inbetween open up to the extensive layers of memory, the dimension of spirit.

In the context of the cinema in particular, the "needs", as addressed above, have to be understood on very subtle levels; when immediate physical needs cease in conscious awareness, perception is still driven by the underlying and more 'immaterial' or spiritual desires that are interlinked with the necessities of the very conditions of the body. In this sense, the body of the spectator in the cinema is not merely in a passive state, as is commonly considered when observed from an externalised or ocular-centered perspective, since internally, various micro-systems are highly stimulated, such as the nervous system, etc. and actively react according to this amplified perceptual condition. On a macro-level the spectators' minds (-bodies) are in a constant modus of 'virtual action', and the more the perceived object is considered as diminishing the distance to the body (and hence a certain danger of intruding or colliding with it is suggested), Bergson (1991: 57) maintained: "... the more does virtual action tend to pass into *real* action". (Emphasis in the original)

Bergson (29) also suggested with reference to ordinary perception: "It might be imagined that the impression received, instead of expanding into more movements, spiritualizes itself into consciousness". This seems to describe exactly what happens in the cinema perception, in the way that it creates "possibles" without the requirement for an externalised action to take place in the moment of perception — although from a perceptual perspective there are nevertheless rather profound reactions (affections) occurring in the body of the spectator. Bergson (1992: 104) defined this "possible" not as something that precedes reality; on the contrary, by taking up a perspective of dynamic memory processes, he asserted that: "We must resign ourselves to the inevitable: it is the real which makes itself possible, and not the possible which becomes real".

In this regard, the focus shifts from a treatment of the relationship between the film and the 'real' and the relationship between the spectators and the screen, to a consideration of those processes that transfer the "virtual" into the "actual", both constituting so-called "reality". The intrinsic quality of the "real" (understood as duration) can only be grasped, according to Bergson, when the flux of intentional creation in preparation for action can momentarily be interrupted and when either or both, a tendency toward "pure perception" or "pure memory", is intuited. According to Bergson (1991: 66), "reality" in its most basic function of the body as a centre for action, is measured by its "degree of utility", it constitutes "undivided growth, progressive invention, duration" (1992: 95-96). He suggested further: "Reality, as immediately perceived, is fullness constantly swelling out, to which emptiness is unknown. It has extension just as it has duration" (96). A debate on 'reality' in cinema theory, in this sense, can be situated within these 'spiritual' processes that unite the virtual with the actual in constant negotiation. Since *images* perceived in the screen can be understood as the same kind as those perceived in the quotidian experience, it could be suggested that the more intense the spectator engages with the film, the more 'real' the perception of a film becomes in the actualisation of the 'virtual'. In other words, 'reality' in the cinema exists in so far, as the spectators enable an actualisation of the virtual (in various degrees reaching toward pure memory or pure perception) during the perceptual processes. Precisely in between these movements of the mind lies the affect, which is created between a perception and an action within an extended continuum of consciousness. Bergson (1991: 57) proposed:

> Suppose the distance reduced to zero, that is to say that the object to be perceived coincides with our body, that is to say again, that our body is the object to be perceived. Then it is no longer virtual action, but real action, that this specialized perception will express, and this is exactly what affection is.

He claimed that perception commonly is always accompanied with affection, since virtual actions overlap with percepts in the body's preparation for action. In this sense, the emotional and affective responses are sensations linked to the sensori-motor reactions of the body and refer to an after-effect of perception. He suggested that:

> Everything will happen as if we allowed to filter through us that action of external things which is real, in order to arrest

and retain that which is virtual: this virtual action of things upon our body and of our body upon things is our perception itself. But since the excitations which our body receives from surrounding bodies determine unceasingly, within its substance, nascent reactions — since these internal movements of the cerebral substance thus sketch out at every moment our possible action on things, the state of the brain exactly corresponds to the perception. It is neither its cause, nor its effect, nor in any sense its duplicate: it merely continues it, the perception being our virtual action and the cerebral state our action already begun. (1991: 232-233)

When memories overlap and supplant the film's content, the 'affect' becomes possible, because the spectator recognises, and empathises or relates in other direct ways to the perception, which consequently can lead to sensori-motor reactions, even when no action is required from an external perspective, yet may still be necessitated through a certain degree of intensity from an internalised point of view. The 'affect' qualifies a potential action in its nascent state, while the consequent action in the cinema perception is usually suspended until the moment when the *images* of the perceived film are recalled as memory-*images* in order to serve future moments of action.

For Bergson, to coincide with the object concerns an extension of consciousness that never leaves the characteristics of an internalised process. The constituting occurrence of perception assigns new qualities to pure perception, which derive from the underlying qualitative states of the infiltrating memory-*images* in the perceptual processes. Consequently, it can be suggested that any meaning or interpretation that derives from this experience can never be assigned to the film as text alone, but necessarily needs to be addressed from an inclusion of at least an awareness of the 'spiritual' (virtual) dimension of the 'human perceptual apparatus'. Bergson (1991: 33) suggested in relation to ordinary perception:

With the immediate and present data of our senses, we mingle a thousand details out of our past experience. In most cases these memories supplant our actual perceptions, of which we then retain only a few hints, thus using them merely as "signs" that recall to us former images. The convenience and the rapidity of perception are bought at this price; but hence also springs every kind of illusion.

This citation can not only be mapped on to the recognised (mechanistic) fact that the apparent movement of still frames in the cinema creates an illusion or simulation to which the spectators deliberately give themselves over and indulge in the pleasure of their own deception. More crucially it also refers to an illusion that is created through the internalised processes within the spectator's consciousness and their qualified individual perception that might be mistaken for a homogeneous 'real'.

It follows that the cinema manifests an ambiguous or double-bind condition; on the one hand it eludes choice due to the cognitively impenetrable effects of its apparatus and the given content of the film, on the other hand, it restores choice in that it provokes a conscious engagement of the spectators' minds. These choices do not immediately lead into actions, but they are nevertheless driven by the desires, needs and necessities of the present moment within the internal processes of recognition and recollection. While Bergson (1991: 180) conceived of the perceptive processes and psychic life as fundamentally oriented towards action, he maintained that:

> A certain margin is, therefore, necessarily left in this case to fancy; though animals scarcely profit by it, bound as they are to material needs, it would seem that the human mind ceaselessly presses with the totality of its memory against the door which the body may half open to it: hence the play of fancy and the work of imagination — so many liberties which the mind takes with nature.

The cinema in its spiritual dimension can, in this sense, be interpreted as a technology for fancy and imagination in that it inspires to open that door to our psychic life that takes a liberty with human nature and liberates the spirit from the material necessities. While this could be said in principle about any entertainment form, the cinema's apparatus creates a specific condition of a cognitively impenetrable experience that exemplifies this threshold in a paradigmatic way and invites to explore this dimension in other forms of artistic expressions. With respect to an understanding of the human condition as oriented toward action, driven by utility and needs, Bergson (184) suggested that:

> The impotence of speculative reason, as Kant has demonstrated it, is perhaps at bottom only the impotence of an intellect en-

slaved to certain necessities of bodily life and concerned with a
matter which man has had to disorganize for the satisfaction of
his wants.

The cinema, in this sense, can be seen as a liberation of just this necessity and constraint of the intellect, since no action is expected or at
stake from an externalised point of view: it is a paradigmatic platform
to transcend the workings of ordinary consciousness and to liberate
the flow of duration (the virtual, memories, the past) from the material
necessities in the creation of new virtual, *imaginary* worlds. This further suggests that the cinema experience provides situations that trigger recollections and sensations from the unconscious past that would
otherwise go unnoticed. Bergson (1991: 171) asserted that:

> ... the more we detach ourselves from action, real or possible,
> the more association by contiguity tends merely to reproduce
> the consecutive images of our past life.

Does this suggest that the cinema mainly replays past experiences, as
a kind of nostalgic regression into the unconscious? While it is certainly resonant with certain comments by Warburg on the *Mnemosyne
Atlas* in that it seems to confirm its effect in activating the powerful
affects of the *pathos formulas* in the perception of the beholder, its
implied passivity would seem as much a one-sided reading of the
cinema experience as the conception of a dream-like state. Instead,
and most significantly, the cinema experience establishes an excess of
an *imaginary,* virtual potential for future actualisation. It opens a conscious engagement with the vast spectrum of both: states of consciousness and of 'non-consciousness', with all possible variations of
psychological, spiritual conditions in between — from illusion to
dream, from automatism to creative imagination.

  While the sensori-motor links are active (differing from the dream-
state in sleep condition), they are restricted in their exercising since
the perception does not require an immediate action through the body
— except on an internalised level of emotions, or sometimes in very
effective or 'moving' movies, through externalised body effects uttered as screams, muscular reactions, tears or other forms of physical
expression. These physical reactions, it could be suggested, are caused
by an awareness of a decreasing of distance between the perceived
object and the subject position, which in the light of Bergson's phi-

losophy strictly has to be regarded as a question of choice. The subject and the object merge instantaneously during the perceptual process occurring in the object to be perceived through an extended conscious act, while the degree of intensity in this expansion (and extension) differs, since perception is ultimately a qualitative event embedded within the complexities of the spiritual (virtual) life of each personality.

It becomes clear that the perception of mediated images, from this perspective, does not differ in kind from the perception of material objects, and consequently reveals the powerful impact of both the cinema apparatus and the *Mnemosyne Atlas* through their involved amplification of ordinary perception. In this context, the *Mnemosyne Atlas* can be seen in a similar light to the interactive engagement of the beholder, which increases and decreases the perceived distance (in terms of qualitative intensity) and subsequently triggers certain affects and emotional states individually. Warburg's notion of a space (or rather time?) for devotion *(Andachtsraum)* adequately describes both the cinema and the *Mnemosyne* in terms of the conception of a philosophical *dispositif* with a focus on the qualitative dimensions of an experience of choice.

For Bergson, action remains the core determinant for the engagement with the virtual life, which determines in how far an active choice is involved in the perceptual processes. This may be, and probably always is, combined with possible habitual reactions to past experiences, since, mapped on to the cinema experience, the density and speed of new stimulations may constrain the spectators to a certain automatism of recollections. In this sense, the cinema experience constitutes an amplification and acceleration of ordinary perception: we see images passing in front of our eyes in 90 minutes or so, at a speed and intensity as if remembering a lifetime[5] — or sometimes several lifetimes in an instant. In this way the cinema can be understood as an apparatus that through a conscious engagement makes us aware of

---

[5] It may seem a far-fetched but not irrelevant analogy recalling the reports of near-death-experiences as accounted for example in the research of Dr. Raymond Moody (2001). Bergson himself referred to this phenomenon in *Matter and Memory* (1991), when he mentioned scientific research into cases of sudden suffocation when visions of forgotten events of life pass before the subject with great rapidity. He referred to this phenomenon in the context of his argument for the existence of forgotten, unconscious memories (on the plane AB) and their reappearance in dreams or somnambulistic states (1991: 155-156).

some of the usually concealed processes of ordinary consciousness in its creative activity. Bergson (1935: 314) reflected:

> The activity of spirit has indeed a material concomitant, but one which corresponds only to part of it; the rest lies buried in the unconscious. The body is indeed for us a means of action, but it is also an obstacle to perception. Its role is to perform the appropriate action on any and every occasion; for this very reason it must keep consciousness clear both of such memories as would not throw any light on the present situation, and also of the perception of objects over which we have no control. It is, as you like to take it, a filter or a screen.[6]

Hence the spectrum of the internal engagement from a relatively 'passive' (in the sense of habitual) to an active modus depends on the present interest and engagement through sympathy or desires with the perceived. A need for action is, in this sense, always necessary for any change and intervention since it derives from the agency of the will and involves an active choice and decision-making. It should further not be forgotten that in the cinema an actualisation (manifestation in perception) of this creative engagement is in any case also enabled through a certain delay until a future action is being prepared, which might be informed by certain qualities associated with the perceived *images* from a past (cinema) experience.

The departure from an active internalised conception of the cinema perception allows us, however, to take an application of Bergson's two tendencies of the mind, intellect and intuition, even further. As the cinema situation does not require any externalised action from the perceiver, and through the gaps that the performance leaves in between both the images and the larger sequential jumps in the editing processes, we could ask: does it not also enable the mind to make a conscious movement into the direction of intuition and pro-actively recreate the self in duration, in its processes of becoming?

According to Bergson it was only through the processes of intuition that time as duration could be grasped. He understood intuition

---

[6] Bergson's elaborations could also bring a fresh perspective to the common notion of so-called out-of-body experiences, one that conceives of the body states as merely diminished in conscious attention. This view would liberate a more conscious engagement with the creative processes of the mind on an experiential, embodied level rather than a shift toward a conceptual transcendental plane.

as a profound introspective action that puts the perceptual process within the flux of psychic states of the deep-seated self (1998: 125).[7] Intuition for Bergson consisted of more than a simple feeling or impulse (as often commonly understood)[8] or a 'vision'; it rather requires almost a reversal of the ordinary direction, a counter movement to the natural bent of the intellect by "… turning thought upon itself in order that it may seize this ability and catch this impulse" that constitutes the very creative activity of our becoming (1992: 94). He claimed:

> When we put back our being into our will, and our will itself into the impulsion it prolongs, we understand, we feel, that reality is a perpetual growth, a creation pursued without end. Our will already performs this miracle. Every human work in which there is invention, every voluntary act in which there is freedom, every movement of an organism that manifests spontaneity, brings something new into the world. (1998: 239)

In intuition we place the mind within the qualitative state of our own duration and through an act of extended consciousness into the duration of the object to be perceived. In this way, accompanied by a certain kind of sympathy, which Bergson also referred to as intellectual sympathy, if only very briefly, we coincide ('co-inside') with the object. This action, Bergson claimed, takes effort and mostly cannot be sustained for long; the mind usually oscillates between the two states, between the movement of the intellect and intuition, which constitute a collaborative, complementary entanglement serving the creative

---

[7] It is significant to remember that Bergson made a distinction between instinct and intuition; in his view intuition could be understood as a further developed capacity of instinct: "… by intuition I mean instinct that has become disinterested, self-conscious, capable of reflecting upon its object and of enlarging it indefinitely" (1998: 176).

[8] This kind of common notion of intuition is frequently reported in relation to the origins of certain scientific ideas and inventions in science, however, these processes have mostly been obscured in the final results and reports. When applying Bergson's concept of intuition it would seem that during the process of analysis by the intellect, for example in scientific experiments, the scientist continuously would go back and forth to this initial intuition to remember the quality he had grasped. This profound part of the processes of the mind is usually excluded, not only because of the scientific positivist paradigm, but also, precisely as Bergson has pointed out, because it is almost impossible to transfer this experience, to express it, because as soon as we take it out from our internal flux of duration, it turns into mere fragmentation, characterised by language and intellectual and social habitus.

evolution of human consciousness. He applied various thought experiments to express these movements, as he also exemplified them schematically in the cone, but they are much fuller developed in *An Introduction to Metaphysics* (1912) from 1903. In this article, originally published in the *Revue de Métaphysique et de Morale,* Bergson (1999b: 25) described intuition as a gradual expanding awareness that moves from the exterior perception, through the affiliated memory-*images* and mental associations and the hereto firmly bound "stir of tendencies and motor habits — a crowd of virtual action" to finally enter a state beyond any representation in *images:* a flux of inner states in becoming, pure duration *(durée).*

Applied to the cinema, it could be suggested that the cinema experience accommodates and enhances both tendencies of the mind — it exemplifies the intellect as well as intuition at work. The intellect makes sense of the montage, the audio-visual structure of the film, through a compilation of a multiplicity of sensory percepts from different perspectives; this is where our intellect feels at home, according to Bergson's analysis. As the spectators always engage with their personal memories and affections in the moment of perception, however, wherever the film structure creates additional meshes in the continuity for these memory-*images* to infiltrate (which Deleuze has located in the 'time-image'),[9] deeper layers of pure memory — duration itself — might be touched. A movement toward intuition may be accommodated since, notwithstanding that the body is in a condition of preparation for a virtual action, the intellect is liberated from certain constraints of sensori-motor necessities. Bergson (1991: 69) proposed in his view on a metaphysics of immanence:

---

[9] Deleuze (1986, 1989) has elaborated on these aspects in relation to the film content, which he has classified in his matrix as the 'movement-image' (in which time is subordinated and the action is driven by the sensori-motor schemata) and the 'time-image' (in which time takes over the drive in action in the direction of film form and leads the intellect astray). When the latter happens, Deleuze corroborated, the spectator directly enters a dimension of time and the dimension of the spirit opens up (see for example 1989: 178). While Deleuze in his analysis mostly excluded the explicit address of the dimension of spirit and intuition, it also remained confined to the predisposition of his matrix of film images. A direct Bergsonian reading of intuition instead shifts the focus away from the screen to the qualitative engagement by the spectator, which can only be favored by certain film images but ultimately always remains a necessary pre-condition for a liberation of the dimension of spirit in the context of any kind of perception.

> Restore, on the contrary, the true character of perception; rec-
> ognize in pure perception a system of nascent acts which plun-
> ges roots deep into the real; and at once perception is seen to be
> radically distinct from recollection; the reality of things is no
> more constructed or reconstructed, but touches, penetrated,
> lived, and the problem at issue between realism and idealism,
> instead of giving rise to interminable metaphysical discussions,
> is solved, or rather, dissolved, by intuition.

It could be posited as a hypothesis that during the cinema experience, processes of intuition are stimulated, if not always explicitly, at least in a latent tendency of an emergent gesture of choice by the mind to grasp 'life' or *durée* beyond the mere appearances of form in the film's content and their suggestive recollections through memory processes. Bergson (1999b: 21-22) claimed:

> But when I speak of an *absolute* movement, I am attributing to
> the moving object an interior and, so to speak, states of mind; I
> also imply that I am in sympathy with those states, and that I
> insert myself in them by an effort of imagination. Then accord-
> ing as the object is moving or stationary, according as it adopts
> one movement or another, what I experience will vary. And
> what I experience will depend neither on the point of view I
> may take up in regard to the object, since I am inside the object
> itself, nor on the symbols by which I may translate the motion,
> since I have rejected all translations in order to possess the ori-
> ginal. In short, I shall no longer grasp the movement from
> without, remaining where I am, but from where it is, from
> within, as it is in itself. I shall possess an absolute.

This could be mapped onto the cinema experience, in the way its amplified perceptual arena carries a potential to bring the spectators in touch with this concrete, enduring self in action. The activity of intuition, which Bergson refers to as an aesthetic or philosophical intuition, enables the subject to enter into a deeper contact with itself and other living beings. Instead of escaping time and place, it enables an immersion in time, in duration itself, in "concrete duration" or "absolute movement" (1998: 363).

Through an application of Bergson's philosophy to the perceptual processes of the spectator as a conceptual, ontological fundament for a further treatment of film content, it can be suggested that the process

of intuition in the cinema consists of grasping a pure moment of duration within the spectator by conjuring up deeper lying memory-
images that merge by way of sympathy through the extended conscious touch of the objects/ action in the screen during the processes
of perception. From this perspective it does not matter if the thing perceived is a material object, a mediated image of a real-life situation, a
computer generated image, the appearance of a phantom or other
forms of hallucination. However, it has of course a particular significance for the audience's share in the perception of for example documentary film, and might provide a philosophical fundament for what
the ethnographic filmmaker and anthropologist David MacDougall
(1998: 271-274) addressed as shared consciousness in his call for an
"anthropology of consciousness". It could be proposed that it is the
qualitative dimension of lived duration that facilitates a sympathetic
immediacy through which the cinema experience becomes intuitive
and 'spiritual'. Bergson (1998: 363) suggested:

> We must appeal to experience — an experience purified, or, in
> other words, released, where necessary, from the molds that
> our intellect has formed in the degree and proportion of the
> progress of our action on things. An experience of this kind is
> not a non-temporal experience. It only seeks, beyond the spati-
> alized time in which we believe we see continual rearrange-
> ments between the parts, that concrete duration in which a
> radical recasting of the whole is always going on. It follows the
> real in all its sinuosities.

According to Bergson (1991: 247), the sensible qualities of matter are
differentiated by their rhythm of duration, and can be regarded as differences of internal tension that can be grasped, when momentarily
interrupting the flow of habit and necessity in the processes of consciousness. This interruption also seems reminiscent of Warburg's
conception of the necessary spaces for reflection in light of the pressure or burden of the recreated affections in the perception of cultural
histories. It follows that in order to enter 'real' movement and becoming, understood by Bergson as 'sensible reality' in contrast to 'intelligible reality', the mind needs to be temporarily released from the

"cinematographical mechanism of thought" (1998: 313-314).[10] Reminiscent of both Bergson's and Warburg's conception of a seismographic activity, it follows that we only perceive enduring movement if we place ourselves *in* the movement itself. In a Bergsonian understanding of the perception processes, we place ourselves within the object to be perceived with a kind of sympathy — to be understood in a relational sense. He suggested: "Install yourself within change, and you will grasp at once both change itself and the successive states in which *it might* at any instant be immobilized" (1998: 308 — emphasis in the original).

Bergson was explicit that duration could be experienced through his conception of philosophical, or as he also called it, aesthetic intuition, but it could never be grasped through concepts in terms of a conceptual representation. He elaborated on how perception turns into concepts when we intellectually attempt to grasp movement and the processes of change — which also could be read as a comment on the method of the *Mnemosyne Atlas* that moves away from an iconological interpretation:

> He who installs himself in becoming sees in duration the very life of things, the fundamental reality. The Forms, which the mind isolates and stores up in concepts, are then only snapshots of the changing reality. (1998: 317)

These stops or halts in time occur, according to Bergson (1998: 312), when we step outside the enduring process of movement itself and intellectually conceptualise it. In this sense, he asserted that: "Infancy, adolescence, maturity, old age, are mere views of the mind, possible stops imagined by us, from without, along the continuity of a process". Similar to the single attitudes in Marey's chronophotography

---

[10] Bergson (1998: 327) compared the "cinematographical method" to Greek philosophy and pointed to the similarity with "modern science" that subordinated "sensible reality": "Finally, it will have on the one hand the system of ideas, logically coordinated together or concentrated into one only, on the other a quasi-nought, the Platonic "non-being" or the Aristotelian "matter". — But having cut your cloth, you must sew it. With supra-sensible Ideas and an infra-sensible non-being, you now have to reconstruct the sensible world". The difference in "ancient and modern science" according to Bergson (330), lay in that: "... ancient science thinks it knows its object sufficiently when it has noted of it some privileged moments, whereas modern science considers the object at any moment whatever".

and Warburg's *pathos formulas,* these concepts belong to the realm of forms that are independent of time since they consist of isolated singularities. Bergson (1998: 339) suggested in a comment, which again could directly be related to the very experience of the *Mnemosyne Atlas,* that: "… for us, conscious beings, it is the units that matter, for we do not count extremities of intervals, we feel and live the intervals themselves". Hence it is not the intervals themselves that count, as some receptions of Warburg's *Mnemosyne Atlas* emphasise, but they merely provide signposts that enable us to experience and live the intervals of a qualitative condition, where change and the momentum of motion turns into a lived experience. In this sense, it can be suggested that through a leap from a conceptual representation to a qualitative experience in time of this same conception, the perception or imagination of *images* during the cinema experience stimulates a tendency toward intuition. Bergson (342) elaborated on this movement with reference to ordinary perception:

> This second kind of knowledge would have set the cinematographical method aside. It would have called upon the mind to renounce its most cherished habits. It is within becoming that it would have transported us by an effort of sympathy. We should no longer be asking where a moving body will be, what shape a system will take, through what state a change will pass at a given moment: the moments of time, which are only arrests of our attention, would no longer exist; it is the flow of time, it is the very flux of the real that we should be trying to follow.

In this comment it becomes apparent why Bergson created the concept of duration *(durée)* as a new definition of 'becoming', which is not aimed toward a predefined outcome or an event in the future, but rather concerns the very experience of the processes of change themselves.

During the event, the cinema experience is almost entirely spiritual, since no action is required; the perception of *images* is spiritualised into consciousness. It may even allow us to slightly open that door against which the mind presses with the totality of its memory in order to engage not merely with fancy and imagination, but possibly with intuition. The agency of the subject, in this view, no longer constitutes an interface between the conscious engagement with the world and an underlying unconscious. It rather *is* the very creative agency that pro-actively plunges into the depths of the 'unconscious', in Bergson's words the "virtual" or "pure memory" — the realm of the spirit — in order to drive forward the creative impulse towards actualisation in every present moment of action: the movement of life itself. As Bergson (199-200, 201) suggested:

> Let us seek, in the depths of our experience, the point where we feel ourselves most intimately within our own life. It is into pure duration that we then plunge back, a duration in which the past, always moving on, is swelling unceasingly with a present that is absolutely new. [...] The more we succeed in making ourselves conscious of our progress in pure duration, the more we feel the different parts of our being enter into each other, and our whole personality concentrate itself in a point, or rather a sharpe edge, pressed against the future and cutting into it unceasingly. It is in this that life and action are free.

If we apply this conception to the cinema perception, we can see that the cinema experience can be understood not only in terms of escapism from time or place — which it does of course when viewed through the filter of an externalised, spatial analysis — but also as a particular relation to a deep immersion within time, as an experience of *durée*. This, at least, happens, when the spectator agrees to enter the qualitative momentum of the cognitively impenetrable experience. In this respect the treatment of the 'spiritual dimension' in cinema theory and technology studies frequently focuses on the issue of teleportation and telepresence, on the simultaneity and synchronicity in terms of place, and rarely explicitly on the immersion in time as enduring momentum that requires a much more subtle approach, which Warburg has so elegantly and effectively addressed in the *Mnemosyne Atlas*. Whereas film content exemplifies time travel mostly in terms of moving the body/ mind into the future and back to the past; in a Bergsonian reading, it is instead the crystallisation of the future and the past in the present perception of the beholder that allows for the intuitive grasping of *durée:* hence the cinema as a time-machine of the enduring present in the becoming within the spectator's consciousness.

In this way the cinema experience provides an amplification of the quotidian processes of the mind, which creates a particular awareness of the introspective movement that is required not merely to understand the meaning of a film, but for actual experience-creation, neither located in the film content alone nor purely internalised. It can rather be conceived as a complex motion almost like a partially externalised introspection whereby internal and external merge and momentarily dissolve the subject-object dichotomy in a continuous fluctuation. This engagement enables the spectator to experience not necessarily pure memory and intuition itself, but at least an awareness of this tendency of the mind as the motion of intuition, in the way that we experience, in order words 'live' the film in relation to our own virtual lives: memories and affections that fuel imagination and desire. As we have seen, intuition, in Bergson's philosophical conception, requires a contrary movement to the intellect that breaks with the sensori-motor, cause-and-effect chain and moves in the opposite direction — a schematic conception (just like Bergson's cone), not to be confused with a spatial indication in terms of inside or outside but in the sense of a qualitative versus a quantitative experience of time. The cinema experience as an amplification of ordinary perception, in this sense, can be regarded as stimulation for introspection, while the films themselves are to our perception not different in kind from any other perception we receive in actual life situations. As the body-memory is not required but notwithstanding in active condition for a delayed actualisation, this particular cinematic *dispositif* stimulates and provides dimensions for experiencing deeper layers of memory-*images* to infiltrate into the perceptual processes, which Bergson classified as the realm of the spirit. The cinema experience can be considered among other things as an amplified experience where a direct, intuitive contact with duration *(durée)* is enabled under certain circumstances, while the engagement with individual *images* allows for experiences of all possible conditions in between pure perception and pure memory — in other words with 'spirit', in the sense that Bergson proposed. He claimed:

> But if, in fact, the humblest function of spirit is to bind together the successive moments of the duration of things, if it is by this that it comes into contact with matter and by this also that it is first of all distinguished from matter, we can conceive an infinite number of degrees between matter and fully developed spirit — a spirit capable of action which is not only undetermined, but also reasonable and reflective. (1991: 221)

The active choice of memory-*images* remains with free will in the conscious engagement with the film, favored by the meshes that the structure of a film creates for a pro-active engagement, whereas the intensity involved depends on the degree of the spectator's relational engagement with the perceptual processes. The more the spectator's consciousness is driven towards curiosity and willingness to engage with and know the world (the universe of the film in this case) and sympathises with it (in terms of establishing relationships that decrease distance), the more this engagement actualises unconscious, associative or even imaginative and consciously recreated memory-*images*. The intensity of these processes concern both the intellect, in the way the single images and scenes are assembled, and the affective engagement with the film content and the intuitive impulse through which memory-*images* actualise and deeper layers of pure memory as well as "pure perception" in the experience of duration may be touched. Because the intensity of the spectators' experience depends on the establishment of certain kinds of relationships with the perceived, Bergson's relational model of the cinema perception empowers the spectators in their individual engagement with the film. The relief and liberation that this perspective further offers lies in the way consciousness is seen as acting between and among both, the material and the immaterial.

When Bergson referred to the creative act in art in his early works — a domain which generally speaking at the time had no place for the populist reception of the cinema as entertainment form — he distinguished between the creative force at work, manifest in the process of the making of an object and the object as a final outcome in its material form. He asserted:

> But this consciousness, which is a *need of creation,* is made manifest to itself only where creation is possible. It lies dormant when life is condemned to automatism; it wakens as soon as the possibility of a choice is restored. [...] For consciousness corresponds exactly to the living being's power of choice; it is co-extensive with the fringe of possible action that surrounds the real action: consciousness is synonymous with invention and with freedom. (1998: 261, 263-264; emphasis in the original)

With view to the cinema experience it follows that as spectators we recreate our 'selves' in each film, as it happens in ordinary situations. The cinema amplifies this continuous creation and recreation of a multiplicity of lives, in ever new forms and reinterpretations. Not only does every spectator perceive the same film differently (beyond the shared points of reference), but also, each time s/he watches the same film again, s/he will experience it differently again, since, as Bergson (5-6; and similarly many other philosophers) has so adequately put it: "... consciousness cannot go through the same state twice. [...] Our personality, which is being built up each instant with its accumulated experience, changes without ceasing". The amplification of the integral processes of becoming can be regarded as constituting one of the intrinsic pleasures of the cinema experience: a moment of transformation and introspection to get in touch with a profound experience of being. Bergson (298-299) asserted:

> We must accustom ourselves to think being directly, without first appealing to the phantom of the nought which interposes itself between it and us. We must strive to see in order to see, and no longer to see in order to act. Then the Absolute is revealed very near us and, in a certain measure, in us. It is of psychological and not of mathematical nor logical essence. It lives with us. Like us, but in certain aspects infinitely more concentrated and more gathered up in itself, it endures.

The "Absolute" for Bergson constitutes life's basic creative force, the *élan vital,* which continuously moulds the matter that is at its disposal. He proposed an understanding of spirit and the *élan vital* beyond the dominance of the intellect and the positivist conception of a "corresponding sensationalistic epistemology, according to which anything knowable is knowable through the physical senses" alone (Griffin 1986: 8) In this manner he paved the way to open a discussion of 'spirit' as an intrinsic constituent of ordinary perception. In this sense, Bergson's (1998: 250) following suggestion could also almost be read as an instruction to the perception of the *Mnemosyne Atlas:*

> Let us try to see, no longer with the eyes of the intellect alone, which grasps only the already made and which looks from the outside, but with the spirit, I mean with that faculty of seeing which is immanent in the faculty of acting and which springs

up, somehow, by the twisting of the will on itself, when action is turned into knowledge, like heat, so to say, into light. To movement, then everything will be restored, and into movement everything will be resolved.

What Bergson here terms movement is not the movement of things or objects external to us in space, but he refers here to "pure movement" as a quality of time experience *in* duration as it is experienced from within, intrinsic to the internal states of consciousness. The apparent discontinuity that the intellect perceives of conscious states is, in Bergson's view, caused by a shifting awareness that appears in seemingly separate acts, and consequently makes these states appear as divided. In a comment that reflects quite adequately Marey's broader research interests and vision, Bergson (3) asserted:

> Our attention fixes on them because they interest it more, but each of them is borne by the fluid mass of our whole psychical existence. Each is only the best illuminated point of a moving zone which comprises all that we feel or think or will – all, in short, that we are at any given moment. It is this entire zone which in reality makes up our state. Now, states thus defined cannot be regarded as distinct elements. They continue each other in an endless flow.

The movement of an ever changing fluid whole, as cited by Bergson above, resituates what Warburg called 'motion' as a persistence of intermediary states in the displacement of the figure revealing the underlying Dionysian principle — the creative disorder of organic life — within the perceptual processes of the beholder. This view resonates with Warburg's attempt to uncover the dimension of the 'spirit' beyond the cultural and religious context of the studied period on an experiential, affective level, for which the *Mnemosyne Atlas* served as the material to momentarily hold the flux of duration in intervals of reflection and conscious awareness of the past impulse in the present. The significance of his intervention can be located in his attempts to straddle these underlying forces as a fundamental activity embedded within the processes of creativity, beyond the surface of visual representation in their forms of appearances.[11] It can be regarded as crucial

---

[11] Michaud's book title *Warburg and the Image in Motion* (2004) gains a profound meaning when it is interpreted from a Bergsonian perspective. The 'image in motion'

intermittent in a discourse that proposes to consider consciousness as key player and instigator of a specific *dispositif,* which includes the spectators' agency as significant constituent in the creative engagement with the dimension of the spirit.

For the scope of this book it can be concluded that the spiritual dimension of the cinema, as it is proposed here, provides not only a platform for various beliefs in other dimensions, as it has been discussed in the literature, but also, most importantly, the fascination with 'spiritual' dimensions in the context of popular culture can also be situated within the cinematic experience itself in which, as Bergson proposed, matter and spirit meet. During these processes, time as duration *(durée)* can be experienced in an amplified way through an awareness of the activated internal psychic states, in which memory extends into the present as a continuous flux. This flow from the past into the future, converging at the present moment in the cinema experience may give some relief in the questionable framework of an exclusive materialism, which gives matter a definite finality and does not allow for spaces or alternative models of immaterial dimensions. This is where Bergson's ontological, immanent approach can be distinguished from purely mechanistic methods and systems of thought that relate to a finalist, reductionist logic concurrent with the predominant positivist paradigms, which he critiqued for their exclusivity in the context of the 19th century scientific epistemology. However, it also provides a relief from phenomenological, idealist conceptions of a supra-reality or dimension behind the perceptual dimension, by liberating matter from a (sometimes involuntary) epiphenomenalism.

For Bergson instead, science and —what he defined as — metaphysics, constitute complementary systems of knowledge practice; an entanglement that can be seen as exemplified in the cinema and the *Mnemosyne Atlas,* both operating as a philosophical *dispositif* although via different modalities, intentions and constituents. From a mechanistic point of view it could be said (similar to Marey's invitation to a reading of stereoscopic images without a lens)[12] that the

---

in this sense may not solely indicate the dynamics beyond the visual representation and perception of an icon in various historical, cultural contexts, instead it could be read as the very motion itself as it is perceived through a time quality in the beholders internalised conscious processes.

[12] Marey invited the reader to an optical exercise that creates a stereoscopic image without a stereoscopical viewer. The two images in his illustration show stereoscopic

Mnemosyne Atlas is a cinema without an external projector — a comparison that only works, when situating movement within the perceptual processes of the beholder. When transferring this reading to technology more generally, the dominating functional, materialist point-of-view that regards technology as mechanistic extension to the body — a reading that in recent theoretical approaches has been altered through the additional immaterial implications of technology (Noble 1997; Peters 1999; Nye 2006) — can in this regard also be reinterpreted by way of a surplus of virtual potentiality in the entertainment situation, constantly seeking a liberation of spirit.

Action not only turns into memory, but also, as virtual actions, memories always already carry a potential to become actualised. From this perspective film perception — any perception — turns into a politicized act. While we might agree that every action is a micro-political act, Bergson's insights go even further in considering every perception as a political act, precisely because of the inherent agency in the beholder's engagement with the present. The more the spectator actively allows memory-*images* to infiltrate through the meshes of necessity, through the filter of a reconsideration and reflection on behalf of the agency of free will in order to create new percepts and meanings, the more her/his spiritual (virtual) life establishes more complex connections and associations with the actuality of the present moment — the more empowerment to act accordingly, beyond the habitual patterns by superseding automatic response and reactionism. Bergson (1991: 56) suggested that:

> Perception, understood as we understand it, measures our possible action upon things, and thereby, inversely, the possible action of things upon us. The greater the body's power of action (symbolized by a higher degree of complexity in the nervous system), the wider is the field that perception embraces.

Simultaneously, when the self-interest of the body retrieves, even if only for split moments, the plausibility of perceiving pure perception

---

trajectories deriving from bright points that in the recording describe abstract curves against a black background. Marey (1895: 22-23) described how the experience of stereoscopy without a technical apparatus occurs simply by placing the focus in the distance between two stereoscopic images and interposing the object between the eyes and the distant point that finally makes the four appearing images melt and turn into a relief.

and pure memory increases, which enables a more profound interconnection with real duration and qualitative conscious states as shared
experience.

Bergson's insights that the higher the degree of complexity in the
nervous system and hence the body's power of action, the wider the
field of perception it embraces, also signifies in relation to the cinema
experience that an amplified and extended field of perception might
increase the complexity in the nervous system and hence increase the
body's power for action. Consciousness for Bergson, in this sense,
presides over action and enlightens choice but is not synonymous with
the whole content of conscious awareness, or past memories. He
claimed:

> But if consciousness is but the characteristic note of the *pres-
> ent,* that is to say, of the actually lived, in short, of the *active,*
> then that which does not act may cease to belong to conscious-
> ness without therefore ceasing to exist in some manner. In
> other words, in the psychological domain, consciousness may
> not be the synonym of existence, but only a real action or of
> immediate efficacy; limiting thus the meaning of the term, we
> shall have less difficulty in representing to ourselves a psychi-
> cal state which is unconscious, that is to say, ineffective. What-
> ever idea we may frame of consciousness in itself, such as it
> would be if it could work untrammeled, we cannot deny that, in
> a being which has bodily functions, the chief office of con-
> sciousness is to preside over action and to enlighten choice.
> Therefore, it throws light on the immediate antecedents of the
> decision, and on those past recollections which can usefully
> combine with it; all else remains in shadow. (1991: 141)

The very special elegance, or trickery and ambiguity, of the cinema
lies in its ability to accommodate a broad spectrum of psychic engagements. It embraces both idealist and realist perspectives and a
spectrum of mental activity within the perceptual processes: from
dreams, illusions, automatisms, technological fancies to realist, materialist or indexical interpretations. It is no surprise, in this light, that
the emerging cinema was received and welcomed so rapidly by heterogeneous audiences around the world, since it seemed to have succeeded in accommodating a great variety of spiritual engagements
beyond the cultural, social or ideological frameworks. One of the
main attractions of the emerging cinema can be seen in its accessible

transparency of internal perceptual and imaginative processes of the human mind as integral to the experience. The spectator in this way turns into a 'participant observer' of her/his own perceptual processes — an 'observing participant' in an immersive experience of time as quality and duration.

It can further be suggested that what media-technologies have created are not only 'databases' of images and sounds, or what Peters (1999: 144) calls "archives of consciousness", but also *images* of shared consciousness, spiritualised into the processes of individual perceptions, recognitions and recollections. Cinema and other technologically enhanced environments more generally, can in this view be seen as philosophical *dispositif,* which within the user's perception and engagement ideally facilitate a liberation of spirit *(esprit)* by accommodating the actualisation of a creative intervention in intimate contact with a perceived 'real', embodied and immanent within the spectrum of the quotidian perceptual processes of the beholder. This perspective provides for an understanding of the cinema experience as an active and creative engagement with spirit *(l'esprit),* located within the framework of an intrinsic quotidian experience of duration. In this way the cinema serves as a paradigmatic platform, where these processes become exemplified and amplified, and not surprisingly, in the popular context, have constantly been interpreted as a subversion of the rationalist paradigm. While the screen time stops after about 90 minutes, and the film images have, instantaneously with perception, turned into memory-*images,* they continue to endure through the vital impulses in the spectator's mind.

Cinema today may be more elaborate in its technological apparatus, techniques and production processes; nonetheless, the emerging cinema of the 1890s already appears as particularly sophisticated in the way it explored and stimulated the vast spectrum of the spiritual dimensions intrinsic to the perceptual processes of the spectators. The *dispositif* alone with its multi-layered performances comprising images, inter-titles, live narration, music accompaniment, sound effects and, in the case of the Hale's tours, a full immersive environment, demanded from the spectators an active engagement and participation, as well as an informed critical response. The intrinsic connection with spiritualist practices and connotations, as they have also been accounted for in the literature, can be regarded no longer as a mere coincidence or naïve gesture of an 'irrational' survival from an archaic worldview or a hysterical response to contingencies of modernism, but rather as part of a sophisticated understanding of the virtual dimensions that the cinematic experience offered as novel 'extra' in its specific arrangement. The spiritual dimension, in this sense, can be regarded as the persistent force that accounts for the cinema's appealing and enduring popularity. The cinema as philosophical *dispositif* not merely activates imaginary thoughts, dreams and illusions, but provides an interface where spirit and matter can meet, intrinsically bound up with the personal histories, drives and imaginary impulses within the spectators' spiritual realms of the mind in anticipation of future actualisation.

In this light, the various restrictions on the spectators' interpretive frameworks must be weighed against the space of freedom in the spectators' conscious engagement that enables them to subvert the ideological framework by liberating, what Bergson called, the spiritual dimension. In this sense, the spectators are situated in a special condition, where the conscious engagement with their 'perceptual apparatus' evokes, provokes and facilitates an engagement with the dimension of 'spirit' — which for Bergson comprised the entirety of all existing conscious states, including the virtual realm of past memories with the potential to actualise in the present. Consequently the cinema in this way can be re-interpreted not merely as an epistemological interface of an establishment of meaning creation, but also as a vehicle that facilitates an amplification of 'spiritual' (mental) experiences, which in a Bergsonian sense need to be understood in a rather political sense as means for action.

Bibliography

Abel, Richard. 2005. *Encyclopedia of Early Cinema*. Abingdon/New York: Routledge.
—. 1996. *Silent Film*. London: Athlone.
—. 1994. *French Ciné Goes to Town: French Cinema, 1896-1914*. Berkeley and Los Angeles: University of California Press.
—. (ed.). 1988. *French Film Theory and Criticism: a History / Anthology, 1907-1939 / Vol. II, 1929-1939*. Princeton, New Jersey: Princeton University Press.

Abel, Richard and Altman, Rick, (eds). 2001. *The Sounds of Early Cinema*. Indiana University Press.
—. 1999. 'Global Experiments in Early Synchronous Sound' in *Film History* 11 (4): 395-498.

Agamben, Giorgio. 2004. 'Warburg', in Giornale di Letterature e Mondo, Giuseppe Genna (ed.), online at: http://www.miserabili.com/2004/07/21/agamben_su_aut_aut_warburg.html (consulted 07.04.2009)
—. 1999. *Potentialities*. Stanford, California: Stanford University Press.

Albright, Ann Cooper. 2007. *Traces of Light. Absence and Presence in the Work of Loïe Fuller*. Middletown, Connecticut: Wesleyan University Press.

Allen, Robert C. and Gomery, Douglas. 1985. *Film History: Theory and Practice*. New York: McGraw-Hill.

Anderson, Joseph and Barbara. 1993. 'The Myth of Persistence of Vision Revisited' in *Journal of Film and Video* 45(1): 3-12.

—. 1980. 'Motion Perception in Motion Pictures' in De Lauretis, Teresa and Heath, Stephen (eds) *The Cinematic Apparatus.* Hampshire, London: The MacMillan Press: 76-95.

Anderson, Joseph and Fisher, Barbara. 1978. 'The Myth of Persistence of Vision' in *Journal of the University Film Association* 30(4): 3-8.

Antliff, Mark. 1993. *Inventing Bergson: Cultural Politics and the Parisian Avant-Garde.* Princeton, New Jersey; Chichester: Princeton University Press.

Aumont, Jacques. 1997. *The Image.* London: British Film Institute. [French original: 1991. *L'Image.* Paris: Nathan.]

Bachofen, Johann Jakob. 1992. *Myth, Religion, and Mother Right: Selected Writings of Johann Jakob Bachofen* (tr. R. Manheim). Princeton: Princeton University Press.
—. 1861. *Das Mutterrecht. Eine Untersuchung über die Gynaikokratie der alten Welt nach ihrer religiösen und rechtlichen Natur.* Stuttgart: Krais & Hoffmann. [English tr. *Mother Right: An Investigation of the Religious and Juridical Character of Matriarchy in the Ancient World.* Basel: s.n.]

Balázs, Béla. 1952. *Theory of the Film: Character and Growth of a New Art* (tr. E. Bone). New York: Dover Publications.

Banks, Marcus and Morphy, Howard. 1999. *Rethinking Visual Anthropology.* Yale University Press.

Barjavel, René. 1944. *Cinéma Total: Essai sur les Formes Futures du Cinéma.* Paris: Les Editions Denoël.

Barnes, John. 1996. *The Beginnings of the Cinema in England: 1894-1901.* Exeter: University Exeter Press.

Barnouw, Erik. 1981. *The Magician and the Cinema.* New York, Oxford: Oxford University Press.

—. 1974. *Documentary: A History of Non-fiction Film.* New York: Oxford University Press.

Baudry, Jean-Louis. 1986a. 'Ideological Effects of the Basic Cinematographic Apparatus' in Rosen, Philip (ed.) *Narrative, Apparatus, Ideology: A Film Theory Reader.* New York: Columbia University Press: 286-298. [French original: 1970. 'Cinéma: Effets Idéologiques Produits par l'Appareil de Base' in *Cinétique* (7/8): 1-8]
—. 1986b. 'The Apparatus: Metapsychological Approaches to the Impression of Reality in the Cinema' in Rosen, Philip (ed.) *Narrative, Apparatus, Ideology: A Film Theory Reader.* New York: Columbia University Press: 299-318.
—. 1975. 'Le Dispositif: Approches Métapsychologiques de l'Impression de Réalité' in *Communications* 23: 56-72. Reprinted in Baudry, Jean-Louis. 1978. *L'Effet Cinéma.* Paris: Albatros. [Translation: 1976. 'The Apparatus' in *Camera Obscura* I: 104-26.]

Bazin, André. 1967. *What is Cinema? Vol. 1.* Berkeley: University of California Press.
—. 1972. *What is Cinema? Vol. 2.* Berkeley: University of California Press.

Bedouelle, Guy. 1985. *Du Spirituel dans le Cinéma.* Paris: Les Editions du Cerg.

Benz, Ernst. 1989. *The Theology of Electricity: On the Encounter and Explanation of Theology and Science in the Seventeenth and Eighteenth Centuries.* Pennsylvania: Pickwick Publications.

Bergson, Henri. 2005. *Essai Sur les Données Immédiates de la Conscience.* Paris: Presses Universitaires de France.
—. [1913] 2001. *Time and Free Will: An Essay on the Immediate Data of Consciousness* (tr. F.L. Pogson). Mineola, New York: Dover Publications. [French original: 1889. *Essai Sur les Données Immédiates de la Conscience.* Paris: Les Presses Universitaires de France].

—. [1968] 1999a. *Duration and Simultaneity: Bergson and the Einsteinian Universe* (ed. R. Durie). Manchester: Clinamen Press. [French original: 1922. *Durée et Simultanéité: À Propos de la Théorie d'Einstein.* Paris: Alcan.]

—. [1912] 1999b. *An Introduction to Metaphysics* (tr. T.E. Hulme). Indianapolis, Cambridge: Hackett Publishing. [French original: 'Introduction à la Métaphysique' in *Revue de Métaphysique et de Morale,* January 1903]

—. [1911] 1998. *Creative Evolution* (tr. A. Mitchell). Mineola, New York: Dover Publications. [French original: 1907. *L'Évolution Créatrice.* Paris: Alcan].

—. [1946] 1992. *The Creative Mind: An Introduction to Metaphysics* (tr. M. L. Andison). New York: The Citadel Press. [French original: 1934. *La Pensée et le Mouvant: Essais et Conférences.* Paris: Alcan].

—. [1911] 1991. *Matter and Memory* (tr. N.M. Paul and W.S. Palmer). New York: Zone Books. [French original: 1896. *Matière et Mémoire: Essai sur la Relation du Corps à l'Esprit.* Paris: Alcan].

—. 1935. *The Two Sources of Morality and Religion* (tr. R. A. Audra and C. Brereton). New York: Doubleday & Company. [French original: 1932. *Les Deux Sources de la Morale et de la Religion.* Paris: Alcan.]

—. 1920. *Mind Energy* (tr. H. Wildon Carr). London: McMillan and Company. [French original: 1919. *L'Energie Spirituelle: Essais et Conférences.* Paris: Presses Universitaires de France].

Berkeley, George. 1975. *Philosophical Works: Including the Works on Vision* (ed. M. R. Ayers). London: J. M. Dent.

Bessy, Maurice and Duca, Lo. 1961. *Georges Méliès, Mage.* Paris: Jean-Jacques Pauvert.

Bijker, Wiebe. 1987. *The Social Construction of Technology.* Cambridge, Massachusetts: The MIT Press.

Blassnigg, Martha. 2006a. 'Clairvoyance, Cinema and Consciousness' in Pepperell, Robert and Punt, Michael (eds) *Screen Conscious-*

ness: Cinema, Mind and World. Amsterdam, New York: Rodopi: 105-122.

—. 2006b. 'Clairvoyance, Cinema and Consciousness' in Meyer-Dinkgräfe, Daniel (ed.) *Consciousness, Theatre, Literature and the Arts.* Newcastle: Cambridge Scholars Press: 387-399.

—. 2000. *Seeing Angels and the Spiritual in Film: An Interdisciplinary Study of a Sensuous Experience.* MA-Thesis. University of Amsterdam.

Bloom, Peter J. 2008. *French Colonial Documentary: Mythologies of Humanitarianism.* University of Minnesota Press: Minneapolis, London.

Boas, George. 1959. 'Bergson and his Predecessors' in *Journal of the History of Ideas* 20(4): 503-514.

Bogue, Ronald. 2003. *Deleuze on Cinema.* New York and London: Routledge.

Böhme, Hartmut. 1997. 'Aby M. Warburg (1866-1929)' in Michaels, Axel (ed.) *Klassiker der Religionswissenschaft: Von Friedrich Schleiermacher bis Mircea Eliade.* München: C.H. Beck: 133-157.

Bordwell, David. 1985. *Narration in the Fiction Film.* Madison: University of Wisconsin Press.

Bordwell, David and Carroll, Noël. 1996. *Post Theory: Reconstructing Film Studies.* Madison: Wisconsin Press.

Bordwell, David and Thompson, Kristien. 1986. *Film Art.* New York: Knopf.

Bragaglia, Anton Giulio. 1970. *Fotodinamismo Futurista.* Turin: Enaudi. [English Tr: 1972. 'Futurist Photodynamism' in Apollonio, Umberto (ed.) *Futurist Manifesto.* New York: The Viking Press.]

Braude, Ann. 1983. *Radical Spirits: Spiritualism and Women's Rights in Nineteenth Century America.* Boston: Beacon.

Braun, Marta. 2006. 'Marey, Muybridge, le Sport et la Race' in Font-Réaulx, Dominique de, Lefebvre, Thierry and Mannoni, Laurent (eds) *E.J. Marey: Actes du Colloque du Centenaire.* Paris: Arcadia: 69-78.

—. 1997. 'The Expanded Present: The Photography of Movement' in Thomas, Ann (ed.) *Beauty of Another Order: Photography in Science.* Ottawa, New Haven: Yale University Press: 150-184.

—. 1996. 'Fantasmes des Vivants et des Morts: Anton Giulio Bragaglia et la Figuration de l'Invisible' in *Études Photographiques* (1): 40-45.

—. 1992. *Picturing Time: The Work of Étienne-Jules Marey (1830-1904).* Chicago University Press.

—. 1984. 'Muybridge's Scientific Fictions' in *Studies in Visual Communication* 10(1): 2-22.

—. 1983. 'The Photographic Work of E.J.Marey' in *Studies in Visual Communication* 9(4): 2-24.

Brenez, Nicole. 2006. 'Étienne-Jules Marey: Modèles et Investissements Problématiques dans le Cinéma Expérimental Récent' in Font-Réaulx, Dominique de, Lefebvre, Thierry and Mannoni, Laurent (eds) *E.J. Marey: Actes du Colloque du Centenaire.* Paris: Arcadia: 121-138.

Breton, André. 1972. *Manifestoes of Surrealism.* Ann Arbor: University of Michigan Press.

Brownlow, Kevin. 1990. 'Silent Films – What Was the Right Speed?' in Elsaesser, Thomas and Barker, Adam (eds) *Early Cinema: Space, Frame, Narrative.* London: British Film Institute: 282-290.

Bruhn, Mathias. s.d. 'Aby Warburg (1866-1929): The Survival of an Idea'. Online at: http://www.educ.fc.ul.pt/hyper/resources/mbruhn/ (consulted 14.03.2009)

Buchanan, Ian. 1997. 'Deleuze and Cultural Studies' in *The South Atlantic Quarterly* 96(3): 515-523.

—. 2000. *Deleuzism: A Metacommentary.* Durham: Duke University Press.

Burch, Noël. 1990. *Life to Those Shadows* (tr. and ed. B. Brewster). London: British Film Institute.

—. 1986. 'Primitivism and the Avant-Gardes: Dialectical Approach' in Rosen, Philip, (ed.) *Narrative, Apparatus, Ideology. A Film Theory Reader.* New York: Columbia University Press: 483-506.

—. 1979. *To the Distant Observer: Form and Meaning in the Japanese Cinema.* Berkeley and Los Angeles: University of California Press.

—. 1973. *Theory of Film Practice.* London: Secker and Warburg.

Burnett, Ron. 2004. *How Images Think.* Cambridge, Massachusetts: The MIT Press.

Canales, Jimena. 2005. 'Einstein, Bergson, and the Experiment that Failed: Intellectual Cooperation at the League of Nations' in *MLN* 120(5): 1168-1191.

Canguilhem, Denis. 2006. 'La Rétine du Savant. La Photographie Scientifique à l'Epreuve du Regard' in Font-Réaulx, Dominique de, Lefebvre, Thierry and Mannoni, Laurent (eds) *E.J. Marey: Actes du Colloque du Centenaire.* Paris: Arcadia: 145-158.

Capek, Miliç. 1971. *Bergson and Modern Physics: A Reinterpretation and Re-evaluation.* Dordrecht: Nijhoff.

Carrel, Alexis. 1931. 'Physiological Time' in *Science* 74 (1929): 618-621.

Carroll, Noël. 1996. *Theorizing The Moving Image.* Cambridge: Cambridge University Press.

Cariou, Marie. 1976. *Bergson et le Fait Mystique.* Paris: Aubier Montaigne.

Chalmers, David. 1996. *The Conscious Mind.* New York: Oxford University Press.

—. 1995. 'Facing up to the Problem of Consciousness' in *Journal of Consciousness Studies* (2): 200-219.

Chanan, Michael. 1990. 'Economic Conditions of Early Cinema' in Elsaesser, Thomas and Barker, Adam (eds) *Early Cinema: Space, Frame, Narrative*. London: British Film Institute: 174-188.
—. 1980. *The Dream that Kicks: The Prehistory and Early Years of Cinema in Britain*. London: Routledge & Kegan Paul.

Charney, Leo and Schwartz, Vanessa R. (eds). 1995. *Cinema and the Invention of Modern Life*. Berkeley: University of California Press.

Cherchi Usai, Paolo. 2001. *Death of Cinema, The History, Cultural Memory and the Digital Dark Age*. London: British Film Institute.
—. 2000. *Silent Cinema: An Introduction* (revised and expanded edition). London: British Film Institute.
—. 1994. *Burning Passions: An Introduction to the Study of Silent Cinema*. London: British Film Institute.
—. (ed.) 1991. *A Trip to the Movies: Georges Méliès Filmmaker and Magician (1861-1938)*. Torino: UTET.

Chéroux, Clément, et al. 2005. *The Perfect Medium: Photography and the Occult*. (Exhibition Catalogue of the Metropolitan Museum of Art in New York) New Haven: Yale University Press.

Claeys, Gregory (ed.). 2005. *Encyclopedia of Nineteenth-Century Thought*. London, New York: Routledge.

Classen, Constance (ed.). 2005. *The Book of Touch*. Oxford: Berg Publishers.
—. 1993. *Worlds of Sense. Exploring the Senses in History and Across Cultures*. London and New York: Routledge.

Clifford, James and Marcus, George E. (eds). 1986. *Writing Culture: The Poetics and Politics of Ethnography*. Berkeley and Los Angeles: University of California Press.

Coates, Paul. [1911] 1973. *Photographing the Invisible*. New York: Arno.

Cœuré, Sophie and Worms, Frédéric. 2003. *Albert Kahn, Henri Bergson, Correspondances*. Paris: Desmaret Edition.

Collier, John. 1986. *Visual Anthropology: Photography as a Research Method.* Albuquerque: University of New Mexico Press.

Comolli, Jean-Louis. 1986. 'Technique and Ideology: Camera, Perspective, Depth of Field (Parts 3 and 4)' in Rosen, Philip (ed.) *Narrative, Apparatus, Ideology: A Film Theory Reader.* New York: Columbia University Press: 421-443.
—. 1980. 'Machines of the Visible' in Lauretis, Teresa de, and Heath, Steven (eds) *The Cinematic Apparatus.* London: Macmillan: 121-142.
—. 1971. 'Technique et Idéologie (I)' in *Cahiers du Cinema* (229) June.

Cook, Pam. 1987. *The Cinema Book.* London: British Film Institute.

Crary, Jonathan. 1988. 'Modernising Vision' in Hall, Foster (ed.) *Vision and Visuality.* Seattle: Bay Press: 29-49.
—. 1990. *Techniques of the Observer: On Vision and Modernity in the Nineteenth Century.* Cambridge, Massachusetts: The MIT Press.

Crawford, Peter I. and Hafsteinsson, Sigurjon Baldur (eds). 1996. *The Construction of the Viewer: Media Ethnography and the Anthropology of Audiences — Proceedings from NAFA 3.* Hojberg: Intervention Press.

Crookes, William. 1897. 'Address by the President' in *Proceedings of the Society for Psychical Research* 12: 338-355.
—. 1874. *Researches in the Phenomena of Spiritualism.* London: J. Burns.
—. 1874. 'Notes of an Enquiry into the Phenomena Called Spiritual During the Years 1870-1873' in *Quarterly Journal of Science,* January.
—. 1871. *Psychic Force and Modern Spiritualism: A Reply to the 'Quarterly Review' and other Critics.* London: Longmans, Green, and Co.

Curl, James Stevens. 1972. *The Victorian Celebration of Death.* London: David and Charles.

Dagognet, François. 1992. *Étienne-Jules Marey: A Passion for the Trace* (tr. R. Galeta, J. Herman). New York: Zone Books.

Debru, Claude. 2004. 'Étienne-Jules Marey: Medical Innovation' in *Bulletin de l'Académie Nationale de Médecine* 188(8): 1413-1421.

DeLanda, Manuel. 1997. 'Immanence and Transcendence in the Genesis of Form' in *The South Atlantic Quarterly* 96(3): 499-514.

Deleuze, Gilles. 2007. *Two Regimes of Madness: Texts and Interviews 1975-1995* (ed. D. Lapoujade, tr. A. Hodges and M. Taormina). New York, Los Angeles: Semiotext(e).
—. 2005. *Cinema 1: The Movement-Image*. London, New York: Continuum.
—. 1997. 'Immanence: A Life...' (tr. N. Millett) in *Theory, Culture and Society: Explorations in Critical Social Science* (London: SAGE Publications) 14(2): 3-7.
—. 1995. *Negotiations. 1972-1990.* New York: Columbia University Press.
—. 1993. *The Fold: Leibniz and the Baroque*. London: Athlone Press.
—. 1991. *Bergsonism* (tr. H. Tomlinson and B. Habberjam). New York: Zone Books. [French original: 1966. *Le Bergsonisme*. Paris: Presses Universitaires de France].
—. 1989. *Cinema 2: The Time-Image*. London: The Athlone Press. [French Original: 1985. *Cinéma 2: L'Image-Temps*. Paris: Les Editions de Minuit].
—. [1983] 1986. *Cinema 1. The Movement-Image*. London: The Athlone Press. [*Cinéma 1: L'Image-Mouvement*. Paris: Les Editions de Minuit].

Deleuze, Gilles and Félix Guattari. 1988. *A Thousand Plateaus: Capitalism and Schizophrenia* (tr. B. Massumi). London: Athlone.

Deutelbaum, Marshall A. 1983. 'Structural Patterning in the Lumière Films' in Fell, John L. (ed.) *Film Before Griffith*. Berkeley: University of California Press: 299-310.
—. (ed.). 1979. *'Image': On the Art and Evolution of the Film*. New York: Dover.

Didi-Huberman, Georges. 2005. *Confronting Images: Questioning the Ends of a Certain History of Art.* University Park: Pennsylvania State University Press. [French original: 1990. *Devant l'Image: Question Posée aux Fins d'une Histoire de l'Art.* Paris: Les Editions de Minuit.]

—. 2002. *L'image survivante: Histoire de l'Art et Temps des Fantômes selon Aby Warburg.* Paris: Les Editions de Minuit.

—. 1982. *Invention de l'Hystérie, Charcot et l'Iconographie Photographique de la Salpêtrière.* Paris: Macula.

Didi-Huberman, Georges and Mannoni, Laurent. 2004. *Mouvements de l'Air: Étienne-Jules Marey, Photographe des Fluides.* (Réunion des Musées Nationaux) Paris: Gallimard.

Dillon, Brian. 2004. 'Collected Works: Aby Warburg's *Mnemosyne Atlas'* in *Frieze Magazine* (80): 46-47.

Dilthey, Wilhelm. 1883. *Introduction to the Human Sciences.* Princeton, NJ: Princeton University Press. Online at: http://www.marxists.org/reference/subject/philosophy/works/ge/dilthey1.htm (consulted 24.02.2009).

Doane, Mary Ann. 2006. 'Real Time: Instantaneity and the Photographic Imaginary' in *Stillness and Time: Photography and the Moving Image.* Green, David and Lowry, Joanna (eds). Manchester: Photoforum and Photoworks.

—. 2002. *The Emergence of Cinematic Time: Modernity, Contingency, the Archive.* Cambridge, Massachusetts; London: Harvard University Press.

Doyle, Arthur Conan. 1926. *The History of Spiritualism* (Vol. 1 and 2). New York: G.H. Doran, Co.

During, Simon. 2002. *Modern Enchantments: The Cultural Power of Secular Magic.* Cambridge, Massachusetts: Harvard University Press.

Durkheim, Émile. [1912] 1965. *The Elementary Forms of the Religious Life* (tr. J. Swain). New York: The Free Press.

Edwards, Elizabeth (ed.) 1992. *Anthropology and Photography 1860-1920*. New Haven: Yale University Press.

Eisenstein, Sergei. 1988. *Selected Works,* Vol.1 (tr. R. Taylor). London: British Film Institute.
—. 1949. *Film Form.* New York: Harcourt, Brace and World.

Eliade, Mircea. 1957. *The Sacred and the Profane: The Nature of Religion.* San Diego, New York, London: A Harvest Book, Harcourt Brace & Company.

Elsaesser, Thomas. 1998. 'Louis Lumière: The Cinema's First Virtualist' in Elsaesser, Thomas and Hoffman, Kay (eds) *Cinema Future: Cain, Abel or Cable?* Amsterdam: Amsterdam University Press.

Elsaesser, Thomas and Barker, Adam (eds). 1990. *Early Cinema: Space, Frame, Narrative.* London: British Film Institute.

Elsen, Albert Edward. 1980. *In Rodin's Studio: A Photographic Record of Sculpture in the Making.* Oxford: Phaidon Press.

Epstein, Jean. 1981. 'On Certain Characteristics of Photogenie' in *Bonjour Cinema* and Other Writings (tr. T. Milne). *Afterimage* (10): 20-23.

Fabian, Johannes. 2007. *Memory Against Culture: Arguments and Reminders.* Durham and London: Duke University Press.
—. 1991. *Time and the Work of Anthropology: Critical Essays, 1971-1991* (Studies in Anthropology and History). London: Routledge, an imprint of Taylor & Francis Books.
—. 1983. *Time and the Other: How Anthropology Makes Its Object.* New York: Columbia University Press.

Fagg, Lawrence, W. 1999. *Electro-Magnetism and the Sacred: At the Frontier of Spirit and Matter.* New York: Continuum.

Faraday, Michael. 1853. 'Experimental Investigation of Table-Moving' in *Athenaeum* (1340), July.

Feilding, Everard.1963. *Sittings with Eusapia Palladino*. New York.

Fell, John L. (ed.). 1983. *Film Before Griffith*. Berkeley and Los Angeles: University of California Press.

Ferguson, Eugene S. 1992. *Engineering and the Mind's Eye*. Cambridge, Massachusetts: The MIT Press.

Fielding, Raymond (ed.). 1967. *A Technological History of Motion Pictures and Television*. Berkeley and Los Angeles: University of California Press.

Fischer, Andreas and Loers, Veit. 1997. *Im Reich Der Phantome: Fotografie Des Unsichtbaren: Fotografie Des Unsichtbaren*. Exhibition Catalogue of the Städtischen Museum Abteiberg Mönchengladbach, Kunsthalle Krems and Fotomuseum Winterthur, Hatje Cantz Verlag.

Flammarion, Camille Nicholas. [1907] 2003. *Mysterious Psychic Forces*. [Boston, Paris] Whitefish, Montana: Kessinger.
—. 1900. *The Unkown*. (reprint of original edition: London, New York: Harpter & Brothers) Whitefish, Montana: Kessinger.
—. 1897. *Lumen*. New York: Dodd, Mead, and Company.
—. 1923. 'Manifestations of the Dead in Spiritistic Experiments' in *Death and Its Mystery:* Vol. 3, *After Death: Manifestations and Apparitions of the Dead: The Soul After Death*. (tr. C. Latrobe). London: T. Fisher Unwin.

Flaxman, Gregory. 2000. *The Brain is the Screen. Deleuze and the Philosophy of Cinema*. Minneapolis: University of Minnesota Press.

Font-Réaulx, Dominique de. 2006. 'Vagues Fixes et en Mouvement, Autour du Film *La Vague* d'Étienne-Jules Marey' in Font-Réaulx, Dominique de, Lefebvre, Thierry and Mannoni, Laurent (eds) *E.J. Marey: Actes du Colloque du Centenaire*. Paris: Arcadia: 49-60.

Foster, Hal (ed.). 1988. *Vision and Visuality.* (Dia Art Foundation: Discussion in Contemporary Culture, Number 2). Seattle: Bay Press.

Frazer, James George. [1890] 1981. *The Golden Bough: The Roots of Religion and Folkore.* (Originally published in in two volumes as *The Golden Bough: A Study in Comparative Religion).* New York, Avenel: Gramercy Books.

Frazer, John. 1979. *Artificially Arranged Scenes: The Films of Georges Méliès.* Boston: G.K.Hall.

Freud, Sigmund. [1913] 1946. *Totem and Taboo.* New York: Random House.
—. 1891. *Zur Auffassung der Aphasien.* Leipzig: Deuticke.

Fuery, Patrick. 2000. *New Developments in Film Theory.* New York: Martin's Press.

Gallagher, Catherine and Greenblatt, Stephen. 2000. *Practicing New Historicism.* Chicago: Chicago University Press.

Gaudreault, André. 1990. 'Film, Narrative, Narration: The Cinema of the Lumière Brothers' in Elsaesser, Thomas (ed.) *Early Cinema. Space Frame Narrative.* London: British Film Institute: 68-75.

Gauld, Alan. 1968. *The Founders of Psychical Research.* London: Routledge & Kegan Paul.

Geertz, Clifford. 1983. *Local Knowledge. Further Essays in Interpretive Anthropology.* New York: Basic Books.
—. 1974. *Myth, Symbol, and Culture.* New York: W.W.Norton.
—. 1973. *The Interpretation of Cultures.* New York: Basic Books.

Geley, Gustave. 1927. *Clairvoyance and Materialisation: A Record of Experiments.* London: T. Fisher Unwin.

Gettings, Fred. 1978. *Ghosts in Photographs: The Extraordinary Story of Spirit Photography.* New York: Harmony.

Gianetti, Louis. 1976. *Understanding Movies.* Englewood Cliffs, New Jersey: Prentice-Hall.

Gibbons, John. 2005. 'Qualia: They're not what they seem' in *Philosophical Studies* 126(3): 397-428.

Gitelman, Lisa. 2006. *Always Already New: Media, History, and the Data of Culture.* Cambridge, Massachusetts: The MIT Press.

Good, Byron J. 1994. *Medicine, Rationality, and Experience: An anthropological Perspective.* Cambridge, New York: Cambridge University Press.

Gombrich, Ernst Hans. 1970. *Aby Warburg: An Intellectual Biography.* London: Warburg Institute.
—. 1999. 'Aby Warburg: His Aims and Methods. An Anniversary Lecture' in *Journal of the Warburg and Courtauld Institute* 62: 268-82.
—. 1982. *The Image and the Eye. Further Studies in the Psychology of Pictorial Representation.* Oxford: Phaidon.

Gouhier, Henri. [1961] 1987. *Bergson et le Christ des Évangiles.* Paris: Vrin-Reprise. [Le Signe].

Green, David and Lowry, Joanna (eds). 2006. *Stillness and Time: Photography and the Moving Image.* Manchester: Photoforum and Photoworks.

Greenaway, Jonathan. 2004. 'Apparent Movement in Motion Pictures'. Online at: www.aber.ac.uk/media/sections/image05.php (consulted 14.03.2009)

Gregory, Richard L. (ed.). 1987. *The Oxford Companion to the Mind.* Oxford, New York: Oxford University Press.

Grieveson, Lee and Kramer, Peter. 2003. *The Silent Cinema Reader.* Routledge: Taylor & Francis.

Griffin, David Ray (ed.). 1986. *Physics and the Ultimate Significance of Time: Bohm, Prigogine, and Process Philosophy.* New York: State University of New York Press.

Griffiths, Phillips A. (ed.) 1987. *Contemporary French Philosophy* (Royal Institute of Philosophy Lecture Series: 21, Supplement to *Philosophy* 1987). Cambridge, New York: Cambridge University Press.

Grimshaw, Anna. 2001. *The Ethnographer's Eye: Ways of Seeing in Anthropology.* Cambridge: Cambridge University Press.

Grosz, Elizabeth. 2004. *The Nick of Time. Politics, Evolution, and the Untimely.* Durham, London: Duke University Press.

Gsell, Paul. 1986. *Auguste Rodin: Art. Conversations with Paul Gsell.* Berkeley, Los Angeles, London: University of California Press. [French original: 1911. *Auguste Rodin: L'Art. Entretiens Réunis par Paul Gsell.* Paris: Grasset.]

Guerlac, Suzanne. 2006. *Thinking in Time. An Introduction to Henri Bergson.* Ithaca, London: Cornell University Press.
—. 2004. 'The 'Zig-zags of a Doctrine': Bergson, Deleuze, and the Question of Experience' in *Pli: The Warwick Journal of Philosophy* 15: 34-53.

Gunning, Tom. 2007. 'To Scan a Ghost: the Ontology of Mediated Vision' in *Grey Room* 26: 94-127.
—. 2003. 'Haunting Images: Ghosts, Photography and the Modern Body' in *The Disembodied Spirit.* Brunswick, Maine: Bowdoin College Museum of Art.
—. 1995. 'Phantom Images and Modern Manifestations: Spirit Photography, Magic Theater, Trick Films and Photography's Uncanny' in Petro, Patrice (ed.) *Fugitive Images: From Photography to Video.* Bloomington: Indiana University Press: 42-71.

Hagen, Wolfgang. 1999. 'Der Okkultismus der Avantgarde um 1900' in Schade, Sigrid, et al. (eds) *Konfigurationen: Zwischen Kunst und Medien.* München: Fink: 338 - 357.

Hall, Trevor N. 1984. *The Medium and the Scientist: The Story of Florence Cook and William Crookes.* Buffalo: Prometheus.

Hammond, Paul. 1974. *Marvellous Méliès.* London: Gordon Fraser.

Hansen, Miriam. 1991. *Babel and Babylon. Spectatorship in American Silent Film.* Cambridge, London: Harvard University Press.

Harding, Colin and Popple, Simon. 1996. *In the Kingdom of the Shadows: A Companion to Early Cinema.* London: Cygnus Arts.

Hardt, Michael. 1993. *Gilles Deleuze: An Apprenticeship in Philosophy.* London: UCL Press.

Harrison, Jonathan. 1976. 'Religion and Psychical Research' in Thakur, Shivesh C. (ed.) *Philosophy and Psychical Research.* London: George Allen & Unwin: 97-121.

Heath, Stephen. 1980. 'The Cinematic Apparatus: Technology as Historical and Cultural Form' in De Lauretis, Teresa and Heath, Stephen (eds) *The Cinematic Apparatus.* Hampshire, London: The MacMillan Press: 1-13.

Henderson, Linda Dalrymple. 1983. *The Fourth Dimension and Non-Euclidean Geometry in Modern Art.* Princeton, New Jersey: Princeton University Press.

Herbert, Stephen. 2009. 'Eadweard Muybridge' (A Chronology). Online at: http://stephenherbert.co.uk/muybCOMPLEAT.htm (consulted 14.03.2009)

Herbert, Stephen and McKernan, Luke (eds). 1996. *Who's Who of Victorian Cinema: A Worldwide Survey.* London: British Film Institute. See also the related website: http://www.victorian-cinema.net (consulted 14.03.2009)

Hinton, Charles Howard. 1912. *The Fourth Dimension.* London: G. Allen.

Hockings, Paul. 1974. *Principals of Visual Anthropology*. The Hague: Mouton.

Holmberg, Jan. 2003. 'Ideals of Immersion in Early Cinema' in *CiNéMAS* 14(1): 129–147.

Hopkins, Albert A. 1898. *Magic: Stage Illusions and Scientific Diversions*. London: Sampson, Low, Marston and Company.

Howes, D. (ed.). 2004. *Empire of the Senses: The Sensual Culture Reader*. Oxford and New York: Berg Publishers.
—. 2003. *Sensual Relations: Engaging the Senses in Culture and Social Theory*. Ann Arbor, MI: University of Michigan Press.
—. (ed.). 1991. *The Varieties of Sensory Experience: A Sourcebook in the Anthropology of the Senses*. Toronto: University of Toronto Press.

Inglis, Brian. [1977] 1992. *Natural and Supernatural. A History of the Paranormal from Earliest Times to 1914*. Dorset: Prism.
—. 1985. *The Paranormal: An Encyclopedia of Psychic Phenomena*. London: Paladin Grafton Books.

James, William. [1920] 1994. *Collected Essays and Reviews*. Bristol: Thoemmes Press.
—. [1886] 1986. 'Essays of Psychical Research' in Burkhardt, F. (ed.) *The Works of William James*. Cambridge, Massachusetts: Havard University Press.
—. [1902] 1982. *The Varieties of Religious Experience*. New York, London: Penguin Books.
—. [1909] 1977. 'Final Impressions of a Psychical Researcher' in McDermott, John J. (ed.) *The Writings of William James: A Comprehensive Edition*. Chicago: University of Chicago Press: 787-799.
—. [1902] 1904. *The Varieties of Religious Experience*. London: Longman, Geen, and Co.
—. [1890] 1950. *Principles of Psychology*, Vol. I-II. New York: Dover Publications.

Janet, Pierre. 1903. *Les Obsessions et la Psychasthénie*. Paris: Alcan.

—. [1898] 1989. *L'Automatisme psychologique: Essai de Psychologie Expérimentale sur les Formes Inférieures de l'Activité Humaine.* Paris: Masson.

—. 1894. *Les Accidents Mentaux.* Paris: Rueff.

Jenkins, Rees V. 1975. *Images and Enterprise: Technology and the American Photographic Industry, 1839-1925.* London: John Hopkins University Press.

Jenn, Pierre. 1984. *Georges Méliès: Cinéaste.* Paris: Albatross.

Jordan, Pierre-L. 1992. *Cinéma: Premier Contact – Premier Regard, Cinema: First Contact – First Look, Kino: Erster Kontakt – Erster Blick.* (Musée de Marseille) Marseille: Images en Manœuvres Editions.

Judah, J. Stilson. 1967. *The History and Philosophy of the Metaphysical Movements in America.* Philadelphia: Westminster.

Kallen, Horace M. 1914. *Mind* (New Series) 23(90): 207-239.

Kant, Immanuel. 1960. *Observations on the Feeling of the Beautiful and Sublime* (tr. J.T.Goldthwait). Berkeley: University of California Press. (First published in 1764).

Kardec, Allan. [1857] 1989. *The Spirit's Book.* Las Vegas: Brotherhood of Life.

Keck, Frederic. 2005. 'The Virtual, the Symbolic, and the Actual in Bergsonian Philosophy and Durkheim' in *Modern Language Notes* 120(5): 1133-1145.

Kellert, Stephen H., Longino, Helen E. and Waters, Kenneth C. (eds). 2006. *Scientific Pluralism.* Minneapolis, London: University of Minneapolis Press.

Kern, Stephen. 1983. *The Culture of Time and Space: 1880-1918.* Cambridge, Massachusetts: Harvard University Press.

Kessler, Frank. 2004. 'Notes on *dispositif*'. Online at:
www.let.uu.nl/~Frank.Kessler/personal/notes%20on%20dispositif.PDF
(consulted 14.03.2009)

Khandker, Wahida (ed.). 2004. 'Lives of the Real: Bergsonian Perspectives'. *Pli, The Warwick Journal of Philosophy,* 15.

Kracauer, Siegfried. 1997. *Theory of Film. The Redemption of Physical Reality.* Chichester: Princeton University Press.

Krauss, Rosalind E. 1993. *The Optical Unconscious.* Cambridge,
Massachusetts: The MIT Press.
—. 1978. 'Tracing Nadar' in *October* 5: 29-47.

Landecker, Hannah. 2006. 'Microcinematography and the History of
Science and Film' in *Isis* 97:121-132.
—. 2005. 'Cellular Features: Microcinematography and Early Film
Theory' in *Critical Inquiry* 31: 903-937.

Lant, Antonia. 1995. 'Haptical Cinema' in *October* 74: 45-73.
—. 1992. 'The Curse of the Pharaoh, or How Cinema Contracted
Egyptomania' in *October* 59: 86-112.

Larsen, Egon. 1947. *Inventor's Scrapbook.* London, Aylesbury: Ha-
zell, Watson & Viney.

Larson, Barbara. 2005. *The Dark Side of Nature: Science, Society, and
the Fantastic in the Work of Odilon Redon.* Pennsylvania: Pennsylvania State University Press.

De Lauretis, Teresa, and Stephen Heath (eds). 1980. *The Cinematic
Apparatus.* Hampshire, London: The MacMillan Press.

Lawlor, Leonard and Moulard, Valentine. 2004. Stanford Encyclopedia of Philosophy. 'On Henri Bergson'. Online at:
http://plato.stanford.edu/entries/bergson/#1 (consulted 14.03.2009)

Leadbeater, C.W. 1920. *Man Visible and Invisible. Examples of Different Types of Men as Seen by Means of Trained Clairvoyance.* London: Theosophical Publishing House.

Lefebvre, Thierry. 2006. 'Film Scientifique et Grand Public. Une Rencontre Différée' in Font-Réaulx, Dominique de, Lefebvre, Thierry and Mannoni, Laurent (eds) *E.J. Marey: Actes du Colloque du Centenaire.* Paris: Arcadia: 159-168.
—. 2005. 'Marey and Chronophotography'. Online at: http://www.bium.univ-paris5.fr/histmed/medica/marey/marey03a.htm (consulted 14.03.2009)
—. 2004. *Le Chair et le Celluloïd: Le Cinéma Chirurgical du Docteur Doyen.* Paris, Brionne: Jean Doyen Editeur.
—. 1997. 'La Lorgnette Humaine: Cinéma et Rayons X à la Conquête de l'Intimité' in *Revue de l'Association Française de Recherche sur le Cinéma* 23: 21-36.

Levesque, Georges. 1973. *Bergson: Vie et Mort de l'Homme et de Dieu.* Paris: Les Èditions du Cerf.

Levie, François. 1990. *Étienne-Gaspard Robertson: La Vie d'un Fantasmagore.* Québec: Préamble.

Lewis, Clarence Irving. 1929. *Mind and the World Order.* New York: C. Scribner's Sons.

Lindsay, A.D. 1911. *The Philosophy of Bergson.* Strand, W.C.: J.M. Dent.

Loizos, Peter. 1993. *Innovation in Ethnographic Film: From Innocence to Selfconsciousness 1955-1985.* Manchester, Chicago: University of Chicago Press.

Lorand, Ruth. 1999. 'Bergson's Concept of Art' in *British Journal of Aesthetics* 5(4): 400-415.

Luckhurst, Roger. 2002. *The Invention of Telepathy, 1870-1901.* Oxford: Oxford University Press.

Lumière, Louis. [1936] 1967. 'The Lumière Cinematograph' in Fielding, Raymond (ed.) *A Technological History of Motion Pictures and Television.* Berkeley and Los Angeles: University of California. [Original printed in *Journal of the SMPE* 27: Dec. 1936]

Lund, E., Pihl, M. and Slok, J. (eds). 1998. *A History of European Ideas.* London: C. Hurst and Company.

MacDougall, David. 2005. *The Corporeal Image: Film, Ethnography, and the Senses.* Princeton, New Jersey: Princeton University Press.
—. 1998. *Transcultural Cinema.* Princeton, New Jersey: Princeton University Press.
—. 1975. 'Beyond Observational Cinema' in Hockings, Paul (ed.) *Principles of Visual Anthropology.* The Hague: Mouton: 109-124.

Maltête-Méliès, Madeleine. 1973. *Méliès l'Enchanteur.* Paris: Hachette.

Mannoni, Laurent. 2006. 'Marey Cineaste' in Font-Réaulx, Dominique de, Lefebvre, Thierry and Mannoni, Laurent (eds) *E.J. Marey: Actes du Colloque du Centenaire.* Paris: Arcadia: 15-36.
—. 2000. *The Great Art of Light and Shadow: Archeology of the Cinema.* Exeter: University of Exeter Press.

Mannoni, Laurent, Nekes, Werner and Warner, Marina (eds). 2004. *Eyes, Lies and Illusions: The Art of Deception.* London: Hayward Gallery Publishing.

Marcus, George E. and Fischer, Michael M. J. 1986. *Anthropology as Cultural Critique: An Experimental Moment in the Human Sciences.* Chicago, London: University of Chicago Press.

Marey, Étienne-Jules. 1901. 'Les Mouvements de l'Air Etudiés par la Chronophotographie' in *La Nature* (7 September): 233-234.
—. 1899. *La Chronophotographie: Nouvelle Méthode Pour Analyser le Mouvement dans les Sciences Physiques et Naturelles.* Paris: Gauthier-Villars.
—. 1895. *Movement: The Results and Possibilities of Photography* (tr. E. Pritchard). London: William Heinemann.

—. 1894. *Le Mouvement*. Paris: Masson.

—. 1888. 'Représentation des Attitudes de la Locomotion Humaine au Moyen des Figures en Relief' in *CRAS* 106: 1635-36.

—. 1886. 'Des Lois de la Méchanique en Biologie' in *Revue Scientifique* 1: 1-9.

—. 1874. *Animal Mechanism: A Treatise on Terrestrial and Aerial Locomotion*. London: H.S.King. New York: Appleton.

—. 1873. *La Machine Animale: Locomotion Terrestre et Aérienne*. Paris: Baillière.

Marey, Étienne-Jules and Demenÿ, Georges. 1893. *Etudes de Physiologie Artistique Faites au Moyen de la Chronophotographie*. Première Série, vol. I. De mouvement de l'homme. Paris: Berthaud.

Marks, Laura U. 2000. *The Skin of the Film: Intercultural Cinema, Embodiment, and the Senses*. Durham and London: Duke University Press.

Marvin, Carolyn. [1988] 1990. *When Old Technologies were New: Thinking About Electric Communication in the Late Nineteenth Century*. New York: Oxford University Press.

Marx, Leo and Smith, Merritt Roe (eds). 1994. *Does Technology Drive History? The Dilemma of Technological Determinism*. Cambridge, Massachusetts: The MIT Press.

Méliès, Georges. 1945. 'Mes Mémoires' in Bessy, Maurice and Duca, Lo (eds) *Georges Méliès, Mage*. Paris: Prisma (reprinted: Pauvert, 1961).

Ménil, Alain. 1995. 'Deleuze et le 'Bergsonisme du Cinéma'' in *Philosophie: Revue Trimestrielle* 9(47) (Les Editions de Minuit): 28-52.

Metz, Christian. 1986a. 'Problems of Denotation in the Fiction Film' in Rosen, Philip (ed.) *Narrative, Apparatus, Ideology*. New York: Columbia: 35-65.

—. 1986b. 'The Imaginary Signifier' (Extract) in Rosen, Philip (ed.) *Narrative, Apparatus, Ideology.* New York: Columbia: 244-280.
—. 1975. 'The Imaginary Signifier' (tr. B. Brewster) in *Screen* 16(2) Summer: 14-76.

Meyer, Birgit and Pels, Peter (eds). 2003. *Magic and Modernity: Interfaces of Revelation and Concealment.* Stanford, California: Stanford University Press.

Meyer-Dinkgräfe, Daniel (ed.). 2006. *Consciousness, Theatre, Literature and the Arts.* Newcastle: Cambridge Scholars Press.
—. 2005. *Theatre and Consciousness: Explanatory Scope and Future Potential.* Bristol: Intellect.

Michaud, Philippe-Alain. 2004. *Aby Warburg and the Image in Motion* (tr. S. Hawkes). Cambridge, Massachusetts: The MIT Press.
—. 2003. 'Passage des Frontières: Mnemosyne Entre Histoire de l'Art et Cinéma' in *Trafic* 45: 87-96.

Mitry, Jean. 1972. *The Aesthetics and Psychology of Cinema.* Bloomington and Indianapolis: Indiana University Press.
—. 1967. *Histoire du Cinéma: Art et Industrie I, 1895–1914.* Paris: Editions Universitaires.

Monaco, James. 1981. *How to Read a Film: The Art, Technology, Language, History, and Theory of Film and Media.* New York, Oxford: Oxford University Press.

Moody, Raymond A. Jr. 2001. *Life After Life: The Investigation of a Phenomenon — Survival of Bodily Death.* San Francisco: Harper.

Moore, F.C.T. 1996. *Bergson: Thinking Backwards.* Cambridge, New York: Cambridge University Press.

Moore, Rachel. 2000. *Savage Theory: Cinema as Modern Magic.* Durham and London: Duke University Press.

Morgan, Lewis Henry. 1877. *Ancient Society: Researches in the Lines of Human Progress from Savagery through Barbarism to Civilization.* London: MacMillan & Company.

Morgan, Michael L. (ed.). 2002. *Baruch Spinoza: The Complete Works* (tr. S. Shireley). Indianapolis: Hackett.

Morin, Edgar. 2005. *The Cinema, or The Imaginary Man* (tr. L. Mortimer). Minneapolis: University of Minnesota Press. [French original: 1956. *Le Cinéma ou l'Homme Imaginaire: Essai d'Anthropologie.* Paris: Les Editions de Minuit.]

Morus, Iwan Rhys. 1998. *Frankenstein's Children: Electricity, Exhibition, and Experiment in Early-Nineteenth-Century.* London, Princeton: Princeton University Press.

Von Mücke, Dorothea E. 2003. *The Seduction of the Occult and the Rise of the Fantastic Tale.* Stanford: Stanford University Press.

Mullarkey, John. 2004. 'Forget the Virtual: Bergson, Actualism, and the Refraction of Reality' in *Continental Philosophy Review* 37(4): 469-493.
—. (ed.) 1999. *The New Bergson.* Manchester: Manchester University Press.

Müller, Jürgen E. (ed.) 1994/1995. *Towards a Pragmatics of the Audiovisual: Theory and History,* Volume 1 and 2. Münster: Nodus Publikationen.

Münsterberg, Hugo. [1916] 1970. *The Photoplay: A Psychological Study and Other Writings.* New York: Dover.
—. 1910. 'Report on a Sitting with Eusapia Palladino' in *Metropolitan* 31(5): 559-572.

Musser, Charles. 1997. *Edison Motion Pictures, 1890-1900: An Annotated Filmography.* Gemona: Le Giornate del Cinema Muto/Smithsonian Institution Press.

—. 1994. *The Emergence of Cinema. The American Screen to 1907: History of the American Cinema, 1.* Berkeley: University of California Press.

—. 1991. *Before the Nickelodeon: Edwin S. Porter and the Edison Manufacturing Company.* Berkeley and Los Angeles: University of California.

Muybridge, Eadweard. 1887. *Animal Locomotion: An Electro-Photographic Investigation of Consecutive Phases of Animal Movements, 1872-1885.* Philadelphia: J.B. Lippincott Company.

—. 1878. 'The gait of horses represented by means of instant photography' in *La Nature* 289 Dec. 14: 23-26.

Nasaw, David. 1993. *Going Out: The Rise and Fall of Public Amusements.* New York: BasicBooks.

Nichols, Bill and Ledermann, Susan J. 1980. 'Flicker and Motion in Film' in De Lauretis, Teresa, and Stephen Heath (eds) *The Cinematic Apparatus.* Hampshire, London: The MacMillan Press.

Noble, David. 1997. *The Religion of Technology: The Divinity of Man and the Spirit of Invention.* New York: Alfred A. Knopf.

Nye, David. 2006. *Technology Matters: Questions to Live With.* Cambridge, Massachusetts: The MIT Press.

—. 1996. *American Technological Sublime.* Cambridge, Massachusetts: The MIT Press.

—. 1990. *Electrifying America: Social Meanings of a New Technology 1880-1940.* Cambridge, Massachusetts: The MIT Press.

Olick, Jeffrey, K. 2006. 'Products, Processes, and Practices: a Non-Reificatory Approach to Collective Memory' in *Biblical Theology Bulletin* 36(1): 5-14.

Opinel, Annick. 2006. 'Cinéma et Recherche à l'Institut Pasteur Dans la Première Moitié du XXe Siècle' in Font-Réaulx, Dominique de, Lefebvre, Thierry and Mannoni, Laurent (eds) *E.J. Marey: Actes du Colloque du Centenaire.* Paris: Arcadia: 169-177.

Oppenheim, Janet. 1985. *The Other World: Spiritualism and Psychical Research in England, 1850-1914.* Cambridge, London, New York: Cambridge University Press.

Ouspensky, P.D. 1931. *A New Model of the Universe.* New York: Knopf.
—. [1912] 1922. *Tertium Organum: The Third Canon of Thought, a Key to the Enigmas of the World.* New York: Knopf, 1922.
—. [1909] 2005. *The Fourth Dimension.* Whitefish, Montana: Kessinger Publications.

Owen, Alex. 1989. *The Darkened Room: Women, Power, and Spiritualism in Late Victorian England.* Chicago, London: The University of Chicago Press.

Panéro, Alain. 2005. 'Matière et Esprit Chez Bergson'. Online at: http://www.ac-amiens.fr/pedagogie/philosophie/PAF/bergson-panero.htm (consulted 14.03.2009)

Pearsall, Ronald. 1972. *The Table Rappers.* London: Michael Joseph.

Pearson, Keith Ansell. 2002. *Philosophy and the Adventure of the Virtual: Bergson and the Time of Life.* London: Routledge.

Pearson, Keith Ansell and Mullarkey, John (eds). 2002. *Henri Bergson: Key Writings.* London: Continuum.

Pepperell, Robert and Punt, Michael (eds). 2006. *Screen Consciousness: Cinema, Mind and World.* Amsterdam, New York: Rodopi.
—. 2000. *The Postdigital Membrane: Imagination, Technology and Desire.* Bristol, UK and Portland, OR, USA: Intellect.

Peters, John Durham. 1999. *Speaking into the Air: A History of the Idea of Communication.* Chicago: University of Chicago Press.

Peucker, Brigitte. 2007. *The Material Image: Art and the Real in Film.* Stanford: Stanford University Press.

Philmus, Robert M. 1969. 'The Time Machine; or, The Fourth Dimension as Prophecy' in *PMLA* 84: 530-35.

Pilkington, Anthony Edward. 1976. *Bergson and His Influence: A Reassessment.* Cambridge; New York: Cambridge University Press.

Pinch, T., Bijker, W., and Hughes, T. (eds). 1987. *The Social Construction of Technological Systems: New Directions in the Sociology and History of Technology.* Cambridge, Massachusetts: The MIT Press.

Pinet, Helen (ed.). 2007. *Rodin et la Photographie* (Musee Rodin). Paris: Gallimard.

Pinotti, Andrea. 2003. 'Memory and Image'. Online at: www.italianacademy.columbia.edu/publications/working_papers/2 003_2004/paper_fa03_Pinotti.pdf (consulted 14.03.2009)
—. 2006. 'Iconography and Ontology of the Image' in *Leitmotiv* 5 (Art in the Age of Visual Culture and the Image). Online at: www.ledonline.it/leitmotiv/allegati/leitmotiv050509.pdf (consulted 14.03.2009)

Pisano, Giusy. 2006. 'L'Instant Choisi et Métamorphosé dans la Matière et l'Instant Quelconque Photographié' in Font-Réaulx, Dominique de, Lefebvre, Thierry and Mannoni, Laurent (eds) *E.J. Marey: Actes du Colloque du Centenaire.* Paris: Arcadia: 91-104.

Pisters, Patricia. 2006. 'The Spiritual Dimension of the Brain as Screen: Zigzagging from Cosmos to Earth (and Back)' in Pepperell, Robert and Punt, Michael (eds) *Screen Consciousness: Cinema, Mind and World.* Amsterdam, New York: Rodopi: 123-137.
—. 2003. *The Matrix of Visual Culture: Working with Deleuze in Film Theory.* Stanford: Stanford University Press.
—. (ed.). 2001. *Micropolitics of Media Culture: Reading the Rhizomes of Deleuze and Guattari.* Amsterdam: Amsterdam University Press.
—. 1998. *From Eye to Brain, Gilles Deleuze: Refiguring the Subject in Film Theory.* Wageningen: Ponsen & Looijen.

Pitkin, Walter B. 1910. 'James and Bergson: Or, Who is Against Intellect?' in *Journal of Philosophy, Psychology, and Scientific Methods* 7: 225-231.

Pitkin, Walter B. and Kallen, H.M. 1910. 'Discussion: James, Bergson and Mr. Pitkin' in *Journal of Philosophy, Psychology, and Scientific Methods* 7: 353-357.

Popple, Simon. 1996. 'The Diffuse Beam: Cinema and Change' in Williams, Christopher (ed.) *Cinema, the Beginnings and the Future: Essays Marking the Centenary of the First Film Show Projected to a Paying Audience in Britain.* London: University of Westminster Press: 97-106.

Popple, Simon and Kember, Joe. 2004. *Early Cinema: From Factory Gate to Dream Factory.* London: Wallflower Press.

Popple, Simon and Toulmin, Vanessa (eds). 2000. *Visual Delights: Essays on the Popular and Projected Image in the 19th Century.* Trowbridge: Flicks Books.

Princenthal, Nancy. 2006. 'Willing Spirits: Art of the Paranormal' in *Art in America* 94(2) February: 104-13, 144.

Punt, Michael. 2005a. 'What the Film Archive Can Tell Us About Technology in the Post-digital Era' in *Design Issues* 21(2): 48-62.
—. 2005b. '?What Shall We Do With All Those Old Bytes? Saving the Cinematic Imagination in the Postdigital Era' in *Design Issues* 21(2): 48-64.
—. 2004. 'd-Cinema – d-Déjà vu' in *Convergence* 10(2): 8-14.
—. 2004b. 'Orai and the Transdisciplinary Wunderkammer' in *Leonardo* 37(3): 201-202.
—. 2003a. 'The Martian in the Multiverse' in *Refractory: A Journal of Entertainment Media* 3: 1-19
—. 2003b. 'The Jelly Baby on My Knee' in Elvers, F., vd Velden, L. and vd Wenden, P. (eds) *The Art of Programming.* Amsterdam: Sonic Acts Press: 40-47.
—. 2001. 'Post Classical Cinema and the Digital Image' in *Convergence* 6(2): 62-76.

—. 2000. *Early Cinema and the Technological Imaginary.* Trowbridge, Wiltshire: Cromwell Press.

—. 1998a. 'Accidental Machines: The Impact of Popular Participation in Computer Technology' in *Design Issues* 14(1): 54-80.

—. 1998b. 'Digital Media, Artificial Life, and Postclassical Cinema. Condition, Symptom, or a Rhetoric of Funding?' in *Leonardo* 31(5): 349-356.

—. 1995a. '"Well, Who You Gonna Believe, Me Or Your Own Eyes?": A Problem Of Digital Photography' in *The Velvet Light Trap* (36): 2-20.

—. 1995b. 'CD-Rom: Radical Nostalgia? Cinema History, Cinema Theory, and New Technology' in *Leonardo* 28(5): 387-394.

Rabinbach, Anson. 1992. *The Human Motor: Energy, Fatigue, and the Origins of Modernity.* Berkeley: University of California Press.

Rabinow, Paul. 1989. *French Modern: Norms and Forms of the Social Environment.* Cambridge, Massachusetts: The MIT Press.

Rampley, Matthew. 2000. *The Remembrance of Things Past: On Aby M Warburg and Walter Benjamin.* Wiesbaden: Harrassowitz Verlag.

—. 1997. 'From Symbol to Allegory: Aby Warburg's Theory of Art' in *Art Bulletin* 79(1) March: 41-55.

Ramsaye, Terry. 1926. *A Million and One Nights: A History of the Motion Picture through 1925.* New York: Simon & Schuster.

Rappl, Werner, et al. (eds). 2006. *Aby M. Warburg Mnemosyne-Materialien.* München, Hamburg: Dölling und Galitz.

Regnault, Félix-Louis. 1897. *Comment on Marche: Des Divers Modes de Progression de la Supériorité du Mode en Flexion.* Paris: Henri Charles-Lavauzelle.

Richet, Charles Robert. 1930. *Our Sixth Sense.* London: Rider & Co. [French original: 1927. *Notre Sixième Sens.* Paris: Montaigne].

—. 1923. *Thirty Years of Psychical Research.* New York: Macmillan. [French original: 1922. *Traité de Métapsychique.* Paris: Alcan].

Richter, Gerhard. 2008. 'Atlas'. Online at: http://www.gerhard-richter.com/art/atlas/ (consulted 14.03.2009)

Rickards, Maurice. 2000. *Encyclopedia of Ephemera*. London: British Library.

Riley, Alexander Tristan. 2002. 'Durkheim Contra Bergson? The Hidden Roots of Postmodern Theory and the Postmodern' in *Sociological Perspectives* 45(3): 243-265.

Rittaud-Hutinet, Jacques (ed.). 1994. *Letters: Auguste and Louis Lumière*. London, Boston: Faber and Faber.

Robinet, André (ed.). 1972. *Henri Bergson, Mélanges* (Correspondances, pièces diverses, documents. Avant-Propos par H. Gouhier). Paris: Presses Universitaires de France.

Rodowick, D.N. 1997. *Gilles Deleuze's Time Machine*. Durham and London: Duke University Press.

Rohdie, Sam. 2001. *Promised Lands: Cinema, Geography, Modernism*. London: British Film Institute.

Rollet, Véronique. 2006. E.-J. 'Marey et N. Bouton: Les Décors Peints de la Classe XII (Photographie) à l'Exposition Universelle de 1900' in Font-Réaulx, Dominique de, Lefebvre, Thierry and Mannoni, Laurent (eds) *E.J. Marey: Actes du Colloque du Centenaire*. Paris: Arcadia: 105-117.

Romanyshyn, Robert. 1989. *Technology as Symptom and Dream*. London: Routledge.

Rony, Fatimah Tobing. 1996. *The Third Eye. Race, Cinema, and Ethnographic Spectacle*. Durham and London: Duke University Press.

Rosen, Philip (ed.). 1986. *Narrative, Apparatus, Ideology*. New York: Columbia.

Rossell, Deac. 1998. *Living Pictures: The Origins of the Cinema.* Albany: SUNY Press.
—. 1995. 'A Chronology of Cinema 1889-1896' in *Film History* 7(2): 115-236.

Roy, Edouard Le. 2004. *A New Philosophy: Henri Bergson.* White-fish, Montana: Kessinger Publications.

Rouch, Jean. [1960] 1989. *La Religion et la Magie Songhay.* Brussels: Editions de l'Universite de Bruxelles.

Ruby, Jay. 2000. *Picturing Culture: Explorations of Film and Anthro-pology.* Chicago: University of Chicago Press.
—. 1995. *Secure the Shadow: Death and Photography in America.* Cambridge, Massachusetts: The MIT Press.

Saxl, Fritz. 1970. *A Heritage of Images: A Selection of Lectures by Fritz Saxl.* Harmondsworth, Middlesex: Penguin Books.

Schade, Sigrid. 1995. 'Charcot and the Spectacle of the Hysterical Body: The 'Pathos Formula' as an Aesthetic Staging of Psychiatric Discourse — a Blind Spot in the Reception of Warburg' in *Art History* 18(4): 499-517.

Schäfer, Hans Michael. 2003. *Die Kulturwissenschaftliche Bibliothek Warburg: Geschichte und Persönlichkeiten der Bibliothek War-burg mit Berücksichtigung der Bibliothekslandschaft und der Stadtsituation der Freien und Hansestadt Hamburg zu Beginn des 20. Jahrhunderts.* (Berliner Arbeiten zur Bibliothekswissenschaft, Vol. 11). Berlin: Logos-Verlag.

Schechner, Richard. 1985. *Between Theatre and Anthropology.* Uni-versity of Pennsylvania Press.
—. 1977. *Performance Theory.* New York: Routledge.

Schivelbusch, Wolfgang. 1995. *Disenchanted Night: The Industriali-zation of Light in the Nineteenth Century.* London: University of California Press.

—. 1986. *The Railway Journey: the Industrialization and Perception of Time and Space.* Berkeley: University of California Press.

Schwartz, Vanessa R. and Przyblyski, J. 2005. *The Nineteenth Century Visual Culture Reader.* London/New York: Routledge.
—. 1998. *Spectacular Realities: Early Mass Culture in Fin-de-Siècle Paris.* Berkeley: University of California Press.

Semon, Richard. 1904. *Die Mneme als Erhaltendes Prinzip im Wechsel des Organischen Geschehens.* Leipzig: Engelmann. (Engl. Tr.: 1921. *The Mneme.* London: George Allen & Unwin.)

Seremetakis, N. 1994. *The Senses Still. Perception and Memory as Material Culture in Modernity.* Boulder: Westview Press Inc.

Shaw, Jeffrey and Weibel, Peter (eds). 2002. *Future Cinema: The Cinematic Imaginary after Film* (ZKM, Zentrum für Kunst und Medientechnologie, Karlsruhe). Cambridge, Massachusetts: The MIT Press.

Shoosmith, F.H. 1918. *Science and Magic.* London: Mills & Boon.

Singer, Ben. 1995. 'Modernity, Hyperstimulus, and the Rise of Popular Sensationalism' in Charney, Leo and Schwartz, Vanessa R. (eds) *Cinema and the Invention of Modern Life.* Berkeley: University of California Press: 72-99.

Solomon, Matthew. 2006. 'Up-to-Date Magic: Theatrical Conjuring and the Trick Film' in *Theatre Journal* 58: 595-615.

Spencer, Frank. 1992. 'Some Notes on the Attempt to Apply Photography to Anthropometry during the Second Half of the Nineteenth Century' in Edwards, Elizabeth (ed.) *Anthropology and Photography 1860-1920.* New Haven and London: Yale University Press: 99-107.

Spradley, James P. 1980. *Participant Observation.* New York: Holt, Rinehart & Winston.

Stafford, Barbara Maria. 2001. *Devices of Wonder: From World in a Box to Images on a Screen.* Los Angeles: Getty Publications.
—. 1999. *Visual Analogy: Consciousness as the Art of Connecting.* Cambridge, Massachusetts: The MIT Press.
—. 1997. *Good Looking: the Virtue of Images.* Cambridge, Massachusetts: The MIT Press.
—. 1994. *Artful Science.* Cambridge, Massachusetts: The MIT Press.
—. 1991. *Body Criticism: Imaging the Unseen in Enlightenment Art and Medicine.* Cambridge, Massachusetts: The MIT Press.

Steinman, Robert M., Pizlo, Zygmunt and Pizlo, Filip J. 2000. 'Phi is not Beta, and Why Wertheimer's Discovery Launched the Gestalt Revolution: a Minireview' in *Vision Research* 40(17): 2257-2264.

Stocking, George W. (ed.). 1989. *A Franz Boas Reader: The Shaping of American Anthropology 1883-1911.* Chicago: University of Chicago Press.
—. 1987. *Victorian Anthropology.* New York: The Free Press.

Stoller, Paul. 1986. *The Taste of Ethnographic Things.* Philadelphia: University of Pennsylvania Press.

Soulez, Philippe. 1989. *Bergson Politique.* Paris: Presses Universitaires de France.

Soulez, Philippe and Worms, Frédéric. 2002. *Bergson.* Paris: Presses Universitaires de France.

Thakur, Shivesh C. (ed.). 1976. *Philosophy and Psychical Research.* London: George Allen & Unwin.

Talbot, Frederick A. 1912. *Moving Pictures: How they are Made and Worked.* Philadelphia: J.B.Lippincott; and London: William Heinemann.

Tesla, Nikola. 1993. *The Fantastic Inventions of Nikola Tesla* (ed. D.H. Childress). Kempton, Illinois: Adventures Unlimited Press.

Thomas, Ann (ed.). 1997. *Beauty of Another Order: Photography in Science.* New Haven, London: Yale University Press.

Toulmin, Vanessa and Popple, Simon (eds). 2000. *Visual Delights: The Popular and Projected Image in the Nineteenth Century.* Trowbridge: Flicks Books.
—. 1996. 'The Fairground Bioscope and Bioscope Biographies' in Harding, Colin and Popple, Simon (eds) *In the Kingdom of Shadows: A Companion to Early Cinema.* London: Cygnus Arts: 191-207.
—. 1994. 'Telling the Tale: The History of the Fairground Bioscope Show and the Showmen Who Operated Them' in *Film History* 6(2): 219-237.

Trutat, Charles-Louis Eugène. 1899. *La Photographie Animée.* Paris: Gauthier-Villars.

Tsivian, Yuri. 1998. *Early Cinema in Russia and its Cultural Reception.* Chicago and London: University of Chicago Press.
—. 1996. 'Media Fantasies and Penetrating Vision: Some Links between X-Rays, the Microscope, and Film' in Bowlt, John E. and Matich, Olga (eds) *Laboratory of Dreams: The Russian Avant-Garde and Cultural Experiment.* Stanford: Stanford University Press: 81-99.

Tunzelmann, G.N. 1889. *Electricity in Modern Life.* London: Walter Scott.

Tylor, Edward Burnett. 1865. *Researches into the Early History of Mankind and the Development of Civilization.* London: John Murray.
—. 1871. *Primitive Culture: Researches in the Development of Mythology, Philosophy, Religion, Art and Custom.* London: John Murray.

Uricchio, William. 2000. 'Technologies of Time' in Olsson, J. (ed.) *Allegories of Communication: Intermedial Concerns from Cinema to the Digital.* Berkeley: University of California Press.

Vaughan, Dai. 1990. 'Let There Be Lumière' in Elsaesser, Thomas (ed.) *Early Cinema. Space Frame Narrative*. London: British Film Institute: 63-67.

Verrips, Jojada. 2007. 'Aisthesis and An-Aesthesia' in *Ethnologia Europaea* 35: 29-36.
—. 2002. 'Haptic Screens and Our Corporeal Eye' in *Etnofoor: Anthropologisch Tijdschrift* (Screens). Amsterdam: Krips Repro, Meppel: 21-46.

Vertov, Dziga. 1984. *Kino-Eye: The Writings of Dziga Vertov* (ed. A. Michelson). Berkeley: University of California Press.

Vischer, Robert. [1873] 1994. 'On the Optical Sense of Form: A Contribution to Aesthetics' in Mallgrave, H. and Ikonomou, E. (tr. and eds) *Empathy, Form and Space: Problems in German Aesthetics 1873-1893*. Santa Monica: Getty Centre for the History of Art and the Humanities: 89-117.

Wainright, Evans. 1963. 'Scientists Research Machine to Contact the Dead' in *Fate* (April): 38-43.

Warburg, Aby M. 2002. *Le Rituel du serpent*. Paris: Macula.
—. 2000. 'Der Bilderatlas MNEMOSYNE' in *Gesammelte Schriften* (ed. M. Warnke in collaboration with Claudia Brink). (Studienausgabe, Band II.1, 2.) Berlin: Akademie Verlag.
—. 1999. *The Renewal of Pagan Antiquity: Contributions to the Cultural History of the European Renaissance* (tr. D. Britt). Los Angeles, CA: Getty Research Institute for the History of Art and the Humanities.
—. 1992. *Ausgewählte Schriften und Würdigungen* (ed. D. Wuttke). Baden-Baden: Valentin Koerner.
—. 1988. *Schlangenritual: Ein Reisebericht*. Berlin: Wagenbach.

Watson, Sean. 1998. 'The New Bergsonism: Discipline, Subjectivity and Freedom' in *Radical Philosophy* (Nov./Dec.) Online at: http://www.radicalphilosophy.com (consulted 14.03.2009)

Wertheimer, Max. [1912] 1961. 'Experimental Studies on the Seeing of Motion' in Shipley, Thorne (ed.) *Classics in Psychology*. New York: Philosophical Library: 1032-1089. [German Original: 1912. 'Experimentelle Studien über das Sehen von Bewegung' in *Zeitschrift für Psychologie* 61: 161-265)

Williams, Alan. 1983. 'The Lumière Organization and 'Documentary Realism'' in Fell, John L. (ed.) *Film Before Griffith*. Berkeley: University of California Press: 153-161.

Williams, Christopher (ed.). 1996. *Cinema: the Beginnings and the Future: Essays Marking the Centenary of the first Film Show Projected to a Paying Audience in Britain*. London: University of Westminster Press.

Williams, Keith. 2007. *H.G. Wells, Modernity and the Movies*. Liverpool: Liverpool University Press.

Williams, Linda (ed.). 1994. *Viewing Positions: Ways of Seeing Film*. New Jersey: Rutgers University Press.

Winston, Brian. 2002. 'Technologies of Seeing' in Shaw, Jeffrey and Weibel, Peter (eds) *Future Cinema: The Cinematic Imaginary after Film*. Cambridge, Massachusetts: The MIT Press.
—. 1998. *Media Technology and Society: A History From the Telegraph to the Internet*. Routledge.
—. 1996. *Technologies of Seeing: Photography, Cinematography and Television*. London: British Film Institute.

Wollen, Peter. 1980. 'Cinema and Technology: A Historical Overview' in De Lauretis, Teresa, and Heath, Stephen (eds) *The Cinematic Apparatus*. Hampshire, London: The MacMillan Press: 14-22.
—. 1969. *Signs and Meaning in the Cinema*. Bloomington: Indiana University Press.

Worms, Frédéric. 2004. *Bergson ou les Deux Sources de la Vie*. Paris: Presses Universitaires de France.

Wundt, Wilhelm. 1874. *Grundzüge der Physiologischen Psychologie,* Vol. I-III.

Yamaguchi, Minoru. 1969. *The Intuition of Zen and Bergson: Comparative Intellectual Approach to Zen; Reason of Divergencies between East and West.* Tokyo, Japan: Herder Agency.

Zielinski, Siegfried. 2006. *Deep Time of the Media: Toward an Archaeology of Hearing and Seeing by Technical Means.* Cambridge, Massachusetts: The MIT Press.
—. 1994a. 'Historic Modes of the Audiovisual Apparatus' in *Iris* 17: 7-24.
—. 1994b. 'Towards an Archaeology of the Audiovisual…' in Müller, Jürgen E. (ed.) *Towards a Pragmatics of the Audiovisual: Theory and History,* Vol. I. Münster: Nodus Publikationen: 181-199.

Zweite, Armin. 1990. *Gerhard Richter: Atlas.* Munich: Sädtische Galerie in Lenbachhaus and Museum Ludwig, Cologne.

Index